'This is a timely and insightful book, which will be of great value to researchers, practitioners and students. It highlights the paradigm shift from car-based to place-based urban planning, and provides a conceptual framing, auditing tools and practical examples of how this transition can be achieved, working closely with local communities.'
   Peter Jones, OBE, Scientific Co-ordinator, CREATE, Professor of Transport and Sustainable Development and Director, University College London, UK

'Reena Tiwari's book is a timely guide for remaking our cities and movement systems into people-oriented places. *Connecting Places, Connecting People* provides a multifaceted assessment of transformative implementation strategies drawn from around the globe that make this book a must have for planners everywhere.'
   GB Arrington, Principal, GB Place Making

'Reena Tiwari's *Connecting Places, Connecting People* is an important contribution to the discourse on how we create sustainable cities in the 21st century. Her thesis enables a paradigm shift in popular urban planning principles by prioritizing people over vehicles to recreate more livable, sustainable cities. The practical audit tool she has developed is rooted in a wealth of good practice from around the globe, and provides a final positive outlook on the future of the city by 2050.'
   Holger Dalkmann, Director, Strategy and Global Policy; EMBARQ Director, WRI Ross Center for Sustainable Cities, World Resources Institute

CONNECTING PLACES, CONNECTING PEOPLE

What is a better community? How can we reconfigure places and transport networks to create environmentally friendly, economically sound, and socially just communities? How can we meet the challenges of growing pollution, depleting fossil fuels, rising gasoline prices, traffic congestion, traffic fatalities, increased prevalence of obesity, and lack of social inclusion?

The era of car-based planning has led to the disconnection of people and place in developed countries, and is rapidly doing so in the developing countries of the Global South. The unfolding mega-trend in technological innovation, while adding new patterns of future living and mobility in the cities, will question the relevance of face-to-face connections. What will be the 'glue' that holds communities together in the future?

To build better communities and to build better cities, we need to reconnect people and places. *Connecting Places, Connecting People* offers a new paradigm for place making by reordering urban planning principles from prioritizing movement of vehicles to focusing on places and the people who live in them. Numerous case studies, including many from developing countries in the Global South, illustrate how this can be realized or fallen short of in practical terms. Importantly, citizens need to be engaged in policy development, to connect with each other and with government agencies. To measure the connectivity attributes of places and the success of strategies to meet the needs, an Audit Tool is offered for a continual quantitative and qualitative evaluation.

Reena Tiwari is a professor of Built Environment at Curtin University, Australia. She has published extensively on space psychology and place making; urban ethnography and community engagement; sustainable transport and urbanism. Fundamental to her work on urban transport and place making is the philosophy of democratic urbanism and a model of enquiry that is ethnographic, collaborative, and trans-disciplinary, and has the goal of facilitating change and adaptation for all involved in the process.

CONNECTING PLACES, CONNECTING PEOPLE

A PARADIGM FOR URBAN LIVING IN THE TWENTY-FIRST CENTURY

REENA TIWARI

NEW YORK AND LONDON

First published 2018
by Routledge
711 Third Avenue, New York, NY 10017

and by Routledge
2 Park Square, Milton Park, Abingdon, Oxon, OX14 4RN

Routledge is an imprint of the Taylor & Francis Group, an informa business

© 2018 Taylor & Francis

The right of Reena Tiwari to be identified as author of this work has been asserted by her in accordance with sections 77 and 78 of the Copyright, Designs and Patents Act 1988.

All rights reserved. No part of this book may be reprinted or reproduced or utilized in any form or by any electronic, mechanical, or other means, now known or hereafter invented, including photocopying and recording, or in any information storage or retrieval system, without permission in writing from the publishers.

Trademark notice: Product or corporate names may be trademarks or registered trademarks, and are used only for identification and explanation without intent to infringe.

Library of Congress Cataloging-in-Publication Data
Names: Tiwari, Reena, 1964- author. Title: Connecting places, connecting people :
a paradigm for urban living in the 21st century / Reena Tiwari.
Description: New York, NY : Routledge, 2018. |
Includes bibliographical references and index.
Identifiers: LCCN 2017010206| ISBN 9781138213050 (hardback) |
ISBN 9781138213067 (pbk.) | ISBN 9781315449241 (ebk)
Subjects: LCSH: Urban transportation. | City and town life. |
Sustainable urban development.
Classification: LCC HE305 .T59 2018 | DDC 388.4--dc23LC
record available at https://lccn.loc.gov/2017010206

ISBN: 978-1-138-21305-0 (hbk)
ISBN: 978-1-138-21306-7 (pbk)
ISBN: 978-1-315-44924-1 (ebk)

Typeset in Univers by
Servis Filmsetting Ltd, Stockport, Cheshire

Printed in Canada

CONTENTS

LIST OF ILLUSTRATIONS	viii
ACKNOWLEDGMENTS	x
PROLOGUE	xi
FOREWORD BY PROFESSOR PETER NEWMAN	xiii
PART I: THE CONCEPT	**1**
Chapter 1: Connecting Places, Connecting People	3
Chapter 2: Connecting Places for Better Communities	13
PART II: MAPPING THE CONTEXT: URBAN RECONFIGURATIONS	**29**
Chapter 3: Reconfiguring Movement	31
Chapter 4: 'Making' Places: Urban and Suburban Transformations	55
PART III: CONNECTING PLACES, CONNECTING PEOPLE: MAKING IT HAPPEN!	**81**
Chapter 5: Remodeling Approaches: Empowering Place Making and Connectivity	83
Chapter 6: Evaluating People, Place, and Transport Connectivity	97
PART IV: THE FUTURE	**125**
Chapter 7: Emerging Challenges: Connected Places in the Global South	127
Chapter 8: Emerging Challenges: Technology Mega-trends and Demographic Shifts	143
EPILOGUE: ETHNOGRAPHY OF PLACE AND MOVEMENT	**163**
INDEX	**165**

ILLUSTRATIONS

Figures

2.1	Agents/indicators of better communities	14
2.2	The negative social consequences of car-oriented city design	15
2.3	Chicanes in place at NE 98th Street, Seattle	16
2.4	A strong pedestrian realm alongside a slow access lane allows activities to flourish in Barcelona	22
2.5	Extending the pedestrian realm: International Boulevard in Fruitvale, CA	22
3.1	Broadway and Euclid intersection before and after construction of the bicycle/pedestrian underpass	34
3.2	Graphics on the street as part of the Heads Up crosswalk safety campaign	35
3.3	Typical 'patch' in Broward County; Quilt-Net formed by the infrastructure corridors; street configuration changes from urban to rural	35
3.4	FUS-ion approach to arterial classification; Manning Road Assessment on FUS-ion Management Model	36
3.5	Octavia Boulevard, San Francisco	38
3.6	Green space in Seoul	39
3.7	Parklets in San Francisco	40
3.8	Compact street network	41
3.9	Green Network of Shanghai proposed for 2020	42
3.10	The High Line: previously disused railtrack transformed into a most popular destination for locals and tourists alike	43
4.1	New development—an extension on the old: Mockingbird Station, Dallas	58
4.2	Open spaces and walkways in and around the Mockingbird development	59
4.3	Map showing the connectivity aspects of the Mockingbird development	60
4.4	Mixed land use development at Mockingbird Station	60
4.5	Map showing the Hoboken Terminal Redevelopment Precinct	61
4.6	Varied height of buildings to avoid the canyon effect	63
4.7	Docklands within the City of Melbourne; nodes and connections	64
4.8	The initial development icons, the stadium and the residential towers at New Quay	65
4.9	Cycle-friendly infrastructure	65
4.10	Travel modal split for Docklands and inner-city Melbourne	66
4.11	Public space and public art at Docklands	67
4.12	Carbon savings in a transit-oriented scenario as compared to a business-as-usual scenario	68
4.13	Place activation at Curtin	69
4.14	Location of the Crossings neighborhood in San Antonio Transit Center change area	70
4.15	A fine grid generates a higher level of connectivity and permeability, as demonstrated by the number of intersections: the Crossings neighborhood before and after redevelopment	71
4.16	Sidewalks, narrow streets, and on-street parking in the Crossings neighborhood	71
4.17	The car-centric city with car yards; residential use being introduced	72
4.18	Tysons Corner Center Plaza; pop-up park at Greensboro Green	74
5.1	Educational engagement through performance	92
6.1	Audit metrics: number of dimensions responding to the three attributes of people, place, and transport connectivity	100
6.2	Land use efficiency and block size	102
6.3	Connectivity maps of a conventional suburb and a traditional suburb	103

6.4	Permeability index and ped-shed accessibility in Indira Nagar, Bangalore, India	103
6.5	Ill-defined and unsafe pedestrian access through car parks; pedestrian accessways and courtyards providing visual and physical permeability	104
6.6	Solid:void ratio for building facade	104
6.7	The impact of height:street-width ratio on 'sense of enclosure'	105
6.8	Public art and graffiti, Melbourne	106
6.9	Geographical setting of King Street and Mission Bay	107
6.10	Diverse block and lot sizes	108
6.11	Diverse rental values reflecting diverse residential quality and typology	108
6.12	Solid:void ratio on building façade	110
6.13	Pedestrian amenity and permeability	110
6.14	Reduced social width on King Street	111
6.15	Building height:street-width ratio changes along King Street, approximately 1:1–1:2	111
6.16	Past remembrance	112
7.1	The corridor system in Cape Town	130
7.2	The conceptual diagram for the corridor system	130
7.3	Cross-section of the Klipfontein Corridor	131
7.4	Factors affecting mode shift	133
7.5	Appropriation of pedestrians' and cyclists' space	135
8.1	A graduated density gradient proposed at Songdo	151
8.2	Benefits and disadvantages for individuals and communities	154
8.3	Using a top-down *and* a bottom-up approach	155

Tables

6.1	Audit Tool showing dimensions of connected places and the variables affecting people, place, and transport connectivity	99
6.2	Types of densities for transit systems	101
6.3	Audit Tool application on King Street, San Francisco	107
6.4	Walking path modal conflict score	114
6.5	Quality of crossing points score	115
6.6	Amenities score	116
6.7	Special needs infrastructure score	117
6.8	Safety from crime score	118
6.9	Motorists' behavior score	119

Box

| 8.1 | Attributes of connecting places, connecting people corresponding with those of digitally enabled future places | 151 |

ACKNOWLEDGMENTS

The idea for this book was first discussed in January 2011 with the late Dr Lee Schipper, to whom I dedicate this work. It has taken me five long years to bring the idea to fruition. From the start, Professor Robert Cervero from the University of California, Berkeley, helped shape this project through innumerable discussions and invaluable feedback.

This book has been a team effort.

Thanks to Rohit Sharma for his excellent research skills, unflagging enthusiasm, and important contribution throughout, and especially for carrying out the literature review and providing writing assistance in Chapters 3, 4, and 7. His contribution in Chapter 8 is especially acknowledged. Thanks to Sneha Rapur for her contribution in Chapter 5. Susan Barrera kept a close watch on the flow of the text, while Tommy Wong assisted in translating ideas graphically. To my excellent editor Christina Houen—thanks for completing this project with me; this was our second in a row! I thank Kamal Yadav, Diya Menon, Tommy Wong, Loveleen Tiwari, Dianne Smith, and Lalima Tiwari for providing pictures at short notice, and acknowledge the financial support provided by the Australia Asia Pacific Institute, Curtin University.

I could not have journeyed through the ups and downs in this project without the continual support and encouragement of my husband Vini. I don't have any words to express my thanks and I am sure he does not need any. My daughters—Lalima and Charleen—helped me to maintain a certain level of sanity and balance with endless cups of chai and, more importantly, some entertaining gossip. And last but not least, thanks to my wonderful parents for being proud of every little thing that I do.

PROLOGUE

Source: Adapted from EMBARQ
Sustainable Urban Mobility by WRI 2016,
retrieved from https://www.flickr.com/
photos/embarq/5226741277/in/album-
72157625516012156.

PROLOGUE

Leonard Mead stands at a city junction in the night. The streets are 'like streams in a dry season, all stone and bed and moon radiance', in contrast to the daytime, when the junction is 'a thunderous surge of cars, the gas stations open, a great insect rustling and a ceaseless jockeying for position as the scarab-beetles, a faint incense puttering from their exhausts, skimmed homeward to the far directions' (Bradbury, 1951, p. 570). Suddenly a police vehicle stops by:

> 'What are you doing out?'
> 'Walking,' said Leonard Mead.
> 'Walking!'
> 'Just walking,' he said simply, but his face felt cold.
> 'Walking, just walking, walking?'
> 'Yes, sir.'
> 'Walking where? For what?'
> 'Walking for air. Walking to see.'

The policeman coerces Mead into the back seat of the car, and he is taken to the Psychiatric Center for Research on Regressive Tendencies (Bradbury, 1951, p. 571).

The above is a satire by Ray Bradbury on the state of the city at the midpoint of the twenty-first century.

Will the supremacy of the automobile make the practice of walking a prohibited act in the not so distant dystopian future? Will the self-imposed cultural curfew due to people's addiction to electronic screens render an 'eerie solitude to the city at night' (Beaumont, 2015, p. 71)? Will our technological existence lead to a self-absorbed, self-masked 'public man' (Sennett, 1977)? Will this worsen the prevalent state of urban alienation in our cities, where people lose connection with the places in which they live, and with each other?

References

Bradbury, R. (1951). *The pedestrian*. New York: Samuel French.
Beaumont, M. (2015). Stumbling in the dark: Ray Bradbury's pedestrian and the politics of the night. *Critical Quarterly 57*(4), 71–88.
Sennett, R. (1977). *The fall of public man*. New York: Alfred A. Knopf.

FOREWORD
Peter Newman[1]

Connecting people and connecting places seems rather obvious. Isn't this what human settlements have always been about? Isn't it something like a human right?

Reena Tiwari has set out the evidence for why we must be better at this 'human right' of connection, or at least the *homo urbanis* right to be connected.

The evidence Reena provides suggests that the era of car-based planning has in fact led to the disconnection of people and place. It is as though a big metal bubble has been wrapped around each of us and disconnected us from the urban place and people. It promised such freedom and gave us a sense that we could actually live anywhere and make connections by ourselves—but the catch was we could only do it by car.

This approach to building cities can work only if a few people or places need such car-based connection. But in the past 20 to 30 years our cities have filled with cars because we made it the only real option for people. Cities became car dependent and instead of freedom we created disconnection.

Place making has been on the agenda for some time but rarely gets put into practice except in the old walking cities where walkable places are built into the city fabric. In most of the other cities, place making is still viewed through the windscreen.

So, we have a problem. How do we now rebuild our cities to reinstate the connections, to rebuild the community, to rebuild the places that attract community through walkability? Is information communications technology going to make us more connected or less connected in terms of place?

Reena has outlined a range of policies and practices that can reconnect people and places. Some are technical design, some are infrastructure-based, some are about changes to behavior. Case studies are given of how it can be done. The results are always inspiring and generate hope for the future. Some seem too easy to be believed. Some seem too difficult. But all will be needed for our cities as we journey along the path to reestablishing connection.

Cities have always been remaking themselves: they never stay the same. This era of city building is to reconnect people and places.

Note

1 Peter Newman is Professor of Sustainability at Curtin University in Australia. He sat on the Board of Infrastructure Australia and is Lead Author for Transport on the Intergovernmental Panel on Climate Change. In 2014 he was awarded the Order of Australia for his contributions to urban design and sustainable transport, particularly related to the saving and rebuilding of Perth's rail system.

Source: Pictures by T. Wong (2015).

PART I

The Concept

Connecting Places, Connecting People asks seemingly simple questions. What is a better community? How can we reconfigure places and transport networks to create environmentally friendly, economically sound, and socially just communities?

These questions are fundamental to our task of grappling with environmental and social challenges. These include growing pollution, depleting fossil fuels, rising gasoline prices, traffic congestion, traffic fatalities, increased prevalence of obesity, and lack of social inclusion (Friel et al., 2011; Litman, 2016; Ribeiro et al., 2007). Analyzing the interactions between urban form and motorized travel provides some important insights for reshaping our environment and our community.

With the worldwide number of cars on the road reaching 907 million (using 2014 data; Statista, 2016), and this number projected to rise to between two and four billion cars by mid-century (Ford, 2011), simply building more roads for more cars and planning cities with more super-highways are not viable options. There is a worldwide movement to reduce the use of private vehicles and the vehicular kilometers traveled per year, to promote healthier communities and more sustainable urban forms (Newman & Kenworthy, 2015; Suzuki et al., 2013). Sadly, these strategies are unlikely to have the necessary impact, largely due to the failure to engage the local communities during their formulation and implementation. Real progress and successful implementation of policies and strategies requires local insight and ownership.

The concept of connecting places, connecting people is offered as a way forward. This concept is truly a paradigm shift. It involves reordering urban planning principles from prioritizing movement of vehicles to focusing on places and the people who live in them. The concept recognizes that people need to reach places and interact, and that movement between places needs to be efficient, environmentally benign, and conducive to healthy communities. The term 'connecting places' conveys this meaning. 'Connecting' indicates that sustainable forms of movement enable interaction between places. 'Places', while being the central focus, implies high-quality areas with a strong sense of locale, within which the community can live, work, shop, learn, and play.

A key distinction between this book and others in the same field is the perspective of place making. Instead of a simplistic reliance on manipulating form and materiality in the creation of a place, the emphasis is on synthesizing physical and cultural components with the needs and aspirations of people. Place making is about making visible people's 'right to their cities' and urban spaces (Purcell, 2002, p. 102).

The book is based on an 'enabling' approach, connecting people to people, people to transport, and people to places.

There is another level of connectivity occurring in our cities. The quest to create 'super-smart' cities with the 'Internet of Things'[1] through smart devices is resulting in a global digital mesh connecting individuals, their homes, and communities. Are the connections made online in isolation more important than connections made socially on the streets? While face-to-face street connections can revitalize urban spaces and local communities, the future for the millennial-driven culture for disruptive change in public spaces could be devoid of difference, vibrancy, and interaction. What is the way forward?

As well as reconfiguring urban morphology and movement to confront a car-induced disconnection, *Connecting Places, Connecting People* offers ways of community-enabled place making to strengthen connections between people, place, and transport.

Note

1 The 'Internet of Things' is visualized as a hyper-connected urban environment—a super-smart city. Sensors provide connectivity to everything from cars, to road infrastructure, to rubbish bins (Perera et al., 2015).

References

All online references retrieved August 17, 2016.

Ford, B. (2011). A future beyond traffic gridlock. Retrieved from www.ted.com/talks/bill_ford_a_future_beyond_traffic_gridlock/transcript?language=en.

Friel, S., Akerman, M., Hancock, T., Kumaresan, J., Marmot, M., Melin, T., & Vlahov, D. (2011). Addressing the social and environmental determinants of Urban Health Equity: Evidence for action and a research agenda. *Journal of Urban Health 88*(5), 860–874.

Litman, T. (2016). *Well measured: Developing indicators for sustainable and livable transport planning.* Retrieved from www.vtpi.org/wellmeas.pdf.

Newman, P., & Kenworthy, J. R. (2015). *The end of automobile dependence: How cities are moving beyond car-based planning.* Washington, D.C.: Island Press.

Perera, C., Liu, C. H., & Jayawardena, S. (2015). The emerging Internet of Things marketplace from an industrial perspective: A survey. Retrieved from https://arxiv.org/pdf/1502.00134.pdf.

Purcell, M. (2002). Excavating Lefebvre: The right to the city and its urban politics of the inhabitant. *GeoJournal 58*, 99–108. Retrieved from http://faculty.washington.edu/mpurcell/geojournal.pdf.

Ribeiro, S. K., Kobayashi, S., Beuthe, M., Gasca, J., Greene, D., Lee, D. S., & Zhou, P. J. (2007). Transport and its infrastructure. In B. Metz, O. R. Davidson, P. R. Bosch, R. Dave, & L. A. Meyer (Eds.) *Climate Change 2007: Mitigation—Contribution of Working Group III to the Fourth Assessment Report of the Intergovernmental Panel on Climate Change* (pp. 323–386). Cambridge: Cambridge University Press.

Statista (2016). Number of passenger cars and commercial vehicles in use worldwide from 2006 to 2014 in (1,000 units). Retrieved from www.statista.com/statistics/281134/number-of-vehicles-in-use-worldwide/.

Suzuki, H., Cervero, R., & Iuchi, K. (2013). *Transforming cities with transit: Transit and land-use integration for sustainable urban development.* Washington, D.C.: World Bank.

CHAPTER 1

CONNECTING PLACES, CONNECTING PEOPLE

Why do we travel? Isn't it to access places so that we can directly manage our everyday affairs? Isn't it to connect with other people?

Connecting [with] people, getting things done—that's what makes the travel worthwhile.

(Tim Finchem, quoted in Shipnuck, 2011)

Yet why do our transportation systems seem more focused on movement between places (mobility) than on safe and easy access to places (accessibility)?

How have we allowed our cities to be dominated by roads and highways and their designs to be dictated by automobiles? What have we lost economically, socially, and environmentally through this myopic vision where the concern has been solely on movement? These are questions we need urgently to address.

Spurred by these questions, and with the aim of providing a more appropriate road map to creating better communities, *Connecting Places, Connecting People* reconfigures the urban environment by replacing mobility-based planning with planning centered on two aspects: accessibility and place making. It deals with the negative economic and environmental repercussions of planning around movement as a dominant approach to transportation planning. A cursory examination demonstrates that the 'mobility first' approach, due to its reliance on segregating 'place' functions and 'movement' functions, has, over time, wreaked havoc on cities by reducing opportunities for social interaction (Appleyard, 1981; DiMento & Ellis, 2013; Giles-Corti, 2006; Jones et al., 2008; Monderman, 2005; Tiwari & Curtis, 2010; Weymouth & Hartz-Karp, 2015). *Connecting Places, Connecting People* refocuses our attention squarely on a fundamental question that has been languishing at the periphery of social awareness over the past half a century. What kind of places do we aspire to live in for the remainder of the twenty-first century, which will lead to healthy, safe, prosperous, equitable, and proud communities?

Perhaps the best place to start is with a review of the current state of urban environments.

The Crisis

The Great Crawl of China . . . Thousands of motorists have been caught up in a 60-mile tailback since August 14—an incredible 11 days ago. And it could last a further three weeks. While many motorists took detours, some ended up trapped for up to five days, sleeping in their cars and taking shifts behind the wheel . . . 400 police were drafted in to ensure the communal road rage was kept in check.

(Bates, 2010)

Imagine being caught in a traffic jam for five long days, not due to any natural disaster, but entirely man-made. Ironically, in this case, caused by roadwork planned to ease traffic congestion. What are the costs? We must include not only loss of productivity and the increased costs to the community and businesses, but also the lost opportunity to spend time with friends and family, the impact on health due to increased pollution, noise, loss of amenity, and driver stress. This one example is reflective of what is happening in urban centers all around the world.

We spend a significant proportion of our available time in the 'in-between spaces'—the streets, highways, transit-stations, and hubs—struggling to move between destinations. This should prompt us to explore the nature of these spaces and the experiential quality they offer to travelers and commuters.

Prior to the automobile era, people used these spaces to meet other people and experience cultural amenities (Glaeser, 2005; Jacobs, 1961; Monderman, 2005). This facility has been largely lost as these spaces have been transformed into movement conduits. Studies show that face-to-face contact or the proximity factor, while important to creativity, innovation, and livability in cities, has always been invaluable in attracting people, firms, and private investments. People-oriented rather than movement-oriented places allow for 'agglomerations' which, studies show, spark innovation and prosperity (Glaeser et al., 1992; Putnam 1995). A smaller carbon footprint is associated with the more intimate scales of people-oriented places (Albrecht, 2005; Cervero, 2010; Shutkin, 2005). Well-designed, livable places can also be more socially inclusive, promoting affordable housing and enabling those with limited budgets to economize on travel by living close to goods, services, and employment opportunities (Cervero, 2010; Newman & Kenworthy, 2015; Renne, 2005). Neighborhoods that promote interaction and everyday face-to-face contact, experiences show, have lower crime rates, promote friendships, and feel safe (Newman, 1972; Putnam, 2000). Highly engaged communities allow natural surveillance, what Jane Jacobs (1961, p. 45) called 'eyes on the street'. Furthermore, with IT advancements, 'formal social capital' is shifting to the virtual realm (Putnam, 2000, p. 49). While this has its attractions, it raises questions about the future roles of streets, plazas, sidewalks, bus stops, train stations, and other parts of the public realm, which formerly encouraged face-to-face interactions. A role repositioning of these spaces—of destinations, and connections between destinations—is more vital than ever. The time is ripe for urban reconfiguration.

Urban Reconfiguration

There are two main ways to reconfigure urban spaces. First, make the connections between destinations stronger, speedier, safer, more equitable, and affordable. Planning policies aimed at bringing destinations closer to each other, thereby reducing the vehicle kilometers traveled, have been put to the test (Cervero, 2004; Iravani et al., 2011). Plans catering for multi-modal traffic and active transport, integration of transport modes, and prioritizing public transport are being forwarded (Appleyard & Lindsey, 2006; Cambridge Systematics, 2009; Laplante & McCann, 2008; Tiwari & Curtis, 2012). A careful placement of these connections cutting through dense, mixed land uses is being laid out for accessing jobs, schools, shops, and housing (Kelly, 2010; Puget Sound Regional Council, 2015; Suzuki et al., 2013). Strategies for linking the needy lower socioeconomic areas of the cities are being planned, and cities like Medellin in Colombia have already implemented them (Bocarejo et al., 2014; Joseph, 2014; Litman, 2016).

As important as these plans, strategies, and policies are, their implementation has been rife with obstacles in many places, while hitting dead ends in others (Cervero & Arrington, 2008; Curtis et al., 2009; Sharma et al., 2015). This brings us to the second level of reconfiguration that needs to happen through community partnership, which is a vital key to success: to transform destinations and connections between destinations into high-quality places with a strong sense of place and of community ownership.

If this transformation into 'places' needs to occur, fostering 'place making' needs to be the guiding planning principle. What exactly is place making? Definitions vary. However, they coalesce around the idea of creating places where we want to 'be', not just 'pass through'. Place making has been defined by the Urban Land Institute (as cited in Legge, 2008, p. 2) as 'the creation of economically vibrant, aesthetically attractive, lively, pedestrian-friendly places'. It can provide an economic stimulus to the once-declining urban precincts (Hall, 1998); high-quality places can be an economic boon by attracting visitors and negating a 'brain and skill-drain' (Markusen & Schrock, 2006), and more importantly they can become magnets for the so-called 'creative class'[1] (Florida, 2002). In a similar fashion, Project for Public Spaces (PPS, 2015) encapsulates the concept as 'creating good public spaces that promote people's health, happiness, and well-being'. Public 'place' evokes community pride, and the quest for place making has sparked urban and suburban transformations in diverse cities of the world. The principles of New Urbanism and Smart Growth in the US (Charter of the New Urbanism, 1993), Compact City in Europe (Dantzig & Saaty, 1973), and Liveable Neighbourhoods in Australia (Western Australian Planning Commission, 2009), among others, are rooted in place making with an objective of encouraging pedestrian- and bike-friendly mixed-use places that facilitate face-to-face interactions and build social capital. As an antidote to urban sprawl, many of these principles have also been forwarded for 'sprawl repair' (Tachieva, 2010, p. 22), and for suburban and urban retrofitting.

Movements like New Urbanism and Smart Growth have been criticized for being overly prescriptive and adopting formulaic approaches to place making (Ellis, 2002). Some accuse such movements of embracing 'cookie-cutter' planning and design as much as the standardized models of suburbanization following the Second World War did (Grant, 2005). These cultural landscapes start 'look[ing] and feel[ing] alike' and are 'experienced through superficial and stereotyped images' (Relph, 1976, p. 118).

Many place-making initiatives have used a recipe that mixes the ingredients of transport and land use in the right proportions to encourage walkability. To remedy 'place-lessness' and engender a sense of community, features of physical form contributing to aesthetic appearance are sprinkled around a fabricated theme like 'old town' or 'urban village' (Harvey, 1997, p. 68). A contextually non-responsive design process is given precedence, and 'begins by creating a tabula rasa onto which the physical features of a traditional conception of community are rolled out' (Parr, 2013, p. 118).

However, 'a Place must not only fit with our bodies, it must fit the way in which our mind works: how we perceive and image and feel' (Lynch, 1984, p. 72). None of these efforts will be effective unless the community connects to its environment holistically, both socially and through aspects of memory and functionality (Tiwari, 2010). This plays an important role in creating high-quality connected places. A better way to generate place making involves identifying and building on that place's distinctive character. This is a creative interaction between the physical setting, the activities that take place there, and the meanings and cultural values created by the individuals and community who inhabit and experience the place in the everyday (Tiwari, 2010). A key finding of the empirical research undertaken by Dovey and Woodcock (2010) at four transit-oriented developments (Subiaco in Australia, Collingwood in Canada, Dalston in Great Britain, and Fruitvale in the US) was that the residents conceptualized the character and image of these places according to their everyday experiences of them. Thus, activities in the everyday, reflective of the lifestyles and sociocultural values of the community, become the primary determinants of place character, rather than physical form and appearance.

Research clearly establishes that high-quality places conducive to walking, cycling, and transit riding can generate many significant mobility, economic, and environmental benefits (Nahlika & Chester, 2014). The greatest challenges, however, lie in building broad-based support for and market acceptance of new urban forms and green alternative modes of travel among increasingly diverse groups of stakeholders. NIMBYs (not-in-my-back-yard) and FRUITs (fear of revitalization, urban infill, and towers), among many other urban protestors, resist alteration to patterns of spatiality and mobility due to their fear of the need to change lifestyles. Implementation strategies must be developed with an understanding of human psychology and social behavior. Done properly, true place making can yield many positive benefits. Community outreach with collaborative and ethnographic approaches are important considerations. The community will mobilize if given the opportunity to 'make their own place' (McCourt, 2013), since 'it's the people who make the place' (Project for Public Spaces, 2015). By injecting their personality and verve, the community will have a heightened sense of ownership and pride (Project for Public Spaces, 2014). Local information, local perspective, smooth implementation, and the legitimacy of the project in the eyes of the community can all make the decision-making process more rationalized, effective, and democratic.

The result will be a connected place—a place that has all of the three key attributes of people, place, and transport connectivity.

Bringing the people and place connections to fruition also depends on an accurate diagnosis of the connectivity attributes and a precise prognosis of the required actions. Can an audit framework be developed that is able to measure how a place performs against the connectivity attributes? Are these attributes still valid in diverse situations and contexts, specifically in the context of the Global South, which is going to be the powerhouse of future growth? Are these attributes also valid in the face of fast-paced mega-trends in disruptive technologies? *Connecting people, connecting places* provides answers to these questions.

What's New?

Research has shown that there are barriers to making connections in three key areas:

1 Professional practices that lack interdisciplinary thinking (Glanz et al., 2016; Munoz & Paget-Seekins, 2016). *Connecting Places, Connecting People* is based on interdisciplinary thinking involving planning, transport, urban design, and sociology to resolve connection issues between transport, people, and place.
2 Community non-acceptance and outrage due to inadequate public outreach and participation (Town of Victoria Park, 2015; Weymouth & Hartz-Karp, 2015). *Connecting Places, Connecting People* puts emphasis on, and proposes ways to engage, the community as decision makers and place managers.
3 The lack of a long-term progressive vision that acknowledges the changing global landscape and lifestyles that are a result of disruptive technologies, shifting demographics, and the rising urban growth in the Global South.[2] *Connecting Places, Connecting People* confronts these challenges and tests the relevance of its design principles for the future urban landscape.

An important contribution of the book is the *Connecting People, Connecting Places* Audit Tool—a practical tool for realizing the paradigm. The tool outlines a range of measures for a continual quantitative and qualitative evaluation of the connectivity attributes. A before and after evaluation of a place using the Audit Tool can measure the success of strategies.

The book adds to the literature and thinking through its comprehensive perspective on place making. A community-led place-making effort, when complemented with the concept of transport accessibility, aspires to achieve community well-being. The focus is shifted towards making better communities through high-quality and accessible places.

The Book: What Lies Ahead?

The book has four parts. The first three parts present the concept and context, and the principles, practices, and methodology for *Connecting Places, Connecting People*. The final part demonstrates the validity of these principles, particularly in the emerging economies of the Global South, and in the face of emerging challenges thrown up by the dynamics of technological and demographic changes.

Since the aim is to create a fertile urban terrain for better communities, Chapter 2, 'Connecting Places for Better Communities', develops the key indicators and measures for these. The chapter also forwards a new way of thinking about transport and planning problems. The creation of safe, healthy, prosperous, and equitable communities becomes the main objective and outcome, while the resolution of transport and planning concerns is the co-benefit.

Reconfiguring movement systems—the in-between spaces—is discussed in Chapter 3. This leads logically to Chapter 4, which is about reconfiguring destinations as places to catalyze urban and suburban transformations. The chapters include case study examples for many different typologies, including streets, corridors, transport hubs, and transit stations, mono-use and redundant industrial zones, unused railyards and abandoned dockyards, edge city retrofits and repurposed 'big-box' shopping malls. Case studies from the US and Australia are over-represented because of these countries' longstanding love affairs with cars and their resultant auto-centric city designs.

Chapters 5 and 6 outline how to 'make the connections happen', with the focus on overcoming implementation challenges. Chapter 5, 'Remodeling Approaches: Empowering Place Making and Connectivity', discusses how to seek public buy-in through inclusive, participatory planning. Hard and soft policy measures are detailed. Collaborative and deliberative approaches are explored through case studies. The chapter describes an ethnographic engagement approach for connecting people to people and people to places. Chapter 6, 'Evaluating People, Place, and Transport Connectivity', outlines a framework to audit places against the connectivity attributes, namely people, place, and transport. Qualitative and quantitative measures emerge from global best-practice examples. An Audit Tool that puts theory into practice, and makes the connecting places, connecting people paradigm realizable, is offered for urban professionals.

Chapter 7, 'Emerging Challenges: Connected Places in the Global South', reflects on the relevance of the concept of connecting places for cities in the Global South. Current theory and practice have explored development challenges for cities in the Global South (formal and informal peri-urban developments, informal collective transport and two-wheelers, and amenities for non-motorized transport) (Feng et al., 2010; Johnston, 2004; Khisty & Arslan, 2005; Samberg et al., 2011; Sclar & Touber, 2013; Zheng et al., 2011). This chapter investigates the success or failure of these practices through the lens of 'people and place'.

The unfolding mega-trends of the twenty-first century and the challenges they pose are discussed in Chapter 8, 'Emerging Challenges: Technology Mega-trends and Demographic Shifts'.

These last four chapters collectively provide an implementation framework for a new paradigm of living in the twenty-first century. As we move into a future shaped by a global mega-trend of disruptive technology, the question to be asked is: can this disruption be turned into innovation? The leap in technological transformation could be an enabler with the end-user—that is, the community—who could be proactively involved in creating a compelling vision for their everyday environment based on shared values.

Notes

1 Because of the push in creative enterprises in the twenty-first century, an economic transformation is taking place. A creative economy is emerging. There is a rise of the creative class—primarily people involved in running small businesses, working in areas of education, architecture, biotech, engineering, theater, and the like.
2 As per the *United Nations Development Program Report 2005*, the Global North refers to the 57 countries that have a Human Development Index (HDI) above 0.8, while the Global South refers to the rest of the countries of the world, most of which are located in the Southern Hemisphere (with the exception of Australia and New Zealand).

References

All online references retrieved August 17, 2016.

Albrecht, V. (2005). Role of environmental regulation in shaping the built and natural environment. In E. Ben-Joseph & T. S. Szold (Eds.) *Regulating place: Standards and the shaping of urban America* (pp. 271–292). New York: Routledge.

Appleyard, D. (1981). *Liveable streets*. Berkeley, CA: University of California Press.

Appleyard, B., & Lindsey, C. (2006, October). At home in the zone: Creating livable streets in the US. *Planning 72*(9), 30–35. Retrieved from http://nacto.org/docs/usdg/at_home_in_the_zone_appleyard.pdf.

Bates, D. (2010, August 26). Great crawl of China: Vendors cash in on 60-mile traffic jam that's lasted 11 days—with no end in sight. *Daily Mail*. Retrieved from www.dailymail.co.uk/news/article-1306058/China-traffic-jam-enters-11th-day-officials-admit-weeks.html.

Bocarejo, J., Portilla, I., Velásquez, J., Cruz, M., Peñaa, A., & Oviedob, D. R. (2014). An innovative transit system and its impact on low income users: The case of the Metrocable in Medellín. *Journal of Transport Geography 39*, 49–61.

Cambridge Systematics. (2009). *Moving cooler: An analysis of transportation strategies for reducing greenhouse gas emissions*. Washington, D.C.: Research study, Urban Land Institute.

Cervero, R. (2004). *Transit-oriented development in the United States: Experiences, challenges, and prospects.* Retrieved from www.scribd.com/document/64040490/Cervero-TOD-in-the-US-2004.

Cervero, R. (2010). Transit transformations. In W. Ascher & C. Krupp (Eds.) *Physical infrastructure development: Balancing the growth, equity, and environmental imperatives* (pp. 165–187). New York: Palgrave Macmillan.

Cervero, R., & Arrington, G. B. (2008). *Effects of TOD on housing, parking, and travel.* Washington, D.C: Transportation Research Board.

Charter of the New Urbanism (1993). The movement. Retrieved from www.cnu.org/who-we-are/movement.

Curtis, C., Renne, J. L., & Bertolini, L. (2009). *Transit oriented development: Making it happen.* Farnham: Ashgate.

Dantzig, G. B., & Saaty, T. L. (1973). *Compact city: Plan for a liveable urban environment.* San Francisco, CA: W. H. Freeman.

DiMento, J., & Ellis, C. (2013). *Changing lanes.* Cambridge, MA, and London: The MIT Press.

Dovey, K., & Woodcock, I. (2010). *The character of urban intensification 2006–2010.* Melbourne, VIC: University of Melbourne.

Ellis, C. (2002). The New Urbanism: Critiques and rebuttals. *Journal of Urban Design 7*(3), 261–291.

Feng, X., Zhang, J., Fujiwara, A., Hayashi, Y., & Kato, H. (2010). Improved feedback modeling of transport in enlarging urban areas of developing countries. *Frontiers of Computer Science in China 4*(1), 112–122.

Florida, R. (2002). *The rise of the creative class.* New York: Basic Books.

Giles-Corti, B. (2006). *The impact of urban form on public health.* Canberra: Australian State of the Environment Committee, Department of the Environment and Heritage. Retrieved from www.environment.gov.au/node/22559.

Glaeser, E. (2005). Review of Richard Florida's *The rise of the creative class. Regional Science and Urban Economics 35*(5), 593–596. Retrieved from http://scholar.harvard.edu/files/glaeser/files/book_review_of_richard_floridas_the_rise_of_the_creative_class.pdf.

Glaeser, E. L., Kallal, H. D., Scheinkman, J. A., & Shleifer, A. (1992). Growth in cities. *Journal of Political Economy 100*(6), 1126–1152.

Glanz, K., Handy, S. L., Henderson, K. E., Slater, S. J., Davis, E. L., & Powell, L. M. (2016). Built environment assessment: Multidisciplinary perspectives. *Social Science & Medicine (SSM)—Population Health 2*, 24–31.

Grant, J. (2005). *Planning the good community: New Urbanism in theory and practice.* New York: Routledge.

Hall, P. (1998). *Cities in civilization: Culture, technology, and urban order.* London: Weidenfeld & Nicolson.

Harvey, D. (1997). The New Urbanism and the communitarian trap. *Harvard Design Magazine 1*(2). Retrieved from http://wsm.wsu.edu/stories/2008/Spring/1harvey.pdf.

Iravani, H., Mirhoseini, A., & Rasoolzadeh, M. (2011). Defining land use intensity based on roadway level-of-service targets. *Journal of Transport and Land Use 4*(1), 59–69.

Jacobs, J. (1961). *The death and life of great American cities.* New York: Random House.

Johnston, R. A. (2004). The urban transportation planning process. In S. Hanson & G. Giuliano (Eds.) *The geography of urban transportation* (pp. 115–141). New York: Guilford.

Jones, P., Marshall, S., & Boujenko, N. (2008). Creating more people-friendly urban streets through 'Link and Place' street planning and design. *IATSS Research 32*(1), 14–25.

Joseph, C. (2014, August 26). Medellín Metrocable improves mobility for residents of informal settlements. Retrieved from www.thecityfix.com/blog/medellin-metrocable-improves-mobility-informal-settlements-low-income-accessibility-equity-development-coby-joseph/.

Kelly, J. (2010). *The cities we need.* Carlton, Victoria: Grattan Institute Report.

Khisty, C. J., & Arslan, T. (2005). Possibilities of steering the transportation planning process in the face of bounded rationality and unbounded uncertainty. *Transportation Research Part C: Emerging Technologies 13*(2), 77–92.

Laplante, J., & McCann, B. (2008). Complete streets: We can get there from here. *Institute of Transport Engineers 78*(5), 24–28. Retrieved from www.smartgrowthamerica.org/documents/cs/resources/cs-ite-may08.pdf.

Legge, K. (2008). *An overview of international place making practice: Profession or ploy*. Paddington, NSW: Place Partners. Retrieved from www.ictcsociety.org/LinkClick.aspx?fileticket=gxhiMdrnhPc%3D&tabid=135&mid=565&forcedownload=true.

Litman, T. (2016, August 24). *Affordable–accessible housing in a dynamic city*. Victoria, BC: Victoria Transport Policy Institute. Retrieved from www.vtpi.org/aff_acc_hou.pdf.

Lynch, K. (1984). *Site planning*. Cambridge, MA: The MIT Press.

Markusen, A. & Schrock, G. (2006). The distinctive city: Divergent patterns in growth, hierarchy and specialization. *Urban Studies 43*(8), 1301–1323.

McCourt, W. (2013, June 11). The people make the place. The World Bank. Retrieved from http://blogs.worldbank.org/governance/people-make-place.

Monderman, H. (2005). *Shared space: Room for everyone: A new vision for public spaces*. Groningen: Fryslân Province. Retrieved from http://shared-space.org/wp-content/uploads/2014/10/Room-for-everyone.pdf.

Munoz, J. C., & Paget-Seekins, L. (2016). *Restructuring public transport through bus rapid transit*. Bristol: Policy Press.

Nahlika, M. J., & Chester, M. V. (2014). Transit-oriented smart growth can reduce life-cycle environmental impacts and household costs in Los Angeles. *Transport Policy 35*, 21–30.

Newman, O. (1972). *Defensible space: Crime prevention through urban design*. New York: Macmillan.

Newman, P., & Kenworthy, J. (2015). *The end of automobile dependence: How cities are moving beyond car-based planning*. Washington, D.C.: Island Press.

Parr, A. (2013). *The wrath of capital: Neoliberalism and climate change politics*. New York: Columbia University Press.

Project for Public Spaces (PPS). (2014, May 13). Why public places are the key to transforming our communities. Retrieved from www.pps.org/blog/why-public-places-are-the-key-to-transforming-our-communities/.

Project for Public Spaces (PPS). (2015, June 10). What is placemaking? Retrieved from www.pps.org/reference/what_is_placemaking/.

Puget Sound Regional Council. (2015). *Transit-supportive densities and land uses: A PSRC guidance paper*. Seattle, WA: Puget Sound Regional Council. Retrieved from www.psrc.org/assets/12239/TSDLUGuidancePaper.pdf.

Putnam, R. (1995). Bowling alone: America's declining social capital: An interview with Robert Putnam. *Journal of Democracy 6*(1), 65–78.

Putnam, R. D. (2000). *Bowling alone: The collapse and revival of American community*. New York: Simon & Schuster.

Relph, E. (1976). *Place and placelessness*. London: Pion.

Renne, J. (2005). *Transit-oriented development in Western Australia: Attitudes, obstacles and opportunities*. Perth, WA: Western Australia Department for Planning and Infrastructure, Planning and Transport Research Centre.

Samberg, S., Bassok, A., & Holman, S. (2011). Method for evaluation of sustainable transportation: Toward a comprehensive approach. *Transportation Research Record: Journal of the Transportation Research Board 2242*, 1–8.

Sclar, E., & Touber, J. (2013). Economic fall-out of urban transport systems: An institutional analysis. In H. Dimitriou & R. Gakenheimer (Eds.) *Urban transport in the developing world: A handbook of policy and practice* (pp. 174–203). Northampton, MA: Edward Elgar.

Sharma, R., Newman, P., & Matan, A. (2015). Urban rail: India's great opportunity for sustainable urban development. London: Association for European Transport. Retrieved from http://abstracts.aetransport.org/paper/index/id/4683/confid/20.

Shipnuck, A. (2011, August 19). PGA tour commissioner Tim Finchem has made a lot of golfers very, very rich—and a few very, very angry. Retrieved from www.golf.com/special-features/pga-tour-commissioner-tim-finchem-has-made-lot-golfers-very-very-rich-151-and-few-v.

Shutkin, W. (2005). From pollution control to place making: The role of environmental regulation in creating communities of place. In E. Ben-Joseph

& T. S. Szold (Eds.) *Regulating place: Standards and the shaping of urban America* (pp. 253–270). New York: Routledge.

Suzuki, H., Cervero, R., & Iuchi, K. (2013). *Transforming cities with transit: Transit and land-use integration for sustainable urban development.* Washington, D.C.: World Bank

Tachieva, G. (2010). *Sprawl repair manual.* Washington, D.C.: Island Press.

Tiwari, R. (2010). *Space–body–ritual: Performativity in the city.* Maryland, WA: Lexington Books.

Tiwari, R., & Curtis, C. (2010). Approaches to arterial road design in Perth: The challenges ahead. In I. Alexander, S. Greive, & D. Hedgcock (Eds.) *Planning perspectives from Western Australia: A reader in theory and practice* (pp. 289–305). Fremantle, WA: Fremantle Press.

Tiwari, R., & Curtis, C. (2012). A three-pronged approach to urban arterial design: A functional + physical + social classification. *Urban Design International 17*(2), 129–143.

Town of Victoria Park. (2015). *Public participation literature review.* Perth, WA: Town of Victoria Park.

Western Australian Planning Commission. (2009). *Liveable neighbourhoods.* Perth, WA: Western Australian Planning Commission. Retrieved from www.planning.wa.gov.au/dop_pub_pdf/LN_Text_update_02.pdf.

Weymouth, R., & Hartz-Karp, J. (2015). Deliberative collaborative governance as a democratic reform to resolve wicked problems and improve trust. *Journal of Economic and Social Policy 14*(1), 4. Retrieved from http://epubs.scu.edu.au/jesp/vol17/iss1/4/?utm_source=epubs.scu.edu.au%2Fjesp%2Fvol17%2Fiss1%2F4&utm_medium=PDF&utm_campaign=PDFCoverPages.

Zheng, J., Atkinson-Palombo, C., McCahill, C., O'Hara, R., & Garrick, N. (2011). Quantifying the economic domain of transportation sustainability. *Transportation Research Record: Journal of the Transportation Research Board* 2242, 19–28.

CHAPTER 2

CONNECTING PLACES FOR BETTER COMMUNITIES

How can better communities be created through place connectivity? This chapter examines current evidence for the many community-based benefits—social, environmental, and economic—of connected places. These include high satisfaction for residents, happiness, social capital, social and cultural diversity, a sense of safety, housing affordability, and civic participation, among others. Key indicators and measures for a better community are marshaled to forward a new way of thinking about planning and transport issues. Case studies are discussed from around the world, but primarily from US and Australian cities, considering that the majority of these are planned around the automobile and have resulted in auto-centric societies with immense social and environmental problems (Jacobs, 1961; McManus, 2005; Putnam, 2001).

There is no simple definition of a 'better community'. The term implies a clean, safe, and healthy community with access to social infrastructure, public spaces, housing, and other neighborhood offerings. Public agencies work in partnership with community members to plan and deliver better services (Tiwari et al., 2014).

A better community is also, to a considerable degree, a 'complete community' in the sense that many day-to-day activities are within easy reach of residents. Moreover, 'completeness' means that everyone who works or in some way is engaged there, whether a well-paid professional or a modestly paid pre-school teacher, has the means to live there. A characteristic trait of better communities, then, is that they embrace diversity, whether in terms of the make-up of land uses, the range of housing costs, or their sociocultural compositions. With a sense of belonging and identity stimulated in such communities, they experience high levels of well-being. Key indicators for a better community are, therefore, safety, health, prosperity, equity, and identity, as demonstrated in Figure 2.1.

Who creates a good community and how is it done? For the last two decades, urban design theorists have discussed the nature of better communities and where responsibility lies. Some conclude that public spaces such as streets and urban squares act as the center of activity within a community. By promoting greater interaction

THE CONCEPT

Figure 2.1 Agents/indicators of better communities

between people, public spaces bind the community together (Gehl, 2010). Other theorists conclude that the way in which people use and colonize public spaces builds a shared sense of belonging and ownership and enhanced communal spirit and identity (Dixon & Durrheim, 2000; Lynch, 1981). All agree that places where people want to be—to live, work, shop, or play—must have high-quality public 'realms', meaning that streets, sidewalks, parks, transit stations, and other public spaces become hubs of shared communal experiences.

A high-quality public realm encourages everyday, routine encounters by 'triangulating' functions. This can be by the mere positioning of a bench, newspaper vending machine, and coffee kiosk near a transit stop (Project for Public Spaces, 2012). Such public places become the best breeding grounds for creativity, where people can meet easily and frequently. They start providing a choice of activity, inclusivity, and user interactivity and promote community engagement and civic participation (Carmona et al., 2003). The Circle in Uptown Normal, Illinois, is an example of a creative breeding ground because of its proximity and connectivity to the Children's Discovery Museum and the bustling Amtrak station, and being within walking distance of Illinois State University. The Circle promotes a microcommunity of students, professors, families, children, and visitors who energize this green space at different times of the day, not only with their everyday activities but also with special events such as arts, festivals, and farmers' markets (US Environmental Protection Agency, 2011).

Triangulating functions can connect places and recover time lost in daily commuting. Evidence suggests that each additional ten minutes lost through commuting decreases an individual's involvement in formal community affairs (public meetings, volunteering, church groups, and so on) by 10 percent. Studies demonstrate that a reduction in informal social interaction is also a consequence of increased

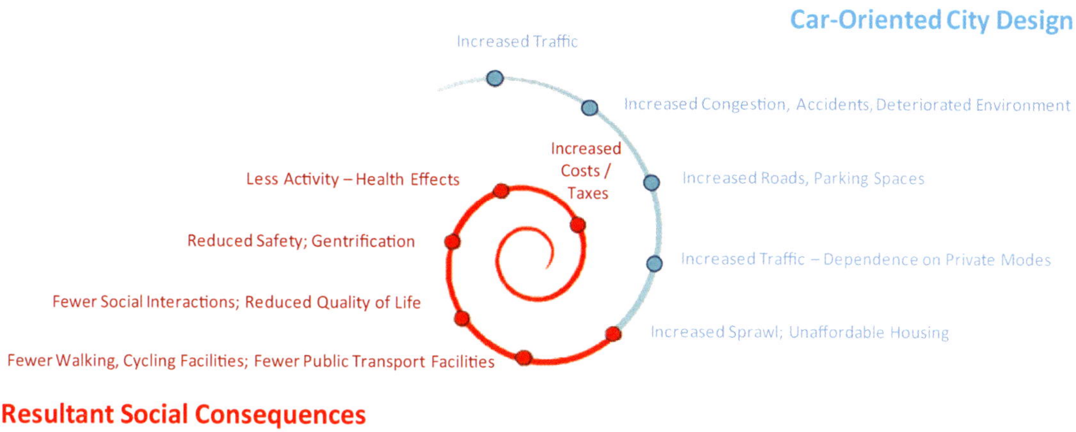

Car-Oriented City Design

(Diagram: spiral showing car-oriented city design consequences)

Outer spiral (blue): Increased Traffic → Increased Congestion, Accidents, Deteriorated Environment → Increased Roads, Parking Spaces → Increased Traffic – Dependence on Private Modes → Increased Sprawl; Unaffordable Housing

Inner spiral (red) – **Resultant Social Consequences**: Increased Costs / Taxes → Less Activity – Health Effects → Reduced Safety; Gentrification → Fewer Social Interactions; Reduced Quality of Life → Fewer Walking, Cycling Facilities; Fewer Public Transport Facilities

commuting time (Putnam, 2001). Further, car-dependent commuting negatively impacts the health of the local and global ecosystems due to air pollution and transport greenhouse gas emissions (André & Rapone, 2009), along with the health of the commuters and the wider community. Short, solitary car commutes in congested traffic, which are common in high-income countries (Bhalla et al., 2007), contribute to road traffic injury. Moreover, the spread of car-based infrastructure is associated with negative social justice outcomes such as gentrified neighborhoods separated by elevated motorways or impoverished enclaves concentrated along congested urban arterials and at urban peripheries (Soja, 1995). Heavy traffic on roads with accompanying noise (Hänninen & Knol, 2011) discourages people from going outside and interacting with their neighbors. Less social interaction, reduced quality of life, reduced safety, and less physical activity are consequences of designing the city to accommodate motorized traffic. This leads to the quality of life deteriorating in a negative spiral, as is illustrated in Figure 2.2.

Growing research over the last decade demonstrates that growing social capital generated by social networks, and associated norms of trust and reciprocity, are pivotal to a safe, healthy, and happy citizenry (Sander, 2002). Connecting places contributes to repairing the state of 'car-disconnect' by rebuilding the social fabric of communities—the fabric that has been slowly but profoundly damaged by car-based infrastructure.

Figure 2.2 The negative social consequences of car-oriented city design

Safe Communities

Safety from Traffic

Globally, over 1.2 million people, mostly pedestrians, die per year in traffic crashes. The number of deaths has been growing every year (Welle et al., 2015). Studies show that the severity of injuries of pedestrians and cyclists in accidents and collisions is directly related to impact speed. The Australian Transport Safety Bureau estimates that for every 10-kph reduction in speed on an urban main road, road crashes and fatalities drop by 30 percent (Commonwealth of Australia, 2008).

THE CONCEPT

Figure 2.3 Chicanes in place at NE 98th Street, Seattle

Source: Adapted from Google Maps by Google, 2015.

Can the behavior of motorists be modified through the physical design of roads? An empirical study shows a correlation between improved visibility and/or increased carriageway width with increasing vehicle speeds (Department for Transport, 2007). On a road 5 meters wide with forward visibility of 10 meters, cars travel at an average speed of 11 mph. Each meter increase in road width provides for visibility improvement of 2–4 meters, resulting in an increase in average speed of 1–5 mph. Disrupting clear sightlines on roads through horizontal displacements, such as chicanes, or vertical displacements, such as speed humps, can dramatically slow cars down. After chicanes were installed at NE 98th Street in Seattle, Washington (Figure 2.3), car speeds reduced by 18–35 percent (Marek & Walgren, 1998). The relationship between visibility, road width, and driver speed also applies at road junctions.

Various traffic-calming measures have been successful in reducing vehicle speeds. These measures include installing traffic management devices and signage, modifying road spaces, reconfiguring the number of lanes devoted to cars, providing street parking, widening sidewalks, planting trees, and installing street furniture. Over the long term, crashes and injuries are reduced by 15–40 percent. A recent before-and-after study showed reduction in collision frequency by 40 percent, and fatalities from one to zero (Anderson et al., 1997; Litman, 1999). Traffic calming, if done throughout the entire residential neighborhood, limits and re-routes traffic out of the neighborhood, resulting in increased safety.

Progressive traffic engineers and designers embrace a radically different approach called 'shared space'. A shared environment for cars, pedestrians, and other transport modes is created by removing the traditional separation between vehicles and other road users. All traffic control devices, street signs, and road markings are removed. The philosophy behind shared space is one of risk compensation, based on the assumption that individual motorists are likely to adjust their driving behavior in response to different levels of perceived risk. By allowing various road users to mingle in the road space, drivers are impelled to drive safely to avoid collision and conflicts (Engwicht, 2005). This strategy has not been popular with pedestrians, especially the elderly and those with a visual handicap (Devon County Council, 1991). Instead, city-wide traffic-calming initiatives in places like Odense in Denmark and Freiburg in Germany have been more successful in reducing car use and hence increasing road safety (Ralph & John, 2011).

Safety against Crime

There is a strong correlation between personal safety against crime and elements of the built environment, such as reduced setbacks, night lightings, front porches, natural surveillance, and active land use (Alfonzo, 2005; Tiwari, 2015). Crime prevention through environmental design (CPTED) links criminology and urban design. The opportunity for crime can be reduced through appropriate design of the built environment (Newman, 1972). After CPTED interventions, the Five Oaks project in Ohio, USA, reported a 26 percent decrease in recorded crime. Residential areas such as Harbordale in Florida, USA, reported a significant reduction in crime rates, as well as a 5.5 percent increase in property values (Schneider & Kitchen, 2002).

Increased perceptions of safety are attributed to increased levels of activity on the streets (Gehl, 2010). Areas with 'movement' and 'place' functions (Kelly et al., 2012), with frequent passers-by, shop owners, and residents who keep an eye on the street (Jacobs, 1961), are perceived as safer. Other factors contribute to perceptions of safety: buildings oriented towards streets so residents can watch the street life; streets with stores, bars, cafés, and restaurants with bustling activity; active frontages with increased openings at ground level and reduced solid:void ratio in a building façade (Carmona et al., 2003),[1] resulting in improved transparency; on-street parking adjacent to mixed uses; and informal street vendors (Tiwari, 2015).

A connected street fabric with a multifaceted mix of uses creates a safe, interesting, lively public realm where community can interact and bond.

Healthy Communities

Walking and cycling are everyday activities recognized as critical for a healthy community (Badland & Schofield, 2005; McCormack et al., 2004; Saelens & Handy, 2008). Obesogenic environments where people walk only from the main door to parking lots minimize physical activity and contribute to recent trends in inactivity and weight statistics. In compact neighborhoods with diverse land use patterns, people spend twice as much time weekly (137 minutes on average) walking to carry out everyday errands (Giles-Corti, 2006). About half as many residents are overweight compared to neighborhoods where activities have been separated and disconnected by modern zoning and design codes (Giles-Corti, 2006; Lehman & Boyle, 2007; Marshall et al., 2014; Saelens et al., 2003). Research further indicates that neighborhoods designed around public transport record more walking trips. A 2005 US travel survey found that 16 percent of all recorded walking trips were part of public transit trips and that these trips tended to be longer than average walking trips (Weinstein & Schimek,

2005). Walking to access public transport demands a high level of street connectivity and destination proximity (measured by density of intersections) (Ewing & Cervero, 2010).

Besides the neighborhood structure, walkability is affected by the quality of the public realm. Public infrastructure such as sidewalks facilitates walking. Residents tend to walk 65 percent more in a neighborhood with sidewalks (Giles-Corti & Donovan, 2002). Safety on sidewalks is another critical factor; 43 percent of people with safe places to walk within ten minutes of home reached recommended levels of physical activity; those without safe places to walk achieved just 27 percent of the recommended level (Powell et al., 2003).

A lack of safe sidewalks discourages children from walking or cycling to schools (US Department of Health and Human Services, 2011). In 1969, 50 percent of children in the US walked or cycled to school; by 2001, this figure had declined to only 15 percent (Hubsmith, 2007), as more parents drove their children to school (Weigand, 2008). Walking or cycling to school helps meet the recommended levels of 60 or more minutes of daily physical activity recommended for children (US Environmental Protection Agency, 2015).

Apart from influencing the physical health of communities, connected places encourage happy and stress-free communities. A high-quality public realm that provides a network of green infrastructure with tree-lined streets and green urban spaces can reduce stress and improve self-esteem and mood disturbance (anger, fatigue, and so on) by connecting people with places.

Prosperous Communities: Jobs, Housing, and Transport

In the metropolitan US, the top six ranked walkable areas have 38 percent higher GDP (Benjamin, 2014) than the lower-ranked walkable metros. This indicates that communities that are economically vibrant and productive are those where people can access services and jobs by walking. To achieve this level of walkability, it is important that these places have the right mix of services, jobs, and housing.

Areas with more jobs than homes can result in high rents. This is evident in metropolitan areas of Austin, Houston, San Francisco, and San Jose, among others. Job gains of 2.4 percent in 2012 saw simultaneous rent increases exceeding 3.5 percent. By contrast, job growth in metros in the US with the smallest rent increases or actual declines averaged just 1.4 percent in 2012. The increases in the costs of land and rent, accompanied by inadequate affordable housing, preclude low-income families from living in these areas. They are pushed out to peripheral areas and forced to spend a large portion of their budgets on transport (Litman, 2016). Owing to the costs of transport and longer commutes, few of these households have sufficient money for healthy food and healthcare, and their ability to accumulate wealth by shifting from rental properties to their own homes is limited (Sanchez et al., 2015). Increased stress levels in these households result in fragile well-being and, in some cases, reduced academic achievement (Litman, 2016). Such households are also vulnerable to the risks of increased costs associated with mortgages, petrol, and inflation (Dodson & Sipe, 2008).

Developing policy guidelines and regulations to incorporate affordable accessible housing into transit-oriented developments, as in the US, is crucial (Center for Transit-Oriented Development, 2009; Chapple, 2009). The focus of many reforms in the US has been to:

- adjust zoning regulations to promote diversity, inclusiveness, and incentive-based development;
- subsidize housing redevelopment and renovation;
- impose rent control;
- implement parking maximums;
- introduce programs to improve transit awareness and knowledge;
- provide greater access to transit discounts;
- provide transit-oriented targeted housing finance; and
- transfer taxes.

An example of incentive-based development is California's 'density bonus', which is offered in exchange for the provision of affordable housing. City jurisdictions can allow developers to extend the normally allowed building envelope to accommodate 35 percent additional units as an incentive for offering affordable housing. Another incentive comes in the form of an efficient and smooth project approval process for projects that incorporate fair labor practices, energy-efficient, affordable housing, and ample open spaces for the community. An example is Berkeley's Voluntary Green Pathway Program. Similar programs are being developed, including the Vancouver EcoDensity Program, Seattle's Multi-Family Tax Exemption Program, and others (Grube-Cavers & Patterson, 2015; Litman, 2016).

Automobile travel costs are significantly higher than those of walking, cycling, or public transit. A study conducted in Queensland, Australia, found that savings achieved by a kilometer walked or cycled instead of vehicular travel are 20.7 cents for decongestion, 168.0 cents towards health, 35.0 cents in vehicle operating costs, 6.8 cents in infrastructure savings, and 5.9 cents towards the environment. Thus, the economy benefits by a total of A$14.30 from a cyclist and A$8.48 from a pedestrian who cycles/walks 20 minutes to work and back (Department of Infrastructure & Transport, 2013, p. 6).

Of course, people's mobility needs and abilities are different; some can walk or cycle and use transit, while others are dependent on automobiles. Cost reduction for lower-income motorists can occur through owning older, low-value vehicles. Usually maintenance and repairs are carried by the owners, and insurance costs are kept to a minimum. However, it still means that they spend a minimum of US$3,200 annually for owning and operating a vehicle (Litman, 2016). Fuel costs can be lowered by reducing the trip length through destination proximity. But more importantly, a modal shift to walking/cycling and transit can be achieved by the provision of good network connectivity, smooth and fast modal transition, and reduced fares. Strategies for connecting places through developing mixed use and walkable places close to each other become critical.

Connected places with high-quality affordable modes of transport and a balance of jobs and inclusive housing options become the linchpin for prosperous communities.

Equitable Communities: Gender, Age, Physically Challenged

As discussed above, access to affordable transport modes, including public transport, is exceedingly important for disadvantaged and excluded social groups (with exclusion based on factors such as low income, age, gender, and physical fitness). Locational disadvantage, discussed in the previous section, is an additional factor working against equitable access to public services such as healthcare facilities, education, shopping, and employment (Department for Transport, 2000).

In many societies, there are no adequate transportation alternatives to the automobile for the elderly. The needs of this sub-group are generally poorly understood. With an increase in age, there is a reduction in overall mobility and a resultant change in transport modes. A study published in 2008 by the Federal Ministry of Transport and Digital Infrastructure in Germany showed a decrease in use of car and an increase in walking after 55 years of age, with a further increase in use of public transport after 75 (INFAS Institute of Applied Social Sciences, 2008).

From an environmental justice perspective, it is important for the elderly to remain mobile (Tacken, 1998). Maintaining mobility minimizes the depression associated with the loss of the ability to drive, so individuals can maintain their quality of life. In research carried out in the area of London, UK, Su and Bell (2009) demonstrated the importance of public transport and walking for older people to remain independent. Connected places provide opportunities for well-designed, accessible, and affordable transport systems, and a pedestrian-friendly environment encourages the elderly to remain mobile.

Family demands on women are different from those on men, and this dictates the way in which they respond to the daily commute. In Nairobi, Kenya, for example, 24 percent of male heads of households used cars compared to 9 percent of female heads (Levy, cited in Peters, 2001, p. 11). In Northern Ireland, 79 percent of men had a full driving licence, compared to 61 percent of women, indicating that women relied less on private vehicles than men (Roads Service, 2003, p. 9). While men are more likely to rely on private vehicles, women tend to access jobs, childcare, education, healthcare, and other services by public transport. This is true in cities of both the developing and the developed world. The need to undertake multiple trips, many at off-peak hours away from main transport routes, and the greater distance between home and work severely limit women's capacity for household and non-household activities. An integrated public transport fare structure, such as in Hong Kong, makes it more convenient and cheaper for women to make multiple short trips (Pardo, 2011).

Another key concern for women using public transport is safety. A high incidence of verbal and physical abuse, pickpocketing, and bag snatching discourages women and girls from using public amenities (Condon et al., 2007; Hamilton & Jenkins, 2000; World Bank, 2014). As a result, they are denied equal access to economic, social, and cultural opportunities.

Addressing concerns of public transport access to services and jobs and improved walkability can encourage women, the elderly, and people with disabilities to participate more fully in economic, social, and political activities. Connected places are therefore critical in reducing the isolation, vulnerability, and dependency of these groups. Effective action would improve the lives of many of the world's most economically weak citizens.

Community Identity, Social Interaction, and Place Making

Much research has shown that social space can be impaired by high-speed car traffic and a car-dominated environment. Appleyard's (1976) study in Ciudad Guayana, Venezuela, was the first of its kind to demonstrate that the sense of community on streets is stronger with less traffic. This is a consequence of greater interaction between neighbors and a better social environment in general.

A similar study in 2008 compared the impact of traffic on a neighborhood located in north Bristol, UK (Hart, 2008). A light-traffic street (140 vehicles per day) had almost three times the number of gathering spots, including cross-street locations, compared with medium-traffic (8,420 vehicles per day) or heavy-traffic (21,130 vehicles per day) streets. Residents on heavy-traffic streets had fewer friends and acquaintances on the same street than residents on light-traffic streets (Hart, 2008). This becomes especially important, since a low crime rate in a neighborhood is correlated to how many neighbors know each other well. Strong social networks benefit people directly by helping them feel that they are safe, that their homes are protected, and that they are looked after. The social capital of the community aids in generating a sense of community well-being (Putnam, 2001).

In their studies of great streets and boulevards around the world, Jacobs et al. (2002) found that the quality of the 'pedestrian realm' within road space plays an important part in the livability and liveliness of the streets (Figures 2.4 and 2.5). The best streets and boulevards establish a pedestrian realm that extends beyond the sidewalks to include tree-lined median and access roads. International Boulevard in Fruitvale, California, is a prime example. By extending the pedestrian realm, a 'slow space' has been created where the vehicle speed automatically reduces due to adjacent pedestrian activities. This helps in making the boundaries between the traffic zone and pedestrian pathways less distinct (Figure 2.5).

The pedestrian realm around spaces oriented to transport functions, such as transit stations and bus stops, can be transformed through place making into community hubs that foster diverse activities. The potential uses for such areas can range from eating places

THE CONCEPT

Figure 2.4 A strong pedestrian realm alongside a slow access lane allows activities to flourish in Barcelona

Source: Picture by R. Tiwari (2013).

Figure 2.5 Extending the pedestrian realm: International Boulevard in Fruitvale, CA, with and without the extended pedestrian realm

Source: Picture by R. Tiwari (2008).

and performance venues to markets and art galleries, especially if there is an adjacent plaza or public space. These activities thrive by attracting new customers from the passing commuter traffic. The commercial value of these neighborhoods is enhanced as a result (Nelson, 2015).

These multi-use spaces offer a choice of activity, social interaction, inclusion, robustness, and legibility, and become communal hubs; and when developed through a process of close community participation and a bottom-up approach, they become successful in instilling a sense of ownership. Community is able to strengthen its own identity around these unique hubs, since questions of 'who we are' are ultimately linked to questions of 'where we are' (Dixon & Durrheim, 2000, p. 27).

Close

This chapter has outlined a case for place connectivity to foster better communities. Health, safety, prosperity, identity, and equity are key measures of stronger, sustainable communities. Connected places can stimulate social interaction and inclusion through a combination of urban design and policy interventions.

A quality public realm with equitable, convenient access promotes a high quality of life in any community. Connected places must promote a mix of housing (including affordable housing), jobs, and services. Developers must have incentives to address social equity concerns, encourage local community spaces and work centers, and incorporate retail centers to cater to all segments of society. These should ideally be within walking distance of mass transit. A mixed-income community is essential to provide the taxation base to subsidize affordable housing. Careful planning can desegregate society, add diversity of experiences, promote tolerance for social and political differences, and enhance democratic practices (Gans, 1961).

Accessibility improvements around transit points through place making can connect people to places. Successful place making encourages people-to-people connectivity and the accumulation of social capital. However, local residents' disapproval of components of accessibility improvements like high density and social diversity has led to a NIMBY (not-in-my-back-yard) attitude that can hinder development that is meant to benefit all sections of society (Machell et al., 2009). There is an urgent need for the developing agencies to conduct public outreach and make the community aware of the pros and cons of development options, thus enabling people to make informed choices. It is critical to engage with all sections of the community and hear the voices of marginalized groups, such as immigrants, the economically weak, people of different ethnic origins, the elderly, and the physically challenged. Engaging constructively with diverse groups in the decision-making process is essential for creating a sense of ownership of new proposals. The heightened sense of community can be considered the software for creating better communities and can only run on the hardware of a high-quality public realm and sustainable infrastructure—hardware that urgently needs reconfiguration.

Note

1   The solid:void ratio in a building façade is the area of the solid wall divided by the area of the façade covered by window and door openings. It is an indicator of the level of opacity versus transparency.

References

All online references retrieved August 17, 2016.

Alfonzo, M. A. (2005). To walk or not to walk? The hierarchy of walking needs. *Environment and Behavior 37*(6), 808–836.

Anderson, R., McLean, A., Farmer, M., Lee, B., & Brooks, C. (1997). Vehicle travel speeds and the incidence of fatal pedestrian collisions. *Accident Analysis and Prevention 29*(5), 667–674.

André, M., & Rapone, M. (2009). Analysis and modelling of the pollutant emissions from European cars regarding the driving characteristics and test cycles. *Atmospheric Environment 43*(5), 986–995.

Appleyard, D. (1976). *Planning a pluralist city*. Cambridge, MA: The MIT Press.

Badland, H., & Schofield, G. (2005). Transport, urban design, and physical activity: An evidence-based update. *Transportation Research D 10*(3), 177–196.

Benjamin, J. (2014). *America's most walkable cities: And what they have in common*. Retrieved from https://urbanful.org/2014/06/20/walkable-cities/.

Bhalla, K., Ezzati, M., Mahal, A., Salomon, J., & Reich, M. (2007). A risk-based method for modeling traffic fatalities. *Risk Analysis 27*(1), 125–136.

Carmona, M., Heath, T., Oc, T., & Tiesdell, S. (2003). *Public places–urban spaces*. Oxford: Elsevier.

Center for Transit-Oriented Development. (2009). *Mixed income housing near transit: Increasing affordability with location efficiency*. Retrieved from www.reconnectingamerica.org/assets/Uploads/091030ra201mixedhousefinal.pdf.

Chapple, K. (2009, August). *Mapping susceptibility to gentrification: The Early Warning toolkit*. Retrieved from http://communityinnovation.berkeley.edu/reports/Gentrification-Report.pdf.

Commonwealth of Australia. (2008). *Transport safety report*. ACT: Commonwealth of Australia. Retrieved from www.atsb.gov.au/media/27749/annual_review_08.pdf.

Condon, S., Lieber, M., & Maillochon, F. (2007). Feeling unsafe in public places: Understanding women's fears. *Revue française de sociologie 48*, 101–128.

Department of Infrastructure & Transport. (2013). *Walking, riding and access to public transport: Supporting active travel in Australian communities*. Retrieved from https://infrastructure.gov.au/infrastructure/pab/active_transport/files/infra1874_mcu_active_travel_report_final.pdf.

Department for Transport. (2000). *Social exclusion and the provision of public transport*. London: Department for Transport. Retrieved from http://citeseerx.ist.psu.edu/viewdoc/download?doi=10.1.1.232.9613&rep=rep1&type=pdf.

Department for Transport. (2007). *Manual for streets*. London: Department for Transport. Retrieved from www.gov.uk/government/uploads/system/uploads/attachment_data/file/341513/pdfmanforstreets.pdf.

Devon County Council. (1991). *Traffic calming guidelines*. Devon: Devon County Council. Retrieved from www.ciht.org.uk/en/knowledge/standards-advice/traffic-calming-guidelines--devon-county-council.cfm.

Dixon, J., & Durrheim, K. (2000). Displacing place-identity: A discursive approach to locating self and other. *British Journal of Social Psychology, 39*(1), 27–44.

Dodson, J., & Sipe, N. (2008). Planned household risk: Mortgage and oil vulnerability in Australian cities. *Australian Planner 45*(1), 38–47. Retrieved from www.academia.edu/2873574/Published_in_Australian_Planner_2008_45_1_pp._38-47_Planned_Household_Risk_Mortgage_and_Oil_Vulnerability_in_Australian_Cities.

Engwicht, D. (2005). *Mental speed bumps (the smarter way to tame traffic)*. Annandale, NSW: Envirobook.

Ewing, R., & Cervero, R. (2010). Travel and the built environment. *Journal of the American Planning Association 76*(3), 265–294.

Gans, H. (1961). Planning and social life: Friendship and neighbor relations in suburban communities. *Journal of the American Planning Association 27*(2), 134–140. Retrieved from http://herbertgans.org/wp-content/uploads/2013/11/4-Planning-and-Social-Life.pdf.

Gehl, J. (2010). *Cities for people*. Washington, D.C.: Island Press.

Giles-Corti, B. (2006). *The impact of urban form on public health*. Canberra, ACT: Australian State of the Environment Committee, Department of the Environment and Heritage. Retrieved from www.environment.gov.au/system/files/pages/4bec898d-d2eb-487b-bf06-103489e46c3c/files/public-health.pdf.

Giles-Corti, B., & Donovan, R. (2002). The relative influence of individual, social, and physical environment determinants of physical activity. *Social Science and Medicine 54*(12), 1793–1812. Retrieved from www.ncbi.nlm.nih.gov/pubmed/12113436.

Grube-Cavers, A., & Patterson, Z. (2015). Urban rapid rail transit and gentrification in Canadian urban centres: A survival analysis approach. *Urban Studies*, *52*(1), 178–194.

Hamilton, K., & Jenkins, L. (2000). A Gender Audit for public transport: A new policy tool in the tackling of social exclusion. *Urban Studies 37*(10), 1783–1800.

Hänninen, O., & Knol, A. (Eds.). (2011). *European perspectives on environmental burden of disease: Estimates for nine stressors in six countries*. Helsinki: University Printing. Retrieved from www.julkari.fi/bitstream/handle/10024/79910/b75f6999-e7c4-4550-a939-3bccb19e41c1.pdf?sequence=1.

Hart, J. (2008). *Driven to excess: A study of motor vehicle impacts on three streets in Bristol, UK*. Bristol: University of the West of England. Retrieved from www.walk21.com/papers/josua_hart.pdf.

Hubsmith, D. (2007, October 1). *Safe routes to school: 2007 state of the states report*. Chapel Hill, NC: National Center for Safe Routes to School. Retrieved from www.saferoutespartnership.org/sites/default/files/pdf/rpt_SRTSstates2007.pdf.

INFAS Institute of Applied Social Sciences. (2008). *Mobilität in Deutschland*. Eschborn: Deutsche Gesellschaft für Internationale Zusammenarbeit. Retrieved from www.mobilitaet-in-deutschland.de/pdf/MiD2008_Abschlussbericht_I.pdf.

Jacobs, A., MacDonald, E., & Rofé, Y. (2002). *The boulevard book: History, evolution, design of multiway boulevards*. Cambridge, MA: The MIT Press.

Jacobs, J. (1961). The *death and life of great American cities*. New York: Random House.

Kelly, J. F., Breadon, P., Davis, C., Hunter, A., Mares, P., Mullerworth, D., & Weidmann, B. (2012, March 1). *Social cities*. Carlton, Victoria: Grattan Institute. Retrieved from http://grattan.edu.au/wp-content/uploads/2014/04/137_report_social_cities_web.pdf.

Lehman, M., & Boyle, M. (2007, July). *Healthy & walkable communities*. Newark, DE: University of Delaware. Retrieved from www.ipa.udel.edu/publications/HealthyWalkable.pdf.

Litman, T. (1999, December 7). *Traffic calming benefits, costs and equity impacts*. Victoria, BC: Victoria Transport Policy Institute. Retrieved from www.vtpi.org/calming.pdf.

Litman, T. (2016, August 24). *Affordable–accessible housing in a dynamic city*. Victoria, BC: Victoria Transport Policy Institute. Retrieved from www.vtpi.org/aff_acc_hou.pdf.

Lynch, K. (1981). *Good city form*. Cambridge, MA: The MIT Press.

Machell, E., Reinhalter, T., & Chapple, K. (2009, August). *Building support for transit oriented development*. Berkeley, CA: University of California. Retrieved from http://communityinnovation.berkeley.edu/reports/Building-Support-TOD.pdf.

Marek, J. C., & Walgren, S. (1998). *Mid-block speed control: Chicanes and speed humps*. Seattle, WA: Seattle Transportation. Retrieved from www.seattle.gov/transportation/docs/ITErevfin.pdf.

Marshall, W., Garrick, N., & Piatkowski, D. (2014). Community design, street network and public health. *Journal of Transport and Health 1*(4), 326–340.

McCormack, G., Giles-Corti, B., Lange, A., Smith, T., Martin, K., & Pikora, T. J. (2004). An update of recent evidence of the relationship between objective and self-report measures of the physical environment and physical activity behaviours. *Journal of Science and Medicine in Sport 7*(1 suppl), 81–92.

McManus, P. (2005). *Vortex cities to sustainable cities: Australia's urban challenge*. Sydney, NSW: University of New South Wales Press.

Nelson, D. M. (2015, June 25). *Project for public spaces*. Retrieved from www.pps.org/reference/thinking-beyond-the-station/.

Newman, O. (1972). *Defensible space: Crime prevention through urban design*. New York: Macmillan.

Pardo, C. F. (2011). *Shanghai manual: A guide for sustainable urban development in the 21st century*. Retrieved from https://sustainabledevelopment.un.org/content/documents/shanghaimanual.pdf.

Peters, D. (2001). *Gender and transport in less developed countries: A background paper in preparation for CSD-9*. London: United Nations Environment and Development Forum. Retrieved from www.socialassessment.com/documents/KudatWorks/2001/2001-Gender-And-Transport-Ayse-Kudat-citations.pdf.

Powell, K., Martin, L., & Chowdhury, P. (2003). Places to walk: Convenience and regular physical activity. *American Journal of Public Health 93*(9), 1519–1521. Retrieved from www.ncbi.nlm.nih.gov/pmc/articles/PMC1448003/.

Project for Public Spaces. (2012, September). *Placemaking and the future of cities*. New York: Project for Public Spaces. Retrieved from www.pps.org/wp-content/uploads/2012/09/PPS-Placemaking-and-the-Future-of-Cities.pdf.

Putnam, R. D. (2001). *Bowling alone: The collapse and revival of American community*. New York: Simon & Schuster.

Ralph, B., & John, P. (2011). Sustainable transport in Freiburg: Lessons from Germany's environmental capital. *International Journal of Sustainable Transportation 5*, 43–70.

Roads Service. (2003). *Travel survey for Northern Ireland*. Belfast: Roads Service, Transportation Unit. Retrieved from www.csu.nisra.gov.uk/Travel%20Survey%20for%20NI%20V2%20.pdf.

Saelens, B., & Handy, S. (2008). Built environment correlates of walking: A review. *Medicine and Science in Sports and Exercise 40*(7), 550–566.

Saelens, B. E., Sallis, J. F., Black, J. B., & Chen, D. (2003). Neighborhood-based differences in physical activity: An environment scale evaluation. *American Journal of Public Health 93*(9), 1552–1558. Retrieved from www.ncbi.nlm.nih.gov/pmc/articles/PMC1448009/.

Sanchez, D., Ross, T., Gordon, J., Edelman, S., Zonta, M., & Schwart, A. (2015, December 16). *An opportunity agenda for renters: The case for simultaneous investments in residential mobility and low-income communities*. Retrieved from http://inequality.stanford.edu/sites/default/files/LowIncomeRenters-report2.pdf.

Sander, T. H. (2002). Social capital and New Urbanism: Leading a civic horse to water? *National Civic Review 91*(3), 213–234.

Schneider, R., & Kitchen, T. (2002). *Planning for crime prevention: A transatlantic perspective*. London: Routledge.

Soja, E. W. (1995). *Postmodern geographies: The reassertion of space in critical social theory*. London: Verso.

Su, F., & Bell, M. (2009). Transport for older people: Characteristics and solutions. *Research in Transportation Economics 25*(1), 46–55.

Tacken, M. (1998). Mobility of the elderly in time and space in the Netherlands: An analysis of the Dutch National Travel Survey. *Transportation 25*(4), 379–393.

Tiwari, R. (2015). Designing a safe walkable city. *Urban Design International 20*(1), 12–27.

Tiwari, R., Smith, D., & Lommerse, M. (Eds.). (2014). *M2 Models and methodologies of community engagement*. Singapore: Springer.

US Department of Health and Human Services. (2011). *Healthy People 2010: Understanding and improving health*. Retrieved from www.healthypeople.gov/2010/document/pdf/uih/2010uih.pdf.

US Environmental Protection Agency. (2011). *Smart growth*. Retrieved from www.epa.gov/smartgrowth/awards/sg_awards_publication_2011.htm.

US Environmental Protection Agency. (2015). *Safe routes to school*. Retrieved from http://epaschools-stage.icfwebservices.com/transportation/saferoutes.html.

Weigand, L. (2008). *A review of literature: The effectiveness of safe routes to school and other programs to promote active transportation to school* (CUS-CTS-08-01). Portland, OR: Portland State University.

Weinstein, A., & Schimek, P. (2005, January 9–13). How much do Americans walk? An analysis of the 2001 NHTS. Paper presented at Transportation Research Board 84th Annual Meeting. Monograph No. 05-2246. Washington, D.C.: Transportation Research Board.

Welle, B., Li, W., Adriazola, C., King, R., Obelheiro, M., Sarmiento, C., & Liu, Q. (2015, July). *Cities safer by design*. Retrieved from www.wri.org/publication/cities-safer-design.

World Bank. (2014, September 8). Sexual harassment: The high cost of being a woman on a bus. Retrieved from www.worldbank.org/en/news/feature/2014/09/08/gender-violence-public-transportation.

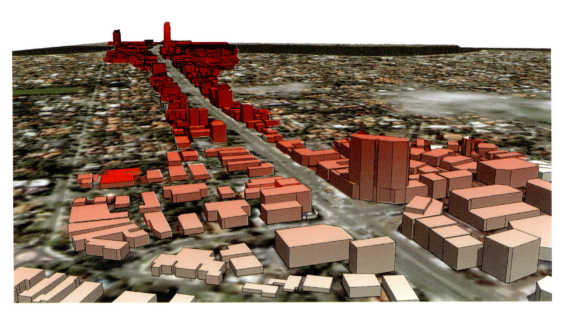

Source: Drawn by T. Seangsong (2010).

PART II

Mapping the Context: Urban Configurations

Part II explores two ways of urban reconfiguration: movement reconfiguration through plans catering for multi-modal traffic, active transport, modal integration, and transit prioritization; and place reconfiguration through the design of dense, mixed-use, economically vibrant, and attractive urban and suburban places that facilitate face-to-face interactions and build social capital. A range of best-practice examples and policies for connecting places in both the developing- and developed-world contexts are discussed. The legacy of the US' and Australia's love for car-centric development has meant an over-representation of these countries in the examples discussed in this part.

CHAPTER 3

RECONFIGURING MOVEMENT

This chapter examines the 'in-between spaces' between origin and destination. These in-between spaces encompass the streets, corridors, transport hubs, and transit stations that can enhance connectivity and place making. The focus shifts from mobility to the quality of neighborhoods. The question asked is: what happens when we reassign the channel-ways used by private cars and trucks to alternative, less disruptive, more people-oriented uses, such as greenways, pedestrian zones, bike lanes, and public parks? Is this part of a solution to the prevalent state of 'car-disconnect'?

Urban growth has a significant impact on connectivity. A successful strategy to manage connectivity is to invest in public transport, which can itself become a powerful city-shaping tool. Vibrant, active, high-density, and mixed-use growth concentrated along high-quality, high-capacity public transport corridors reaps economic benefits. However, to achieve this growth, the hurdles of land acquisition, high capital costs, and a lack of leadership and policy frameworks must be overcome. That this can be done successfully is demonstrated by the selected case studies.

The Nature of In-Between Spaces

The character of a city is most revealed by those elements that do not belong to the citizens yet are most frequented by them. These elements include streets, corridors, and transport hubs. These spaces are neither origins nor destinations. They are recognized as intermediate or in-between spaces. The functional character of these spaces can invite users to interact and get a feel of the place or the neighborhood, and even of the mobility priorities of the city. The qualitative interactions can reveal how 'friendly' or otherwise the city is. The anatomy of such spaces is therefore crucial. As they are an integral part of a city's mobility network or movement system, their design can significantly assist or hinder the creation of connected places.

The twentieth-century movement system was a response to powered movement (Hebbert, 2005). Conventional road design practice attempted to accommodate the 'average user'. For decades, the average user was assumed to be a motorist. This assumption has governed the composition of intermediate spaces, with the largest share of the space devoted to carriageways and parking lots.

Hierarchical road design, implemented in new post-war towns, produced movement systems that separated strolling pedestrians from speeding cars. This was in response to the assumption that drivers behind the wheel became more aggressive and foolhardy, and less sociable, rational, or kind (Ritter, 1964). As segregation of motorized and non-motorized transport became the only acceptable basis for urban reform, a law of inverse correlation of access and movement developed,[1] which persisted until recent decades. This practice exacerbated the carbon footprint of motorized transport, supported by a generous supply of roadways and parking. A study conducted by Brown et al. (2009) on the 100 largest metropolitan areas of the US revealed that, in 2005, transportation was responsible for 33 percent of the US' carbon footprint, and road transport accounted for almost 80 percent of that.

By the end of the twentieth century, the philosophy of segregation was replaced by the concept of 'social inclusion'. Reviving the quality of life in physically isolated environments became an urban concern that demanded rearrangement of intermediate spaces (Hebbert, 2005). Post-modern global competition also impelled cities to the realization that the public realm had become a wasted asset and had the potential to become safe and attractive for everyone (Oc & Tiesdell, 1997). The turn of the twenty-first century saw the advent of the boulevard, as cities across the world rediscovered major roads as complex urban spaces rather than mere traffic conduits. The pavement along the Champs Élysées in Paris, for example, was widened from 12 to 24 meters. Through considerable reordering, pedestrians gained a clear line of vision. Since then, the imperative of equitable access to places has been recognized as one of the primary objectives in the design of movement systems (Hebbert, 2005; UN Habitat, 2013).

The priority given to motor vehicles has waned as roads dedicated exclusively to arterial purposes are being transformed to accommodate coexisting parking, pedestrians, cyclists, and traffic streams of variable speed (Tiwari & Curtis, 2010). The reassignment of intermediate spaces has been done to reduce parking minimums, widen pavements, reduce carriageway, and so on. Redistributing public spaces allows greater access for more people, provides more mobility options, and encourages more functions. The changes are not detrimental to mobility, but in fact complement non-motorized mobility and quality of place.

As contemporary trends lead lifestyles in new directions, it is necessary to reimagine the in-between spaces to maximize their function and quality. The aim of *Connecting Places, Connecting People* is to balance the functional efficiency and place-making aspects of these in-between spaces.

Reconfiguring In-Between Spaces

Three typologies of in-between spaces based on functional classification are discussed: streets and corridors, green connectors, and transit hubs and transit stations. The intention is to explore ways of shrinking the footprint of movement systems while increasing efficiency and quality. The approach presented here is to reconfigure in-between spaces as people-oriented spaces rather than movement-centric spaces.

Reconfiguring Streets and Corridors: Theoretical Underpinnings

Giving priority to operating speed and traffic-carrying capacity results in urban roadways that divide neighborhoods, destroy local businesses, and create sterile, inhospitable streetscapes (Laplante & McCann, 2008). With increased traffic volumes, residents retreat from public streets, relocating their activities to quieter parts of their houses, thus encouraging anonymity and its disadvantages (Appleyard, 1981).

As a response, the notion of Livable Streets was introduced, and became a precursor for a shifting paradigm in the way in which streets and arterials are conceived. The Dutch government used the *woonerf* concept[2] in 1976 to prioritize pedestrians and cyclists over motorists. Similarly, the Home Zones Program in the UK operated to ease traffic and reduce accidents on residential streets (Appleyard & Lindsey, 2006). However, the regulation and standardization of *woonerf* as merely another category in the road hierarchy to be applied in residential areas subdued the enthusiasm for this concept, and Home Zones suffered the same fate in the UK (Hamilton-Baillie, 2008).

In the Dutch province of Friesland, the Shared Space Project (Monderman, 2005) revived the concept of integrated movement and place. This project involved the rather radical intervention of removing traffic signage and redesigning the street as shared space. In his work, Monderman (2005) adapts social protocols to design the streets and public spaces of small towns and villages (Hamilton-Baillie, 2008). He distinguishes between traffic behavior, social behavior, and social traffic behavior, and fosters their coexistence in shared public space without any one becoming dominant (Monderman, 2005, pp. 10, 11). The first example of shared space was in the village of Oudehaske. This resulted in a 40 percent reduction of vehicle speed, compared to a 10 percent reduction through conventional traffic calming (Hamilton-Baillie, 2008). The project was based on the philosophy that slow and fast networks were mutually reinforcing. The slow network, a fine meshed path and lane network, made the public spaces safe and easily accessible to pedestrians and cyclists. The fast network consisted of high-quality thoroughfares engineered to enable motorized traffic to reach destinations (Monderman, 2005). This example demonstrated that people were willing to change their behavior; such changes later came to be known as 'psychological traffic calming' (Engwicht, 1999). The project also illustrated the integration of movement and place which could be applied to busy non-residential roads.

The New Urbanism movement in the US is founded on similar ideas (Ellis, 2002). The aim of the street design model, The complete Streets Thoroughfare Assemblies SmartCode Module (Duany Plater-Zyberk et al., 2003), is to create walkable environments with a typology of streets to suit different built forms, from rural to urban. The module divides the rural to urban transect into different zones determined by their level of physical and social intensity and character, and is based mainly on a linear progression of rural to urban thoroughfares. Thoroughfare cross-sections in different transects have been established solely on vehicles per day and have ignored multi-modality or person capacity (Tiwari & Curtis, 2012).

In contrast to the above, person capacity rather than vehicle capacity was used to determine arterial street design in the Context Sensitive Solutions in Designing Major Urban Thoroughfares for Walkable Communities (CSS; Institute of Transportation Engineers, 2006). CSS also shifted the focus from roads to the surrounding context and forwarded the notion that the road design depends on more than simply the road itself (Tiwari & Curtis, 2012). A project-based approach, it provided a guide for safe environments for all users (Laplante & McCann, 2008). In the late 1990s, the city of Boulder, Colorado, decided to improve the streets. Boulder has a population of about 100,000 and is in a region dominated by car commuting. The project aimed to integrate the context-sensitive design and aesthetics and enhance multi-modality (Rauf, 2010). Instead of focusing on improving vehicle capacity, the city made a concerted effort to fund transit, thus emphasizing person capacity (the 'Hop', 'Skip', and 'Jump' shuttles). There was an increase in the alternative modes from 35 percent in 1993 to 47 percent in 1997 (City of Glendale, 2007). Faulty areas in the roads were redesigned and reconstructed in a cost-effective manner, new bike networks were created and extended, and a high-frequency bus Community Transit Network was implemented. 'Super Stops', which retrofitted the intersection or underpass as a pedestrian- and cycle-friendly, high-quality place with a strong connection to the community and the surroundings, were planned (American Association of State Highway and Transportation Officials, 2005). The Broadway, which carried more than 2,500 vehicles during peak hours, was retrofitted to increase traffic capacity. An example is the Euclid intersection, where a new bicycle and pedestrian underpass was created to benefit all transport modes, while providing a public gathering space with public art and landscaping integrated into the surrounding area (Figure 3.1). In total, forty-two prioritized corridors were retrofitted and landscaped for better user-centric functionality

Figure 3.1 Broadway and Euclid intersection before (left) and after (right) construction of the bicycle/pedestrian underpass

Source: Reprinted from Safe Streets Boulder Report (p. 15), by Transport Division, 2016, Boulder, CO: City of Boulder, Colorado, USA.

RECONFIGURING MOVEMENT

Figure 3.2 Graphics on the street as part of the Heads Up crosswalk safety campaign

Source: Reprinted from *Safe Streets Boulder Report (p. 17)*, by Transport Division, 2016, Boulder, CO: City of Boulder, Colorado, USA.

(Rauf, 2010). These projects, along with initiatives on safety education (Figure 3.2), helped to reduce traffic fatality rates significantly. Pedestrian fatalities declined from four in the period 2009–2011 to one in 2011–2014. Bicycle fatalities declined from five in 2009–2011 to zero in 2011–2014 (Transport Division, 2016).

In Broward County, Florida, the proposed Quilt-Net approach considers the urban arterial as a system at different scales ranging from rural to urban, and is able to respond to the particularity of place by developing a context-specific built-form vocabulary (Abbate, 2007; Figure 3.3). Downtown skylines, buildings, heritage sites, and natural features provide identity cues that give a sense of place and an effective system of way finding (Abbate, 2007). A grid network of 1 × 1 mile stitches together the varied patches of the quilt (Abbate, 2007; Figure 3.3). Community preferences and needs drive the

Figure 3.3 Typical 'patch' in Broward County; Quilt-Net formed by the infrastructure corridors; street configuration changes from urban to rural

Source: Based on *County-wide Community Design Guidebook* by A. Abbate, 2007, n.p. Broward, FL: Broward County.

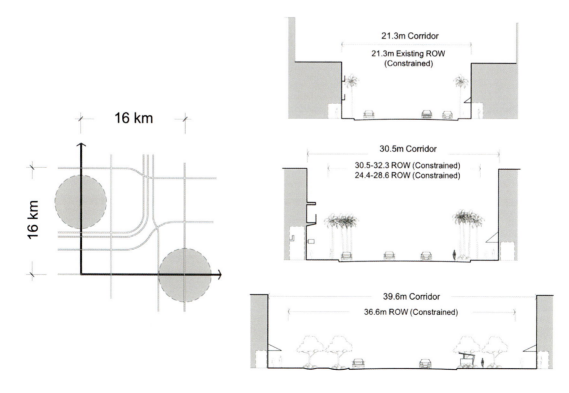

| 35

MAPPING THE CONTEXT

variations in different patches. The core design components revolve around: accommodating regional and local transit, park-and-ride facilities, and interconnected walkway systems; green tunnels and promenades; a mix of housing types, mixed uses, and coherent public places with local landmarks; and an emphasis on adaptation of the existing infrastructure. With the Quilt-Net approach's roots in the concept of sense of place, a place-based design emerges. However, the movement hierarchy is overlooked, with freight traffic left unconsidered (Tiwari & Curtis, 2012).

The FUS-ion (Function, Universality, Scale) model, based on the multi-functional Activity Corridors concept (Curtis & Tiwari, 2008; Tiwari & Curtis, 2012), considers the needs of freight and through-traffic movement. A three-pronged approach of Function, Universality, and Scale of place and traffic (Figure 3.4a) brings the community and stakeholders (People Axis) to agree on the current and future status of the arterial, based on factors outlined on the Transport Axis and the Built Form Axis. The emphasis to be given to the arterial as a multi-modal activity corridor, environmental corridor,3 or freight corridor is decided by using the Management Tool (Figure 3.4b). The current status for Manning Road in the Australian city of Perth, for example, is assessed as a high-volume, controlled-access, low-speed arterial. Its future was agreed in the stakeholder workshop as a multi-modal arterial that has a fast public transit, thus maintaining a high people-carrying capacity. At the same time, it retains low speeds for other modes, has a human scale with intense activity, and place-based design. By incorporating functional, physical, and social aspects, the model demonstrates how stakeholders (including residents) could agree on the current and future status of the arterial (Tiwari & Curtis, 2012).

Figure 3.4 *(a) FUS-ion approach to arterial classification; (b) Manning Road Assessment on FUS-ion Management Model*

Source: Adapted from 'A three-pronged approach to urban arterial design: A functional + physical + social classification,' by R. Tiwari, and C. Curtis, 2012, Urban Design International, 17(2), 129-143.

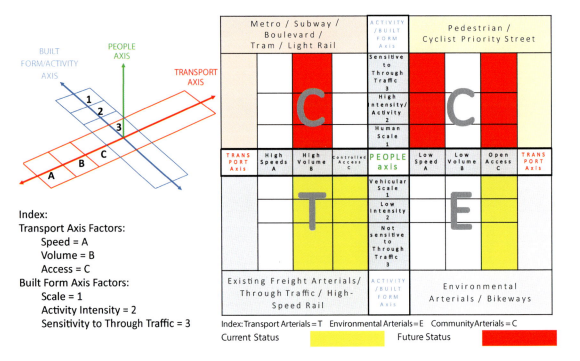

Index:
Transport Axis Factors:
    Speed = A
    Volume = B
    Access = C
Built Form Axis Factors:
    Scale = 1
    Activity Intensity = 2
    Sensitivity to Through Traffic = 3

Birmingham City Council in the UK has used a similar concept termed Place and Link[4] (Jones et al., 2008). The publication *Birmingham Connected* classifies the entire street network in terms of Link and Place functions to determine appropriate street space allocation and design solutions for different contexts (University College London, 2016). These principles have been adopted by the Mayor of London's Roads Task Force (Transport for London, 2014), which has led to refined analysis and planning for investment as compared to the previous analysis based on a traditional road user hierarchy model. Boroughs are required to use the new 'street family' classification in all new street funding submissions.

Reconfiguring Streets and Corridors: Intervention Tools

Integrating place and mobility function requires retrofitting or rebuilding arterials. Cervero (2006, p. 2) calls freeways 'grade-separated' structures, from an era when high priority was given to efficient automobile movements. This priority resulted in multi-level freeways with negative consequences for residents, such as barriers, visual blight, noise, and air pollution. Faith in multi-level freeways has waned now, as cities grapple with traffic jams and a polluting environment. With all the issues associated with these massive structures, many cities have opted for at-grade facilities following the deconstruction of freeways. The infrastructure involves creating more human-scale facilities with improved transit, landscaped urban parks, attractive boulevards, and new public spaces, including quality pedestrian and bikeway facilities.

The deconstruction of the Central Freeway and its transformation into Octavia Boulevard in San Francisco has been supported by the Hayes Valley citizen activists. The freeway was initially planned as part of an ambitious spiderweb of freeways through San Francisco, but the 1989 Loma Prieta earthquake made it unsafe. Deconstructing and reconfiguring the freeway into a multi-modal arterial resulted in new parks, housing, commercial space, and community markets (Municipal Transportation Agency, 2015a). The main challenge was to accommodate new buildings along the eastern side of the boulevard while still maintaining width requirements for multi-modal lanes. Lane-width compromise between urban designers, engineers, and the Fire Department resulted in central lanes, access lanes, and parking lanes being 11 feet, 10 feet, and 8 feet, respectively. Clever placement of median trees near the central roadway and the provision of a mountable curb along the access roadway side of the median meant that a fire engine could enter the access road with one wheel on the median (Figure 3.5). Another design issue around boulevard termination at Fell Street, to allow for the through traffic to turn west, was resolved by inserting a small neighborhood park within the boulevard's right of way (Macdonald, 2006). This open space has become the local community hub and demonstrates an effective way of complementing local-level use with a city-scale infrastructure (Figure 3.5).

Intense collaboration occurred with residents, especially the Hayes Valley Neighborhood Association, though the use of physical models

MAPPING THE CONTEXT

Figure 3.5 Octavia Boulevard, San Francisco

Source: Plan adapted from Building a boulevard (p. 5) by E. Macdonald, 2006, Berkeley, USA: University of California Transport Center. Copyright by UCTC, USA. Picture by R. Tiwari (2008). Image Adapted from Google Maps by Google, 2015.

and video simulations (Macdonald, 2006). Neighborhood associations agreed to advocate planning design that would reduce traffic fatalities and injuries, lead to zero congestion, and replace liquor stores and mechanics shops with trendy restaurants and high-end boutiques (Municipal Transportation Agency, 2015b). The positive outcomes of Octavia Boulevard have been significant increases in jobs (up to 23 percent) and property values (up to 25 percent) as well as a 75 percent increase in transit trips (Congress for the New Urbanism, 2015).

Freeway deconstruction has not evolved from a spontaneous desire for livability; rather, it has been a consequence of the extensively reported freeway revolts in the US during the 1960s and 1970s. Expansion of road infrastructure to accommodate the growing demand of suburban in-commuters resulted in a blanket displacement and destruction of inner-city neighborhoods. This mobilized grassroots opposition, where community groups argued that freeways mainly advantaged suburban dwellers over city inhabitants, who were less likely to own a car (Cervero et al., 2009). The resulting federal and state environment laws increased costs of freeway construction and removed the appetite for more. Dismantling freeways was seen as a demobilization strategy focused on reducing car travel and promoting more sustainable forms of travel, emphasizing the pedestrian-friendly principles of New Urbanism (Cervero et al., 2009).

In South Korea, Seoul's urban freeway deconstruction project over the Cheonggyecheon stream became famous after the freeway was torn down. The dried stream bed under the freeway had been buried under concrete, but was restored by a comprehensive project redevelopment, including new parks, public spaces, pedestrian infrastructure, landscaping, and bus rapid transit (BRT) lanes (Rao, 2011; Figure 3.6). To alleviate possible congestion due to the freeway closure, the Seoul Metropolitan Government opened 68 kilometers of rapid bus-only lanes in the median strips of major arterials. Shopkeepers and merchants along the former elevated freeway were financially compensated and relocated to a newly constructed market featuring easy accessibility (Kang & Cervero, 2008). Most importantly, the redevelopment connected the residents to the city's

past. Forgotten treasures were revealed, including historical bridges, carvings, and relics, and these helped to strengthen place identity (Figure 3.6). The project also significantly reduced the urban heat island effect. Ambient temperatures along the green parkway were 3.3–5.9 degrees centigrade lower than along the parallel arterial road surface just five blocks away (Hwang, quoted in Rao, 2011).

Retrofitting arterials passing through community neighborhoods has allowed the installation of traffic-calming measures such as road dieting and intersection treatments. Road dieting, also known as right-sizing, is the reallocation of road space to non-vehicular purposes to serve a wider range of street users. This term is associated with the Complete Streets movement (Laplante & McCann, 2008, p. 26). A 1.2-mile section of Stone Way North in Seattle underwent a road diet (Woldeamanuel, 2016, p. 89). The road diet section of the four-lane roadway, carrying 13,000 vehicles per day, was modified to a two-lane roadway that included roadside parking on both streets, bicycle lanes, and a center-turn lane. Total crashes decreased by 14 percent, while bicycle volume increased by 35 percent. Fifteen percent of the increased number of cyclists were previously peak-hour motorists (Woldeamanuel, 2016). The US Department of Transportation concluded that road diets have the potential to reduce traffic crashes by an average of 29 percent and in some smaller towns up to 50 percent (Tan, 2010).

Road diets that convert road space or parking lots into a temporary park or seating area are known as parklets (Figure 3.7). Parklets are

Figure 3.6 Green space in Seoul: what was once a looming, congested elevated freeway is now a haven for pedestrians

Source: Pictures by T. Wong (2015).

MAPPING THE CONTEXT

Figure 3.7 Parklets in San Francisco

Source: Adapted from San Francisco Parklet Manual version 2.2 (pp. 3, 6) San Francisco Planning Department, 2015, San Francisco, CA: City of San Francisco.

a grassroots initiative in San Francisco. The aim is to encourage non-motorized transportation, pedestrian safety, and activities, to foster neighborhood interaction, support local business, and improve overall livability and neighborhood quality (San Francisco Planning Department, 2016). The first parklet was established in 2010. As of March 2015, the city had more than 50. These spaces include amenities such as seating, planting, bicycle parking, and art. While parklets are funded, managed, and established by neighboring owners, they are open for public use. Establishing a parklet involves an application process with a design proposal. The City of San Francisco evaluates the technical and operational parameters of the proposal prior to approval. Open-house and community meetings are hosted around the project applications for knowledge sharing and project design. The process of establishing parklets goes beyond a bottom-up approach and leads to alliance formation between local and independent businesses who also sponsor the project (Steinmuller, 2015). This engenders a sense of local autonomy due to the multi-stakeholder ownership of the targeted public realm.

The parklet program thus brings the community into conversation while simultaneously working towards reducing traffic speed. Traffic-calming measures can sometimes provoke the community and become controversial. Motorists dislike the restrictions imposed by one-way streets, banned turnings, and obstacles like road humps. A collision that occurs after a calming measure is put in place can result in a backlash from drivers.

Liability for accidents can be a murky area, subject to conflicting interpretations. In New Jersey, for example, Belmar's Ocean Avenue is usually packed with vehicles that most often disregard the 25 mph speed limit, making it hard for the large number of pedestrians to cross the road safely. Frequent fatalities prompted the Borough of Belmar to take action towards making the street safer. Sand-filled plastic barrels were placed at busy intersections to slow motorists down. Ironically, the borough was sued by Monmouth County (Kemp & Stephani, 2015), as the barrels were seen as hazardous for drivers. It is important that drivers are educated to understand that traffic calming aims to encourage slow and careful driving, thus making streets safer for both drivers and pedestrians (City of Hobart, 2008).

RECONFIGURING MOVEMENT

As much as urban professionals and public administrations would wish it, eliminating cars altogether is not feasible. Restricting car use can work only if the city or district has appropriate infrastructure. Vauban, a small neighborhood to the south of the town center in Freiburg, Germany, which used to house military barracks, was able to remove cars from its streets. The compact geometry of the street network articulates efficiently with the active transport modes and transit and filters out cars (Raphael, 2009; Scheurer, 2001; Figure 3.8). Every house is within 400 meters of the transit line, which encourages residents to walk or cycle within administrative limits. This leaves the residential pockets as car-free zones that limit residential parking space at the periphery (Field, 2014; Linck, 2008, p.13).

Figure 3.8 Compact street network where cars are driven below 30 km/h only on main roads shown in yellow

Source: Based on data from Car free experience in Vauban, Frieburg (p. 13), by Hannes Linck, 2008, Frieburg: Verein für autofreies Wohnen e.V.

Reconfiguring Green Connectors

Green connectors, when networked as a circulation system, enable access to local public spaces with active modes of 'feet and pedal' (walking and cycling), while still providing region-wide connectivity to recreational parklands, conserved wetlands, and ecological greenways.

Abandoned railway rights of way and wasted urban assets like underutilized back lanes and utility corridors are, over time, retrofitted as green connected public places and eventually help to expand the soft mobility network beyond conventional sidewalks (Toccolini et al., 2006). Non-motorized travel becomes safer and more pleasant (San Francisco Planning Department, 2016). Developed as a network, these green connectors contribute to the rationalization of irrigation requirements and the maximization of drainage functions while enhancing amenity and reducing pollution. In fact, the integration of water-sensitive urban design techniques like vegetative control (over-

MAPPING THE CONTEXT

Figure 3.9 *Green Network of Shanghai proposed for 2020*

Source: Based on Urban ecosystem services—Assessing green infrastructure in Shanghai, by J. Breuste, 2015.

land flow and grassed channels), detention (wet basins and wetlands), retention (infiltration basins), xeriscaping,[5] and windbreaks helps to make the green connectors respond to the local particularities. Thus, besides conserving water, they contribute to place identity for the neighborhood that they pass through (Vernon & Tiwari, 2009).

Environmental green corridors are under construction in Shanghai as a response to increased urbanization and resultant serious environmental pollution. Green corridors based on a ring-road system are at the outer and middle rings of Shanghai (He, 2007; Figure 3.9). Green belts 100 meters wide along expressways, 50 meters for major roads, and 25 meters for secondary roads are intended to reduce noise, eliminate the vibration effect to nearby residential dwellings, and control the suspended particulate matter (Breuste, 2015). While tree plantations on the outer parts of the city running along the outer circle highway provide a stable environment for ecological communities, the middle circle highway incorporates a combination of small green patches like street parks and community open spaces (Li et al., 2014). The north–south corridor along the Huangpu River has amalgamated cultural, recreational, and ecological aspects. By 2020, the target is to increase green area per capita to 6.5 square meters downtown and 10 square meters in urbanized areas (Breuste, 2015). The system focuses on the structure of natural habitats and builds an artificial, environmental community that lays a foundation for biodiversity and habitat conservation (Xiu, 2014).

In the US, green rail trails have become popular in a number of cities. The above-ground High Line Park in New York has been built on a disused railroad track, originally designed for easy delivery of freight by cutting through blocks. Local activists rescued it from demolition and it was retrofitted as an aerial greenway, providing a natural habitat to a variety of birds and small animals (Levere, 2014). The High Line attracts about five million visitors annually (Wolcha et al., 2014). Home values within one-third of a mile of the park increased 10 percent immediately following its opening, generating additional property taxes that exceeded the cost of constructing the park. While new businesses have opened in the area (Levere, 2014; Wolcha et al., 2014), the 'essence of the place' as a vibrant urban arts and manufacturing cluster has been retained primarily by maintaining a manufacturing designation for the blocks associated with

RECONFIGURING MOVEMENT

galleries. Allowed floor area ratio (FAR) was reduced for the High Line-encumbered properties, which could sell their 'air rights'— unbuilt transferable development rights—away from the High Line towards the business end in the north (Broder, 2012). What was once a wasted piece of transportation infrastructure has been transformed into one of the US' most important pieces of civic infrastructure (Broder, 2012; Figure 3.10).

Recognizing the adaptive value of wasted infrastructure as a green connector system becomes critical in achieving social and environmental benefits for local communities.

Figure 3.10 The High Line: previously disused railtrack transformed into a most popular destination for locals and tourists alike

Source: Picture by T. Wong (2015).

Reconfiguring Transport Hubs and Transit Stations: Investing in Development around Public Transit

While the above sections focused on resolving the barriers between motorized private transport and other modes of transport, and between movement and place function through reconfiguration of the movement network, this section focuses on how investing around public transport hubs can in itself become a powerful city-shaping tool for a high-quality public realm.

The economy of a city depends on transferring and sharing knowledge. This in turn requires efficient communication technology and dense urban form that encourages person-to-person interaction. Public transport is a great enabler of dense urban form, with rail 20 times more spatially efficient than cars (McIntosh et al.,

| 43

2014; Newman, 2012). However, the investment becomes worthless if access to public transport is through an unsafe, sterile environment.

Transit-oriented developments (TODs) in Hong Kong did not initially receive much attention, as transport planners focused on developing only the transit network. After realizing hazardous walking conditions and sterile station area environments were making users reluctant to use the transit system, the Mass Transit Railway Corporation (MTRC) commenced integrating transit with TOD land use strategies (Cervero, 2010). The improved station area environment increased transit ridership. A study showed that the pedestrian-friendly design of MTR stations (commercial shops along pedestrian paths, place making, and so on) added 2.84 rail trips per weekday for each additional household within 500 meters of the station, compared to 1.75 trips for an MTR without place-making initiatives (Cervero & Murakami, 2009). A greater proportion of green areas in TODs resulted in decreases in noise and air pollution.

Research shows that greater access to public transport increases the value of adjacent land. This is true in both developing and developed countries (McIntosh et al., 2014; Singh & Sharma, 2012). This is demonstrated by a study on the impact of BRT on land values in Seoul between 2001 and 2007: residences within 300 meters of BRT stops obtained land price premiums of between 5 and 10 percent (Cervero & Kang, 2011). This occurred within a few years of the BRT enhancements. Shops and other non-residential uses within 150 meters of the nearest BRT stop experienced more varied premiums, from 3 to 26 percent.

Zoning is critical in allowing TODs to become mixed-use, dense centers with minimal parking and substantial affordable housing (Gorowitz, quoted in Curtis et al., 2009, p. 20). The Seoul Metropolitan Government proactively encouraged land densification through regulatory and zoning reforms and neighborhood enhancement strategies. FAR in Seoul ranges from 10 in the central business district (CBD), to 4–8 in sub-centers, and 1.5–4 in residential areas (Vision Mumbai, n.d.). These high densities are supported by the highly used mass rapid transit network (Ahluwalia, 2014).

At a macro scale, the Seoul BRTs are well integrated with other public transport modes. Common fare cards, integrated information, and physical and network integration allow seamless movement. At a micro scale, the stations incorporate enhanced pedestrian facilities. Unfortunately, until recently, bicycle facilities were ignored in the TOD planning. There were no parking slots or bicycle paths to link with the BRTs. Despite this, the overall system provided a successfully implemented transit system.

In cities without coordination between land use and transport planning, transit projects remain more as mechanisms for mobility between two points. A case in point is the Janmarg BRT initiative in Ahmedabad, India. It has been one of the first few examples of BRT in India. Low and fairly uniform FARs (1.8–2.25) have limited growth around transit stations. The local government is cautious about higher FARs, since the aim is to decongest the city. As a result, there are no dense developments around BRT stations. Some efforts to increase the FAR to 4 around station areas have been made, but progress has been limited (Suzuki et al., 2013).

Reconfiguring Transport Hubs and Transit Stations: Challenges

The main challenges in implementing TODs revolve around considerations of markets, land consolidation, and leadership (Utter, 2009). TODs cost more than conventional developments. High upfront capital costs, long development timelines, and longer payback periods are a few among myriad constraints towards developing rail and metro (ITF/OECD, 2008). Developers therefore seek sites in higher-income areas, as higher rent rates can cushion high costs and potentially realize greater profits. There have been mechanisms to encourage private partnership in middle- and low-income areas, where there is greater need for accessibility. Inducements for private developers to promote affordable TODs in Austin, Texas, under the SMART (safe, mixed-income, accessible, reasonably priced, transit-oriented) housing program included expedited development approvals, zoning incentives, fee waivers, and smoother regulatory processes (Newman et al., 2011). The Dudley Village Project in Dorchester, Boston, was a privately developed project where 100 percent affordable housing was offered (City of Boston, 2009). Critical to the project's success was a new state-fundinded scheme providing financial support for active transport infrastructure and affordable housing development within a quarter of a mile of transit stations.

The costly and time-consuming process of land acquisition, especially for brownfield developments,[6] makes greenfield sites[7] more attractive for TODs. This works contrary to development and rejuvenation of the inner city. Scarcity of finances results in basing the selection of routes for infrastructure development on the acquisition costs of the right of way instead of on the long-term development potential of the areas (Suzuki et al., 2013). This issue has been addressed through land consolidation techniques. The Tokyo Corporation has used land consolidation techniques to provide landowners with fully serviced parcels. Landowners form a cooperative to amalgamate irregularly formed properties, resulting in smaller but fully serviced parcels. The sale of 'extra' reserved land is used to fund roads, sewerage, and other infrastructure.

The benefit to the private rail company responsible for the development of transport infrastructure in such projects is the reduction in the upfront burden and land acquisition and development risks. Transit value capture has historically been used at a regional scale for rail and property development and has in turn ensured the viability of railway operations and a built form that is highly transit oriented (Cervero, 2010; Suzuki et al., 2013). An important example is the East Japan Railway Company's real estate project, Tokyo Station City. This is being developed jointly with other private interests in conjunction with the Tokyo Metropolitan Government (Suzuki et al., 2013). The damaged, early twentieth-century station was restored to its original architectural form. Multiple functional centers at Tokyo Station City, including high-rise office buildings, retail centers, and hotels, are being developed. Extensive buildable area above depots and high pedestrian traffic volumes provide an opportunity for a large-scale redevelopment project. The proposal blends tradition, innovation, and inner-city redevelopment (Maeda, 2010). With pathways at grade connecting to the imperial gardens, the place is pedestrian friendly. Such projects symbolize the movement of cities towards integrated city spaces involving all stakeholders, and responding in a sustainable way to market demand (Suzuki et al., 2013; Zacharias et al., 2011).

Land consolidation can also provide financing for TODs through public–private partnerships (PPPs), particularly in lower-income areas where the need for accessibility is greater (Suzuki et al., 2013). In India, Gujarat's Town Planning Scheme (TPS) acquired 13 kilometers of peripheral land from the 63-kilometer-long Ahmedabad Ring Road. This was achieved through land pooling via active community participation and with no money paid for the land (Ballaney, 2010). In theory, poorer fringe areas can be developed in this fashion. When the fringe landowners are wealthier business owners or politicians rather than poor farmers, the objective of the exercise can be deviated.

Yet another area that can be targeted for supporting TODs is the underutilized parking area within the inner city. At least one-third of the space in US cities is dedicated to parking (Ben-Joseph, 2012). Besides encroaching on valuable real estate, each parking spot costs a city an average of US $1,000 in annual lost tax revenue (Burns, 2014).

Chicago's sale of three city-owned parking lots for the purpose of TOD demonstrates the financial benefit provided to people and government. The City of Chicago indicated its intention to sell city-owned parking lots adjacent to a transit station. Selling such parcels was good for the budget, 'bringing in $12.4 million from three separate buyers—far more than the $7 million appraisal', according to Freemark (2015), as well as increasing long-term tax revenues (Brasuell, 2015). Development on the parking lots had the potential to add US$358,000 in annual new property tax revenues (Freemark, 2015).

Los Angeles County, California, demonstrates the additional benefits of converting surplus parking lots to TODs. Serving 113 stations, the TOD consists of six rail lines, including two rapid transit subway lines and four light rail lines. The Metropolitan Transportation Authority has facilitated TOD of 17 stations on Metro-owned land through a joint development (JD) program (Hornstock, 2014). Under this program, 2,077 new units of housing, 305 hotel rooms, 820,000 square feet of retail, and 650,000 square feet of office space have been developed (City of Centennial, 2012). These developments promote equity by providing 35 percent of affordable housing with covenants (Metro Joint Development Program, 2015).

As part of Metro's TOD program, the Hollywood/Vine station became a primary target for rejuvenation. Around 4.7 acres of parking area owned by Metro and others have been developed for hotels, condominiums, apartments, and street retail space (Metro Joint Development Program, 2014). The extra benefit that the community has gained from this project is the re-creation of place identity. This station is the most attractive and fun station in the entire Metro system. Features include a movie screen flanked by large curtains with reference to the movie industry. Pillars replicating palm trees and musical notes for a famous song beneath the handrails add to the excitement. Pedestrians follow the hand-painted art tiles and are reminded of the Yellow Brick Road from *The Wizard of Oz*. Los Angeles's car culture is resonated through the carefully sculpted benches placed on the platform. The place picks on Hollywood symbols and is able to connect closely with passers-by.

Another challenge in the implementation of TODs, highlighted by Utter (2009), is finding the right leadership for the vision of sustainable development. To be successful, these projects require visionaries such as Jaime Lerner, who placed Curitiba, Brazil, on the world map as a model for TOD (Hidalgo, 2014).

In the 1960s, Curitiba's city authorities formulated a master plan to guide the city towards growth, order, and extra room for the automobile (Adler, 2016). To solve the problem of traffic congestion, the master plan envisaged replacing historic buildings in the downtown area with new traffic lanes. Lerner, a young architect at the time, argued against this vision and initiated an opposing movement from which sprang a vision of dense urban form along mass transit corridors. This meant a reining-in of sprawl, expansion of green spaces, and preservation of historic districts (Adler, 2016; Schwartz, 2004). Lerner's approach was consistent with the core concepts of TOD. Over the next two decades, first as planner then as mayor, his vision transformed Curitiba through a plan that integrated land use, transport, living, leisure, and other elements of the city (Adler, 2016).

His first proposal to pedestrianize downtown streets was opposed by shopkeepers, who believed that the car was the transport mode of choice for their customers. To demonstrate that this was not the case, Lerner implemented the project only on weekends (Hollis, 2013). The ultimate success of the project resulted in shoppers demanding more pedestrianized streets, and there were petitions for car-free streets from different parts of the city (Adler, 2016; Hollis, 2013).

The BRT system, another of Lerner's inspiring ideas, combined land use regulations with cohesive street networks and strong public transit (Irazábal, 2004). By zoning land within two blocks of the transit arteries as high density and tapering densities based on the distance from transit ways, a higher-transit ridership per square foot was achieved. Very limited downtown public parking was provided, with most employers offering transportation subsidies, especially to low-skilled and low-paid employees.

These far-sighted policies have paid off over the last half century, and the BRT system now serves over 31 million passengers per day in Curitiba (Hidalgo, 2014). Other policies include: the right to develop forests in exchange for development rights; 10 percent discount towards the city tax if the private landowner has a Parana pine tree on their land; and financial support through a federal grant if the issue of flooding is addressed by creating lakes that overflow into parklands (Suzuki et al., 2010). As a result, Curitiba's green space has increased from 1 square meter per inhabitant to 52 square meters (Hidalgo, 2014). The community was actively engaged in this process. Numerous ethnic groups were allowed to fit out parks according to their cultural preferences. The results include a path symbolizing the Italian ritual of strolling, a Ukrainian church constructed in timber, a

Bavarian forest environment where tales are told by witches, and a Japanese oasis deep among the skyscrapers (Mikesh, 2007).

The context of municipal governance and the system in which Lerner worked were important to his ability to implement innovative ideas. During two of his three terms as mayor, Brazil was ruled by a military dictatorship. The state was highly centralized and Lerner was appointed by a strong central government. Innovative urban development strategies were possible due to the institutional structure present in Brazil at that time. Lerner had overall responsibility for transport and land use development that was inclusive of zoning, building codes, public space, and park development. This responsibility extended to social development in areas of education, childcare, *favela* (slum) improvement, and healthcare (Instituto de Pesquisa Planejamento Urbano de Curitiba, quoted in Tadamun, 2014). Lerner also had discretion in policy making, administering, and financing. This provided a holistic context for him to make and implement decisions.

Lerner tackled the city's problems by giving due weight to the citizens' preferences, and to the quality of life and habitability. These had largely been ignored or given a low priority during previous administrations. Lerner's success stemmed from an effective mix of leadership, innovation, and institutions. The result was job creation, accessible public transport, housing development, and improvement in waste management. The ensuing TOD accentuated the significance of consolidating urban uses around transport corridors. Curitiba is now recognized as the most successful example of TOD (WRI, 2014). This success is evidenced by data: from 1975 to 1995, Curitiba's GDP increased 75 percent more than that of the total state of Paraná, and 48 percent more than that of the country as a whole. The interventions during these decades transformed the city into a location that attracted multinational industries, including automotive manufacturing and information technology (WRI, 2014).

That leadership instigated from the bottom up is crucial is demonstrated in the Chicago Adopt-a-Station Project, which is a partnership of community organizations, local businesses, and individuals. The partnership adopts a station and is involved in developing it to reflect the history and diversity of the community it is serving (Village Well, 2006). The result has been a high-quality place developed as an iconic 'gateway' to the locality (Village Well, 2006).

Platform for Art is a public art program on the London Underground. The permanent installations and changing exhibitions are coordinated through community engagement. Schoolchildren, youth ethnic groups, the elderly, and community artists in theater, the visual arts, and music are encouraged to participate. The program works closely with the local community. This is evidenced in the way in which the curated exhibitions become intercultural expressions, especially of marginalized groups (Village Well, 2006).

These programs, by being inclusive, ensure that citizens have a stake in their environment, consequently ensuring their success. Citizens, for their part, benefit directly from the programs. Research from the US shows that residents in neighborhoods around transit hubs spend 16 percent less on transportation, and the value of these neighborhoods increases by as much as 50 percent compared with locations away from transit stops (City of Winnipeg, 2012, p. 8). TOD housing generates 50 percent less traffic and can reduce new infrastructure costs by up to 25 percent through more compact and infill development (City of Winnipeg, 2012, p. 9). Prioritizing developments that support public transport over auto-centric developments not only leads to high-quality connected places but also generates economic benefits for the community.

Close

A paradigm shift to reconfigure movement systems is occurring worldwide. Considering streets as places, removing elevated freeways, using urban green connectors for active mobility, and prioritizing efficient public transport through transit-supportive development are some ways to respond to residents' desire for improved livability, and to pave the way for connected places. Travel is a derived demand that can be kept in check by developing connected places where people live, work, shop, and play. These places drive economic growth and community development with key transport and place-making investment. Developing connected places does not preclude profiting from real estate. More importantly, connected places can generate environmental benefits through shrinking the footprint of movement space dedicated to private transport modes. The movement system needs to be seen as a means to an end, not an end in itself.

Notes

1 Achieving uninterrupted and high-speed movement on the roads has meant ignoring requirements for access to adjacent land uses. Higher access results in lower speeds (Tiwari & Curtis, 2010).
2 In the 1970s, the term *woonerf* ('living yard')—a residential street—was formally recognized by the Dutch government to design low-speed residential roads. On a *woonerf* street, the speed is restricted to walking pace, with legal priority given to pedestrians and cyclists over motorists (MVW, 2006).
3 The term 'environmental corridor' here refers to roads that pass through or are adjacent to environmentally sensitive green parklands or water bodies. It demands low speed, low traffic volume, low urban activity intensity, open access, and preferably active transport modes (see Figure 3.4b).
4 As a Link, a street provides a conduit for through movement for all transport modes and forms an integral part of urban networks. Its essential purpose is to minimize travel time by following a continuous path with minimum disruption and a seamless connection from the beginning to the end of the journey (Jones et al., 2008). As a Place, a street becomes a location where activities occur on or adjacent to the street. A Place user is someone who wishes to use some of the features on that particular street, and will usually do so on foot (Jones et al., 2008).
5 Xeriscaping conserves water through creative landscaping. The landscaping, which involves water-wise gardening techniques, reduces the need for supplemental water from irrigation.
6 'Brownfield' describes abandoned (and possibly contaminated) land previously used for industrial or commercial purposes.
7 'Greenfield' describes undeveloped land within or at the periphery of the city or rural area that is used for agriculture.

References

All online references retrieved August 17, 2016.

Abbate, A. (2007). *Broward County county-wide community design guidebook*. Florida: Broward County. Retrieved from www.broward.org/PlanningAndRedevelopment/DemographicsAndEconomics/Pages/UrbanDesign.aspx.

Adler, D. (2016, May 6). How radical ideas turned Curitiba into Brazil's 'green capital'. Retrieved from www.theguardian.com/cities/2016/may/06/story-of-cities-37-mayor-jaime-lerner-curitiba-brazil-green-capital-global-icon.

Ahluwalia, I. J. (2014). *Planning for urban development in India*. Retrieved from http://icrier.org/Urbanisation/pdf/Ahluwalia_Planning_for_Urban_%20Development.pdf.

Allen, H. (2013). *Bus reform in Seoul, Republic of Korea*. Retrieved from http://unhabitat.org/wp-content/uploads/2013/06/GRHS.2013.Case_.Study_.Seoul_.Korea_.pdf.

American Association of State Highway and Transportation Officials (2005). Revitalizing communities and corridors creating statewide strategies for land use and transportation. Retrieved from http://environment.transportation.org/pdf/2004_smart_growth_competition.pdf.

Appleyard, D. (1981). *Livable streets*. Berkeley, CA: University of California Press.

Appleyard, B., & Lindsey, C. (2006, October). At home in the zone: Creating livable streets in the US. *Planning* 72(9), 30–35. Retrieved from http://nacto.org/docs/usdg/at_home_in_the_zone_appleyard.pdf.

Ballaney, S. (2010). Town Planning Scheme mechanism Gujarat. Paper presented at the Annual Bank Conference on Land Policy and Administration, Washington, D.C. Retrieved from http://siteresources.worldbank.org/INTHOUSINGLAND/Resources/339552-1272658002920/Ballaney.pdf.

Ben-Joseph, E. (2012). *Re-thinking a lot: The design and culture of parking*. Cambridge, MA: The MIT Press.

Brasuell, J. (2015). The outsized benefits of transforming parking lots to TOD. Retrieved from www.planetizen.com/node/81208/outsized-benefits-transforming-parking-lots-tod.

Breuste, J. (2015). *Urban ecosystem services: Assessing green infrastructure in Shanghai*. Retrieved from www.bfn.de/fileadmin/BfN/internationaler naturschutz/Dokumente/8._Dt.Cn.WS/2015_Sino-GermanWS_12_Breuste.pdf.

Broder, J. M. (2012). Deconstructing New York City's High Line Park: The how, why and wherefore. *Journal of Transportation Law, Logistics, and Policy* 79(3), 245. Retrieved from http://search.proquest.com/openview/f9b42545b2c7bd08dacdbf19fa582aec/1?pq-origsite=gscholar.

Brown, M. A., Southworth, F., & Sarzynski, A. (2009). The geography of metropolitan carbon footprints. *Policy and Society* 27(4), 285–304. Retrieved from www.academia.edu/11555249/The_geography_of_metropolitan_carbon_footprints.

Bukowski, B., Boatman, D., Ramirez, K., & Du, M. (2013). *A comparative study of transit-oriented developments in Hong Kong*. Hong Kong: Institute of Education. Retrieved from https://web.wpi.edu/Pubs/E-project/Available/E-project-022713-065611/unrestricted/Comparative_Study_of_TOD_in_Hong_Kong.pdf.

Burns, R. (2014). Multistorey car park in US transformed into designer microapartments. Retrieved from www.theguardian.com/cities/2014/jul/09/multistorey-car-park-us-designer-micro-apartments-affordable-housing.

Cascetta, E., & Pagliara, F. (2009). Rail friendly transport and land use policies: The case of the regional metro system of Naples and Campania. In C. Curtis, J. L. Renne, & L. Bertolini. (Eds.) *Transit oriented development: Making it happen* (pp. 49–65). Farnham: Ashgate.

Cervero, R. (2004). *Transit-oriented development in the United States: Experiences, challenges, and prospects*. Retrieved from www.scribd.com/document/64040490/Cervero-TOD-in-the-US-2004.

Cervero, R. (2006, October). Freeway deconstruction and urban regeneration in the United States. Paper presented at the International Symposium for the 1st Anniversary of the Cheonggyecheon Restoration, Seoul. Retrieved from www.uctc.net/research/papers/763.pdf.

Cervero, R. (2010). Transit transformations. In W. Ascher & C. Krupp (Eds.) *Physical infrastructure development: Balancing the growth, equity, and environmental imperatives* (pp. 165–187). New York: Palgrave Macmillan.

Cervero, R., & Kang, C. D. (2011). Bus rapid transit impacts on land uses and land values in Seoul, Korea. *Transport Policy 18*(1), 102–116.

Cervero, R., & Murakami, J. (2009). Rail and property development in Hong Kong: Experiences and extensions. *Urban Studies 46*(10), 2019–2043.

Cervero, R., Kang, J., & Shively, K. (2009). From elevated freeways to surface boulevards: Neighbourhood and housing price impacts in San Francisco. *Journal of Urbanism: International Research on Placemaking and Urban Sustainability 2*(1), 31–50.

City of Boston (2009, August 8). Mayor Menino celebrates grand opening of Dudley Village Homes. Retrieved from www.cityofboston.gov/NEWS/DEFAULT.ASPX?ID=4316.

City of Centennial (2012). I-25 Corridor Subarea plan corridor economic analysis. Retrieved from www.plancentennial.com/wp-content/uploads/2012/12/Phase-2-Market-Analysis-Draft-sm.pdf.

City of Fresno. (2016). Traffic engineering: Road diets. Retrieved from www.fresno.gov/Government/DepartmentDirectory/PublicWorks/TrafficEngineering/RoadDiets.htm.

City of Glendale (2007). Downtown mobility study. Retrieved from www.glendaleca.gov/home/showdocument?id=20134.

City of Hobart. (2008). Traffic calming. Retrieved from www.hobartcity.com.au/Transport/Managing_the_Transport_Network/Traffic_Management/Traffic_Calming.

City of Winnipeg. (2012). *Winnipeg transit-oriented development handbook*. Retrieved from www.winnipeg.ca/ppd/planning/TOD/pdf/Handbook.pdf.

Congress for the New Urbanism. (2015). Octavia Boulevard: Creating a vibrant neighborhood from a former freeway. Retrieved from www.pps.org/reference/octavia-boulevard-creating-a-vibrant-neighborhood-from-a-former-freeway/.

Curtis, C., & Tiwari, R. (2008). Transitioning urban arterial roads to activity corridors. *Urban Design International 13*(2), 105–120.

Curtis, C., Renne, J. L., & Bertolini, L. (Eds.) (2009). *Transit oriented development: Making it happen*. Farnham: Ashgate.

Duany Plater-Zyberk, Chellman, C., Hall, R., & Swift, P. (2003). *Complete Streets Thoroughfare Assemblies SmartCode*. Retrieved from http://transect.org/docs/CompleteStreets.pdf.

Ellis, C. (2002). The New Urbanism: Critiques and rebuttals. *Journal of Urban Design 7*(3), 261–291.

Engwicht, D. (1999). *Street reclaiming: Creating liveable streets and vibrant communities*. British Columbia: New Society.

Field, S. (2014). *Case study: Vauban, Frieburg, Germany*. Retrieved from www.itdp.org/wp-content/uploads/2014/07/26.-092211_ITDP_NED_Vauban.pdf.

Freemark, Y. (2015). Chicago is selling parking lots, and the payoff is bigger than the sales price. Retrieved from www.metroplanning.org/news/7219/Chicago-is-selling-parking-lots-and-the-payoff-is-bigger-than-the-sales-price.

Hamilton-Baillie, B. (2008). Shared space: Reconciling people, places and traffic. *Built Environment 34*(2), 161–181. Retrieved from www.solaripedia.com/files/1233.pdf.

He, X. (2007). Celebrating green infrastructure in Shanghai, China. Retrieved from http://courses.umass.edu/greenurb/2007/he/green%20map%20goals.htm.

Hebbert, M. (2005). Engineering, urbanism and the struggle for street design. *Journal of Urban Design 10*(1), 39–59.

Hidalgo, D. (2014). Urbanism hall of fame: Jaime Lerner—the architect of Curitiba. Retrieved from http://thecityfix.com/blog/urbanism-hall-fame-jaime-lerner-architect-curitiba-dario-hidalgo/.

Hollis, L. (2013). *Cities are good for you: The genius of the metropolis.* London: Bloomsbury.

Hornstock, J. (2014). *Metro's Joint Development Program.* Retrieved from www.smartgrowthamerica.org/documents/hornstock-locus.pdf.

Institute of Transportation Engineers. (2006). *Context Sensitive Solutions in Designing Major Urban Thoroughfares for Walkable Communities.* Retrieved from http://contextsensitivesolutions.org/content/reading/ite 036_css/resources/ite_css/.

Irazábal, C. (2004). *City making and urban governance in the Americas: Curitiba and Portland.* Chippenham: Routledge.

ITF/OECD. (2008). *Transport infrastructure investment: Options for efficiency.* Retrieved from www.oecd-ilibrary.org/transport/transport-infrastructure-investment_9789282101568-en.

Jones, P., Marshall, S., & Boujenko, N. (2008). Creating more people-friendly urban streets through 'Link and Place' street planning and design. *IATSS Research 32*(1), 14–25.

Kang, C. D., & Cervero, R. (2008). *From elevated freeway to linear park: Land price impacts of Seoul, Korea's CGC Project.* Retrieved from www.its.berkeley.edu/sites/default/files/publications/UCB/2008/VWP/UCB-ITS-VWP-2008-7.pdf.

Kemp, R. L., & Stephani, C. J. (2015). *Urban transportation innovations world-wide.* Jefferson, NC: McFarland.

Laplante, J., & McCann, B. (2008). Complete streets: We can get there from here. *Institute of Transport Engineers 78*(5), 24–28. Retrieved from www.smartgrowthamerica.org/documents/cs/resources/cs-ite-may08.pdf.

Levere, M. (2014). *The High Line Park and timing of capitalization of public goods.* Retrieved from http://econweb.ucsd.edu/~mlevere/pdfs/highline_paper.pdf.

Li, W., Bai, Y., Zhou, W., Han, C., & Han, L. (2014). Land use significantly affects the distribution of urban green space: Case study of Shanghai, China. *Journal of Urban Planning and Development 141*(3), A4014001.

Linck, H. (2008). *Car free experience in Freiburg-Vauban.* Retrieved from www.atr.fc.it/admin/PagPar.php?op=fg&id_pag_par=1317&fld=file.

Lo, H. K., Tang, S., & Wang, D. Z. (2008). Managing the accessibility on mass public transit: The case of Hong Kong. *Journal of Transport and Land Use 1*(2), 23–49. Retrieved from http://hdl.handle.net/1783.1/8685.

Macdonald, E. (2006). Building a boulevard. *ACCESS Magazine 1*(28). Retrieved from https://escholarship.org/uc/item/94h4j1r4.

Maeda, A. (2010). *Aiming for the creation of new space: Development of Tokyo Station City.* Tokyo: JR East.

McIntosh, J., Trubka, R., & Newman, P. (2014). Can value capture work in a car dependent city? Willingness to pay for transit access in Perth, Western Australia. *Transportation Research Part A: Policy and Practice 67*, 320–339.

Metro Joint Development Program. (2014). *Completed projects.* Retrieved from http://media.metro.net/projects_studies/tod/images/TOD_completed projects.pdf.

Metro Joint Development Program. (2015). *Policies and process.* Retrieved from http://media.metro.net/projects_studies/joint_development/images/JDP_policies_process_2015-07.pdf.

Mikesh, N. (2007). *Curitiba case study.* Retrieved from https://depts.washington.edu/open2100/Resources/1_OpenSpaceSystems/Open_Space_Systems/Curitiba%20Case%20Study.pdf.

Ministerie van Verkeer en Waterstaat (MVW). (2006). *Road traffic signs and regulations in the Netherlands.* The Hague: MVW.

Monderman, H. (2005). *Shared space: Room for everyone: A new vision for public spaces.* Groningen: Fryslân Province Retrieved from http://sharedspace.org/wp-content/uploads/2014/10/Room-for-everyone.pdf.

Municipal Transportation Agency. (2015a). *Octavia Boulevard enhancement project.* Retrieved from www.sfmta.com/projects-planning/projects/octavia-boulevard-enhancement-project.

Municipal Transportation Agency. (2015b). *Octavia Boulevard enhancement project.* Retrieved from www.sfmta.com/sites/default/files/projects/2015/Open%20House%20Board_1.pdf.

Newman, P. (2012). *Why do we need a good public transport system?* Retrieved from www.curtin.edu.au/research/cusp/local/docs/pb-cusp-research-paper-section-abcd.pdf.

Newman, P., Bachels, M., & Scheurer, J. (2011). *The knowledge arc light rail: Sections F and G*. Perth, WA: Curtin University. Retrieved from www.curtin.edu.au/research/cusp/local/docs/cusp-arc-lrt-tod-hr.pdf.

nMotion. (2015). *Nashville MTA strategic plan, transit strategies: Transit-oriented development*. Retrieved from http://nmotion2015.com/wp-content/uploads/2016/08/MTA_RecommendedPlan-Draft.pdf.

Oc, T., & Tiesdell, S. (1997). *Safer city centres: Revivng the public realm*. London: Paul Chapman.

Rao, K. (2011). Seoul tears down an urban highway and the city can breathe again. Retrieved from http://grist.org/infrastructure/2011-04-04-seoul-korea-tears-down-an-urban-highway-life-goes-on/.

Raphael, C. (2009). Car-free German town captures American imagination. Retrieved from www.pps.org/blog/car-free-german-town-captures-american-imagination/.

Rauf, R. (2010). *Complete streets: A case study of Boulder, Colorado, and the great streets initiative*. Retrieved from www.uc.edu/cdc/niehoff_studio/programs/great_streets/w10/ppt/complete_streets_ppt.pdf.

Ritter, P. (1964). *Planning for man and motor*. Oxford: Pergamon Press.

San Francisco Planning Department. (2015). *San Francisco parklet manual version 2.2*. Retrieved from http://pavementtoparks.org/wp-content/uploads//2015/12/SF_P2P_Parklet_Manual_2.2_FULL1.pdf.

San Francisco Planning Department. (2016). Green connections. Retrieved from http://sf-planning.org/green-connections.

Scheurer, J. (2001). *Urban ecology, innovations in housing policy and the future of cities: Towards sustainability in neighbourhood communities*. Doctoral dissertation, Murdoch University Institute of Sustainable Transport, Perth, WA. Retrieved from http://trove.nla.gov.au/work/24548674?q&versionId=29633940.

Schwartz, H. (2004). *Urban renewal, municipal revitalization: The case of Curitiba, Brazil*. Alexandria, VA: Higher Education Publications.

Singh, M., & Sharma, R. (2012). Financing options for a transit system through real estate. Paper presented at the European Transport Conference 2012, Glasgow, UK. Retrieved from http://abstracts.aetransport.org/paper/index/id/4005/confid/18.

Steinmuller, A. (2015). Beyond bottom-up in San Francisco: Public–private initiatives and the potential for proactive citizenship. Retrieved from www.part-urbs.com/anthology/beyond_bottom_up_in_san_francisco.

Suzuki, H., Cervero, R., & Iuchi, K. (2013). *Transforming cities with transit: Transit and land-use integration for sustainable urban development*. Washington, D.C.: World Bank.

Suzuki, H., Dastur, A., Moffatt, S., Yabuki, N., & Maruyama, H. (2010). *Eco2 cities: Ecological cities as economic cities*. Retrieved from https://openknowledge.worldbank.org/handle/10986/2453.

Tadamun. (2014). Mayors and innovation: Examples for Egypt from Curitiba. Retrieved from www.tadamun.info/2014/10/02/mayors-innovation-comparing-curitiba-cairo-2/?lang=en.

Tan, C. (2010, June). *Evaluation of lane reduction 'road diet' measures on crashes*. Retrieved from www.fhwa.dot.gov/publications/research/safety/10053/.

Tiwari, R., & Curtis, C. (2010). Approaches to arterial road design in Perth: The challenges ahead. In I. Alexander, S. Greive, & D. Hedgcock (Eds.) *Planning perspectives from Western Australia: A reader in theory and practice* (pp. 289–305). Fremantle, WA: Fremantle Press.

Tiwari, R., & Curtis, C. (2012). A three-pronged approach to urban arterial design: A functional + physical + social classification. *Urban Design Inernational 17*(2), 129–143.

Toccolini, A., Fumagalli, N., & Senes, G. (2006). Greenways planning in Italy: The Lambro river valley greenways system. *Landscape and Urban Planning 76*, 98–111.

Transport Division. (2016). *Safe Streets Boulder report*. Retrieved from www-static.bouldercolorado.gov/docs/2016_Safe_Streets_Boulder_Report_FINAL-1-201605241239.pdf.

Transport for London. (2014). *Street types for London*. Retrieved from https://tfl.gov.uk/info-for/boroughs/street-types.

UN Habitat. (2013). *State of the world's cities 2012/2013: Prosperity of cities*. Retrieved from https://sustainabledevelopment.un.org/content/documents/745habitat.pdf.

University College London. (2016). A new approach to urban street planning and design. Retrieved from www.ucl.ac.uk/impact/case-study-repository/new-approach-to-urban-street-planning.

Utter, M. A. (2009). Developing TOD in America: The private sector view. In C. Curtis, J. L. Renne, & L. Bertolini. (Eds.) *Transit oriented development: Making it happen* (pp. 209–225). Farnham: Ashgate.

Vernon, B., & Tiwari, R. (2009). Place-making through water-sensitive urban design. *Sustainability 1*(4), 789–814.

Village Well. (2006, July). *Train stations as places for community wellbeing*. Retrieved from www.vichealth.vic.gov.au/~/media/ProgramsandProjects/PlanningHealthyEnvironments/Attachments/Train_Stations_Community_Wellbeing2.ashx.

Vision Mumbai. (n.d.). *Policy Note #4: New approaches to development control regulations and alternative spatial strategies for setting FSI values*. Retrieved from www.visionmumbai.org/images/projects/Document_DCR%20Options%2008x%20abscvk031313042241.pdf.

Wolcha, J. R., Byrne, J., & Newell, J. P. (2014). Urban green space, public health, and environmental justice: The challenge of making cities 'just green enough'. *Landscape and Urban Planning 125*, 234–244.

Woldeamanuel, M. (2016). *Concepts in urban transportation planning: The quest for mobility, sustainability and quality of life*. Jefferson, NC: McFarland. Retrieved from www.mcfarlandbooks.com/book-2.php?id=978-0-7864-9966-3.

WRI. (2014). *Mobility policies and planning*. Retrieved from http://wricitieshub.org/aggregator/sources/6?page=1.

Xiu, N. (2014). Do urban green corridors 'work'? In *The nature of cities*. Retrieved from www.thenatureofcities.com/2014/10/05/do-urban-green-corridors-work-it-depends-on-what-we-want-them-to-do-what-ecological-andor-social-functions-can-we-realistically-expect-green-corridors-to-perform-in-cities-what-attributes-defi/.

Zacharias, J., Zhang, T., & Nakajima, U. D. (2011). Tokyo Station City: The railway station as urban place. *Urban Design International 16*(4), 242–251.

CHAPTER 4

'MAKING' PLACES
Urban and Suburban Transformations

A place embodies both the tangible and the intangible attributes of the built environment: its natural landscape and architecture, the events and occurrences within it, and its history and memory. This chapter explores a palette of urban and suburban place typologies that integrate movement and place functions. The aim is to make places that can be easily accessed and that provide their users with a collective meaning and identity.

The Industrial Revolution of the late eighteenth to early nineteenth century brought more people to already established inner-city areas. The intensity of activities in urban cores led to overburdened basic services and gave rise to pollution, unhygienic living conditions, and unplanned development. Previously prosperous centers experienced urban decline, resulting, in extreme cases, in outright abandonment of them. At this time, the modern car was in many ways viewed as a savior, and received with open arms. It became a means of freedom (Nyström, 2001), enabling people to escape the oppressive, polluted, and overcrowded inner-city areas. In most developed cities, automobile-oriented living has become synonymous with urban life in the post-Second World War era. The automobile significantly impacted urban morphology, its scale, and its experience. The primacy of the old city center was diffused over multiple suburban hubs, business parks, suburban gated estates, and shopping malls, leading to an incoherent and dispersed city morphology (Jacobs, 1961). While the scale of buildings shifted from a human scale to giant malls and office complexes, the experience of streetscape and urbanscape became high paced. The automobile compelled the city to be experienced or viewed as a panorama (Boyer, 1994, p. 40) where the suburbanites could navigate around the city without encountering the lives of the residents of the inner city. A disconnection between people emerged, removing any opportunity for them to engage with each other (Boyer, 1994) or to connect with the city closely—what I term a state of *car-disconnect*.

This rapid development of a new suburban morphology has occurred in parallel with inner-city decline the world over, demanding that the issues within the urban cores and suburban developments are addressed simultaneously. In city centers, the earlier congestion caused by the confluence of horses, carriages, bicycles, and streetcars has been replaced by automobile congestion. A further challenge has been to accommodate motorized traffic in cities that were designed for walking and horse-drawn carts.

With an efficient, less damaging transportation network, can decayed inner-city areas become 'places' served by and connected to other places? Can transport connectivity and place making feed off and reinforce each other and enhance livability in these areas?

While the above questions need to be asked in the context of inner-city or urban transformation, consideration should simultaneously be given to the fundamental transformation occurring in suburbs. In the US, the once affluent, middle-class suburbs of 30 years ago are being gentrified. New immigrants, the elderly, singles, and childless households are over-represented in the suburban populace (Tachieva, 2010). This is also true for suburbs in Australian cities, where an investigation of the socioeconomic impact of rising fuel prices and general price inflation revealed the gentrified outer and fringe suburban zones to be the most vulnerable (Dodson et al., 2006). How far can 'business-as-usual' planning with more emphasis on a car culture (Schiller et al., 2010) and less investment in transit provision go towards addressing social inequity and giving universal accessibility to jobs and services?

Jane Jacobs (1961) argues that modernist urban planning destroyed communities and decimated their economies by creating isolated, inefficient, and unnatural urban spaces as well as car-dependent urban growth. The capital and operational costs of sprawled suburban developments, she argues, outweigh the costs of inner-city redevelopment. Although these costs are area specific, the evidence suggests that the cost difference between the two development forms can be 50 percent (SGS Economics & Planning, 2003). A study done on Australian cities by Roman Trubka, Peter Newman, and Darren Bilsborough (2010, p. 1) concludes that 'the savings in transport and infrastructure for 1000 dwellings are in the order of $86 million up-front for infrastructure and $250 million for annualised transportation costs over 50 years'. The most significant cost is road transport, followed by water and sewerage infrastructure. The higher-density inner city consumes between four and ten times less transport energy than the lower-density outer suburbs (Newman, 2014). Moreover, the socioeconomic toll of living in suburban areas is sometimes increased by poor access to education, healthcare, and employment opportunities (NSW Parliamentary Library, 2014).

The New Climate Economy Project of the Global Commission on the Economy and Climate suggests that by 2030 the world's 724 largest cities could reduce annual greenhouse gas emissions by up to 1.5 billion tonnes of carbon dioxide equivalent through more compact urban growth (Global Commission on the Economy and Climate, 2014, p. 30).

Local governments, urban practitioners, and academics have recognized a need for a twofold strategy for compact urban growth: the need to focus on reinvesting in and regenerating inner cities; and the need to make connections to the suburbs stronger and more affordable while making them attractive and livable.

Redeveloping inner cities according to the concept of connecting places means managed re-densification or strategic residential infill by first rebuilding the physical fabric and eventually rebuilding lost social diversity and the local economic base. This process invites higher-density, proximate development with functionally and socially diverse neighborhoods, walkable streets, public transport, and human-scale local urban environments (OECD, 2012). The result is a heightened sense of community.

Inner-city areas with the potential to be transformed as connected places tend to be areas where the initial land use has become redundant. These areas have been through a 'land use shock', are economically obsolete due to the closure or shrinkage of major industry or docks, or are no longer self-sustainable. The shutting down of major employment centers also has a profound impact on local shops and services, and on neighborhood life in general. Examples are redundant industrial zones, unused rail yards, and redundant dockyards.

In the case of suburbia, traditional zone-based regulations (Talen, 2013) that have historically led to single-use and fragmented developments are under revision. They are being replaced by Form-Based Codes or Smart Codes (Parolek et al., 2008), where the emphasis is on urban form, pattern, and mixed use in an effort to retrofit and repair the low-density, single-use suburbs. The biggest challenge lies in tapping opportunities for transforming auto-oriented shopping malls, mono-zoned institutional campuses, and edge city typologies into mixed-use, compact developments with ample open spaces encouraging public transit, walking, and cycling (Kotharkar et al., 2012).

Redundant Industrial Zones

Most cities of the developed world and a few in the developing world were once important centers with a dynamic industrial and cultural character. The prosperity these cities enjoy today is a result of past industrial activities (Smith, 2008). Industries were usually located on valuable land in the city center. In the next phase—post-industrialization—the service sector emerged and manufacturing declined. De-industrialization of the inner core led to urban decay with high unemployment, poverty, and a degraded physical environment. A number of public and private funding initiatives have been devoted to redeveloping such areas. The principles of New Urbanism (in the US and Australia) and Urban Renaissance (in Europe) have guided such urban redevelopment (Congress for the New Urbanism, 2015; Council of Europe, 1986; Duany Plater-Zyberk, 2016; Government of Western Australia, 2015; Pearson, 2012; Zetter, 1982).

An example of an industrial ruin that once had a function is a vacant Western Electric warehouse building in Dallas, Texas. It was transformed in 1997 into Mockingbird Station, a mixed-use retail, office, and rental loft TOD. The warehouse, a concrete building of three stories with high ceilings built in 1947, was in an extreme state of disrepair (Boroski & Arrington, 2002). Architects and developers resisted pressures to demolish the historic structure, and instead mined and reused its components to house 180 dwelling types (Pitts, 2008). Renovating the structure added to the place value of the area. Most importantly, by working with the fabric of the warehouse and responding to the envisaged activities, the design aesthetics remained faithful to the former essence. Most of the old brick walls have been left exposed and the jalousie windows have been retained. The bowstring truss of the original building is remembered through a distinctive arched roof that caps the structure (Figure 4.1). This leads to a heightened sense of place that in itself acts as an attractor.

The private developer, Ken Hughes, who initiated the project, was able to take advantage of the building's proximity to Dallas' CBD (an eight-minute train ride) and the expanding Dallas Area Rapid Transit (DART) rail line (Boroski & Arrington, 2002). The project was planned to integrate with the transit system. The new pedestrian bridge to the station and the improved bus stops and new parking areas near the station have improved accessibility. The landscaped pedestrian bridge introduces the development by leading the pedestrian through a series of gardens and a public courtyard with a water feature. Public open space becomes a hub for social activities, increasing the opportunity for Mockingbird Station to be a 'node-place'.[1] Extensive landscaping, streetscaping, and use of native materials, such as Austin

Figure 4.1 New development—an extension on the old: Mockingbird Station, Dallas

Source: Drawn on Google Maps by Google, 2016.

URBAN AND SUBURBAN TRANSFORMATIONS

Figure 4.2 Open spaces and walkways in and around the Mockingbird development
Source: Pictures by D. Menon (2016).

stone, provide connection to the context (Boroski & Arrington, 2002; Figure 4.2). By choosing the option of orienting the central plaza towards the transit line rather than placing it adjacent to the entries from the highway and arterial, the project emphasizes its preference for transit users (Creed et al., 2013).

According to Ken Hughes,

> Once people see how closely we are identified with DART's Mockingbird Station, they see the potential for taking the train instead of driving. I take people over to Mockingbird Station and show them the BMWs and Volvos parked there; these people are using mass transit because they like it.
> (Quoted in Boroski & Arrington, 2002, p. 6)

The project has attracted tenants due to its proximity to transit, and there are strong indications from both the current and prospective tenants that there will be an increase in transit ridership in the future.

The high-density zoning permits mixed land use, with 211 loft apartments, a movie theater, 150,000 square feet of office space, and 183,000 square feet of restaurants and boutiques in the former warehouse (Dittmar & Ohland, 2004, p. 159). Mixed land use made it possible for the developer to apply a reduced parking credit (Boroski & Arrington, 2002), while the intensified activities increase the efficiency of the transit system and promote a dense neighborhood.

However, there are a few barriers that need to be overcome in order for Mockingbird Station to be a connected place. The connectivity to the adjacent land uses is a cause for concern. The residential, retail, and commercial functions are destinations that are not yet accessible for pedestrians from the surrounding neighborhoods, due to the highway and heavily trafficked arterial that presently tend to isolate the areas from each other (Figure 4.3). Additionally, the pedestrian link that leads from the Mockingbird development across the railway line ends up in a sea of car parks, making pedestrians highly vulnerable to unsafe situations. Pedestrian amenities have been installed in a fragmented fashion, with discontinuous and narrow sidewalks. The design of public spaces is still car-centric. The built form and street interface can be improved by buffering activities occurring on pavements from street-side parking (Figure 4.4).

The rent for retail space at Mockingbird Station (as of 2002) was $40 per square foot, about $15 more than average Dallas retail rents.

MAPPING THE CONTEXT

Figure 4.3 Map showing the connectivity aspects of the Mockingbird development

Source: Drawn on Google Maps by Google, 2016.

Figure 4.4 Mixed land use development, at Mockingbird Station

Source: Adapted from Google Street View by Google Earth 2016.

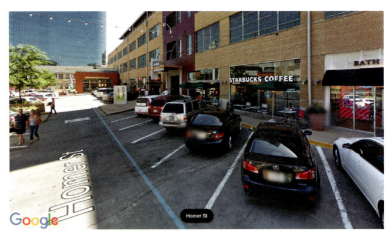

Residential rent was also higher: $1.52 per square foot, compared to $1.25 in neighboring apartments (Boroski & Arrington, 2002). The higher rent in the redeveloped area raises concerns about potential gentrification in such projects, where people with money are able to exercise their 'right to buy'. This results in weakening local networks and a loss of the sense of belonging—aspects that are critical for the development of a connected place. This should be a consideration for the next phase of the Mockingbird project.

Unused/Underutilized Rail Yards

Many railway yards servicing the industrial system became redundant and abandoned brownfields in post-industrial cities; others were left isolated when the surrounding land uses became defunct. These yards were strategically located within the inner-city core, so the challenge is to redevelop them as connected places by minimizing gentrification and creating inclusive and equitable places.

The Hoboken Yard Redevelopment Area was deemed to be an 'area in need of redevelopment' by the City of Hoboken, New Jersey

URBAN AND SUBURBAN TRANSFORMATIONS

Figure 4.5 Map showing the Hoboken Terminal Redevelopment Precinct

Source: Drawn on Google Maps by Google, 2016.

(City of Hoboken, 2014a). A relocation of the rail operations to the Rail Operations Center in Meadowlands has occurred, and although some zones within the complex are functionally efficient, others are dysfunctional, underutilized, and/or in need of an overhaul. A long history of ownership changes has resulted in many structures being demolished, transportation modes being eliminated, and facilities being relocated (Phillips Preiss Shapiro Associates, 2006). The lack of a sense of community is induced by the way in which the neighborhood block to the north comes to a halt at the rail yards, resulting in poor pedestrian connectivity (Figure 4.5).

The Hoboken Terminal and Yard within the area identified for redevelopment is of great locational value, as it connects Hoboken and Jersey City. With this in mind, the 2003 master plan called for the area to be developed as a gateway for the city, a destination for the regional area. The area also boasts historic structures that have the potential to offer a strong sense of place. This historic character was not reflected in the 2008 plan prepared by the City and New Jersey Transit, however, and hence was not adopted. To address place making, the city decided to embark on a redevelopment plan in 2011; for this, considerable input and consensus from the community, stakeholders, and property owners was sought through surveys, meetings, and workshops. All feedback was posted on the City of Hoboken website, and community feedback was incorporated in the redevelopment plan. An updated economic analysis and amended 2014 redevelopment plan incorporated the post-Hurricane Sandy flood mitigation considerations for a resilient and sustainable community (City of Hoboken, 2014b). Land proposed for parklands in the Coastal High Hazard area was purchased, and strategies of stormwater retention and management through the use of rain gardens, sea walls, and flood barriers are being developed (Bailin, 2014).

The 2014 master plan recommended a mixed-use, integrated transit center as a gateway to the Hudson waterfront. The proposal connects the area with other parts of the city by railroad, light rail, PATH commuter rail, the Trans-Hudson ferry service, and the regional bus service. About 50,000 commuters pass through Hoboken

Terminal on a typical weekday morning. This provides a base support and accessibility for all economic development projects in the redevelopment area, and an opportunity for TOD as a world-class multi-modal transportation hub (City of Hoboken, 2014a, 2014b).

Diversity of land uses has been achieved through an interplay of three precincts: the heritage precinct, which includes the historic terminal, office, transportation-related uses, and ground-floor retail uses, in the vicinity of the terminal facilities; the commercial mixed-use district (C-MU), proposed to be an office and commercial TOD within walking distance of the terminal building; and the residential mixed-use district (R-MU), with the proposed residential uses congruent with existing residential areas on the north side of the highway (Figure 4.5). The blurring of the edges between these three precincts is essential for tangible infrastructure connections and for the intangible connections required for a strong sense of community.

Such redevelopment can be prone to gentrification, as discussed in the case of Mockingbird Station. Social diversity and equity as key elements of a connected place should be encouraged through mandatory affordable housing. Keeping this in mind, the Hoboken redevelopment is providing at least 10 percent affordable units in this area. Different public transport modes in the area will contribute further to diversity and equity by attracting various segments of population to the area. The reconstruction of the bus terminal is proposed, while the infrastructure for other transit modes will be restored. A bicycle network link will connect the redevelopment area with other parts of the city.

Place making is an important component. A variety of public spaces, including indoor space, a piazza, and green roofs, will create a vibrant pedestrian environment. The plan proposes parks and pedestrian plazas, with a minimum of 4.5 acres of public spaces in the redevelopment area. The public spaces will feature street furnishings, lighting, landscaping, seating, public art, and green infrastructure that contributes to water management. To avoid canyon effects at street level, the heights of the buildings in the redevelopment area will vary throughout for all land uses (City of Hoboken, 2012; Figure 4.6).

The synthesis of old and new architectural aesthetics is planned through the rehabilitation and restoration of historic buildings, and the construction of a mixed-use development with modern office, retail, and residential spaces. This will enhance and build on the existing heritage footprint of the area.

As an economically sustainable connected place, the redevelopment is envisaged to provide 11,000 new permanent jobs, millions of dollars of revenue for the authorities, US $ 50 million of annual consumer spending, and upgraded infrastructure to protect against natural disasters (Pappas, 2016).

Redundant Docklands in Melbourne

Urban ports were the economic heart of cities and countries in the 1960s. A port was a place of commerce and industry. Seed industries and distribution-intensive enterprises were offered

URBAN AND SUBURBAN TRANSFORMATIONS

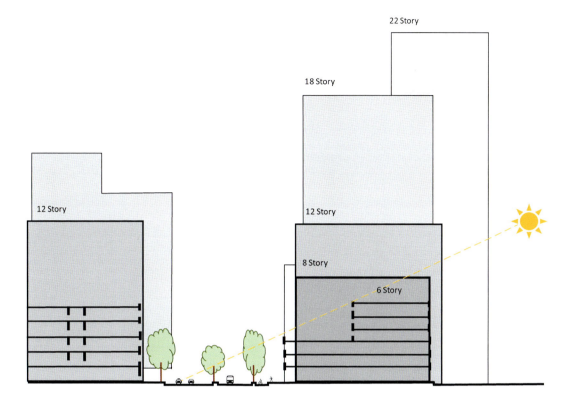

Figure 4.6 Varied height of buildings to avoid the canyon effect

attractive locations. Either through targeted development or the unplanned growth of interdependent industries, many ports developed as industrial clusters. Eventually, steamships replaced sailing ships, requiring larger docks and deep-water berths. With technological advances and dramatic increases in vessel sizes, inner-city ports could no longer handle the port functions (Bird, 1971; Slack, 1975, 1980). Today, larger ports that are multi-modal and efficient are being developed beyond the city limits as replacements for the deteriorated and abandoned within-city ports. These abandoned areas are ready to be transformed as connected places due to their location and an already established infrastructure.

An example is the Melbourne Docklands area (Places Victoria & City of Melbourne, 2012), which was Melbourne's largest and busiest port from the 1950s to the 1990s. This area covered nearly 190 hectares of land, including 44 hectares of water and more than 7 kilometers of waterfront (State Government of Victoria, 2016). Wharves, warehouses, and rail yards were the dominant land uses throughout the mid-1800s (Wood, 2009). By the late 1980s, however, Docklands had become a redundant inner-city industrial wasteland, located west of Melbourne's CBD (Figure 4.7a).

Aware of the desirability of inner-city living and the growth in Melbourne's population, the Victorian Government took the opportunity to extend the western edge of Melbourne's CBD to its historic Docklands (State Government of Victoria, 2016). The proximity of Docklands to Melbourne's main transport networks, including

MAPPING THE CONTEXT

Figure 4.7 (a) Docklands within the City of Melbourne (top); (b) nodes and connections (bottom)

Source: Drawn on Google Maps by Google, 2016.

Southern Cross Station, increased the accessibility and locational value of the area (Figure 4.7b). An attempt to connect the CBD to the east was made by introducing a bridge across the railways. An arterial thoroughfare, Wurundjeri Way, next to the football stadium, fed the traffic to and from the motorways (Shaw, 2013; Figure 4.7b).

URBAN AND SUBURBAN TRANSFORMATIONS

Figure 4.8 The initial development icons, the stadium and the residential towers at New Quay

Source: Pictures by L. Tiwari (2015).

The nearby football stadium, which was a potential dead space, initiated the development of the area as a destination (Figure 4.8). Anticipated in the plan was a dense development with the conversion of industrial wasteland into a modern visitor destination with diverse activities. Initially the plan was devoid of social housing, community facilities, and environmental initiatives, and these factors were included in the new mandate from 2000 onwards. 'For all people and their needs', 'focused on the public realm', 'ecologically sustainable', and 'creative and innovative' were the themes that were introduced (Docklands Authority, 2000, p. 66).

The redevelopment transformed Docklands into a modern residential, commercial, and visitor destination in inner-city Melbourne. From 2001 to 2015, the residential population grew from 658 to 10,000, while its working population grew from 600 to 53,000 — a rapid increase. In recent years, tram lines and bus routes have been introduced, and the bicycle infrastructure and pedestrian pathways improved (Figure 4.9). A study in 2011 on modal split revealed 30 percent of Docklands residents travel by car and 34 percent walk, as compared to 41 percent and 13 percent in inner-city Melbourne (Places Victoria & City of Melbourne, 2013, p. 18; Figure 4.10). The improved infrastructure has also made the area more accessible from other parts of the city and paved the way for TOD.

Figure 4.9 Cycle-friendly infrastructure

Source: Redrawn using data from Access Docklands (p. 33), by Places Victoria and City of Melbourne, 2013.

Figure 4.10 Travel modal split for Docklands and inner-city Melbourne

Source: Picture by L. Tiwari (2015).

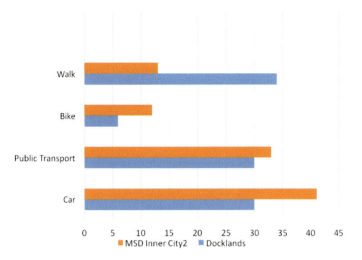

Despite these improvements, the Docklands area has largely been considered unsuccessful from a place-making perspective (Ansett & Singline, 2012). It is described as an example of 'ideal-type place-less neoliberalism' (Hackworth & Moriah, 2006, p. 510). Its high-rise glass and metal structures located within big blocks and network of suspended walkways do not belong to the Melbourne grid people know—the three-tiered, human-scale, intricate grid of criss-crossing streets and laneways that lend diversity and authenticity while providing a ground for spontaneous pop-up creative events (Shaw, 2013).

The key to place making for a successful connected place is the involvement of the community in planning and development. Efforts are now under way to create public space through people-centered planning at Docklands. The Docklands Public Realm Plan (2012) and the Docklands Community and Place Plan (2012) describe the key community infrastructure projects that could create 'place' for the people in the Docklands area. The existing Docklands Community Garden, the Docklands Sports Court, the newly opened library, and the 42 artwork installations across its parks, promenades, and public spaces are some of the interventions for creating community spaces (Lucas, 2014; Figure 4.11). Public spaces at Docklands are lined with urban art. There is a piazza with two permanent screens in which up to 10,000 people congregate. However, the recent (April 2015) approval by the City of Melbourne, after no consultation with the Docklands Community (Docklands Community Association, 2016), of a 17-story residential tower to be built on the piazza could destroy this open event area (Docklands News, 2015).

The government is planning further place-making activities in the Docklands area, including the interpretation of heritage elements in public space, the infilling of major movement corridors with activated laneways, and the extension of public transport. Short-term creative art and performance spaces, temporary uses, such as pop-up vending stores and busking, and a variety of land- and water-based activities should address place activation concerns of the public domain (Figure 4.11).

URBAN AND SUBURBAN TRANSFORMATIONS

Figure 4.11 Public space and public art at Docklands
Source: Picture by L. Tiwari (2015).

The absence of a mix of ages, social, and economic diversity and a lack of affordable housing continue to plague the Docklands development and hinder the people-focused principles of connecting places. This mainly stems from a lack of community participation and strategic planning in the initial stages of development, which allowed the commercial side to dominate in the development.

Considered within the framework of connecting places, the historic Docklands area enjoys an ideal location near the CBD, with access via Southern Cross Station, part of the city's main transport network. Recent improvements in bicycle infrastructure, pedestrian pathways, and tram lines are examples of demand management (Figure 4.11 a, b), adding to the mobility convenience of the community and reducing the use of private vehicles and carbon emissions (Figure 4.11 c, d).

Although the Docklands development will achieve a high density under the existing approach, policies need to focus more on the mix of uses, a human-scale urban form, and equity through greater participation of diverse groups in the decision-making process. With recent governance changes, these issues are being addressed, and Docklands has the potential to become an example of a connected place in the future.

Mono-use Zones: Curtin University Campus

Many university campuses were originally conceived as mono-use areas peripheral to the city, but now they find themselves within the inner-city core as a result of city expansion. How can such destinations be transformed into connected places?

Curtin University, located in the car-oriented city of Perth, Western Australia, is one such example. The university area, formerly a pine plantation, is dedicated chiefly to education, research, and development. The university is seen as a destination and not as a place to live, work, and play. Due to the lack of a permanent population in the area, there is little activity after university hours. The high reliance on private vehicles for transport, narrow-focused employment prospects for students and surrounding residents, and the limited night-time and day-time activities all add up to an unfriendly place for the young and the elderly, while the underutilization of space contributes to Perth's sprawl (Tiwari et al., 2011).

Although 8,000 international students attend Curtin University, only 1,175 can be accommodated on campus. The lack of affordable housing on campus or in the immediate neighborhood could be a major barrier to attracting students in future. Reducing the level of motorized transport and congestion in the area is also a challenge, as students commute over long distances.

A study conducted in 2009 revealed that in a business-as-usual (BAU) scenario, the transport emissions around residential and office/student uses and around retail/commercial/service uses would jump over 130 percent and 500 percent respectively by 2031 as compared to 2009 figures. A TOD-based scenario could halve the amount of carbon dioxide produced as compared to a BAU scenario (Tiwari et al., 2011; Figure 4.12). This could be achieved using the Avoid, Shift, Improve, and Finance (ASIF) paradigm (Dalkmann & Brannigan, 2007) in combination with a Density, Diversity, and Design model. As the biggest trip generator is the university, increasing student housing would reduce trip generation, while a simultaneous focus on sustainable urbanism (higher densities, diversity, and rich design that ensures a high-quality place) and multi-modal transport would help in *avoiding* the projected increased carbon emissions. 'Carrots' (integrated transport and land use, active transport infrastructure) and 'sticks' (car-only areas and increased parking charges) would lead to a *shift* in travel behavior and patterns. Infrastructure and amenities for transit passengers would be *improved* with real-time passenger information, provision of shade, and shelter, and *financing* invested heavily in BRT.

The Greater Curtin Master Plan 2031 (2014) has been developed along the above lines, with the aim of attracting 44,000 students and 73,000 daily visitors, to become an employment hub for 20,000

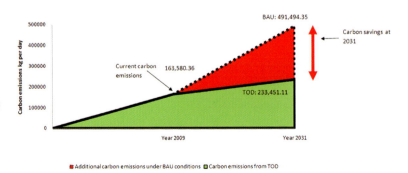

Figure 4.12 Carbon savings in a transit-oriented scenario as compared to a business-as-usual scenario

Source: 'Driving CO2 reductions by integrating transport and urban design strategies,' by R. Tiwari, R. Cervero, & L. Schipper, 2011, Cities, 28(5), p. 403.

URBAN AND SUBURBAN TRANSFORMATIONS

jobs and a place of residence for 20,000 staff and students by 2031. The vision is for a vibrant urban environment that is 'responsive and respectful to the land and cultures it is built on' (Curtin University, 2014, p. 21) and contributes about A$4.5 billion to the local and state economies.

As a connected place, Greater Curtin will be home to a diverse and integrated community. The goal is to provide a boundless and adaptable urban context that supports engagement between industries, businesses, governments, and researchers, and forges partnerships where new thoughts will be conceived and knowledge and innovation will extend beyond the buildings. Businesses will be able to locate within the university area so students will study in real-life environments. Living at Curtin would mean driving 79 percent fewer kilometers, and carbon dioxide emissions would be reduced by 54 percent (Curtin University, 2014).

The integration of public art with daily activities at the campus has already commenced and is promoting a stimulating and creative place. Workshops and student assignments have moved out of the classroom and into the public space, making it more activated, engaging, and safe (Figure 4.13). New buildings have been planned, ensuring the preservation of the existing pine plantation and other trees. The retention of local flora will preserve the genius loci. A living stream connected to the nearby Canning River is proposed as an urban amenity and a stormwater treatment facility.

The Greater Curtin Master Plan incorporates various features appreciated by current campus users and demonstrates effective place making. Being a university of technology, Curtin needs to ensure that the digital tools of communication, information delivery, maintenance, and systems efficiency are developed in an integrated manner for the development of a connected environment at all levels of transport, place, and people.

Figure 4.13 Place activation at Curtin

Source: Pictures by Place Activation, Curtin University (2015) and R. Tiwari (2015).

MAPPING THE CONTEXT

Breaking the Big-Box Shopping Center: The Crossings at Mountain View, California

Promoted by the Garden City movement and a hike in consumerism, the dense, socially heterogeneous consumption space of city centers has been replaced by the suburbs' clean, sprawling, socially and visually homogeneous shopping centers, known as galleria or malls (Zukin, 1998). The malls—or big boxes—generated myriad problems. How can these big boxes be broken?

The Urban Land Institute at Washington, D.C. reconceptualizes these areas around changes that have happened in shopping preferences (such as internet shopping), family work patterns (both parents at work), traffic congestion, and so on (Beyard et al., 2006). Currently, there is a process of reversal towards dense, mixed-use, pedestrian-oriented street retail. Examples such as the Washington Center in Gaithersburg, Maryland, and Bella Terra in Huntington Beach, California, create hybrid indoor–outdoor spaces, engendering a deeper sense of connection between customers, their community, culture, climate, and daily lives (Beyard et al., 2006).

The neighborhood of Crossings around San Antonio transit station in Mountain View, California, has replaced a failed strip mall occupying 18 acres of land with residential and commercial projects concentrated along the commuter rail line (Kaiser, 2010; Figure 4.14). To address diminishing business, the development policy for the neighborhood included improved accessibility, expansion of community space, and enhanced livability with a mix of uses (City of Mountain View, 2012).

Figure 4.14 Location of the Crossings neighborhood in San Antonio Transit Center change area—a station node on the Bus Transit and Caltrain corridors

Source: Drawn on Google Maps by Google, 2016.

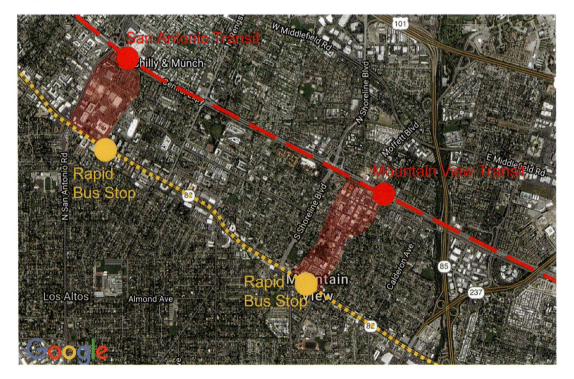

URBAN AND SUBURBAN TRANSFORMATIONS

Infilling with residential use is targeted to a population looking for relatively affordable housing in the high-cost Silicon Valley real estate market, and creates a tax base for the city (US Environmental Protection Agency, 2016). Affordability comes with the compact design, where residential density is at 30 units per net acre in comparison to 7–10 units per net acre in the city. The typology ranges from single-family bungalows, smaller cottages, and townhouses to condominium apartments.

The Caltrain station and San Mateo Transit buses provide regional and intra-city connectivity, respectively (US Environmental Protection Agency, 2016). The parking lots and shopping mall have been replaced with a new fine grid of streets providing neighborhood-level connectivity (Figure 4.15). The number of intersections post-redevelopment are 46, as compared to 25 prior to redevelopment. Residents are less than a five-minute walk to open space or parking from anywhere in the development. The network of tree-lined, narrow streets, sidewalks, and pocket parks emphasizes walkability and bikeability (Figure 4.16). The narrowness of the streets helps in slowing down vehicular traffic, to such an extent that the planned street width does not meet the required minimum standards for emergency access as per the local fire code. However, this was allowed, since the local community (Homeowners Association) was invited to own several identified roads as private driveways (Kaiser, 2010). This concept has

Figure 4.15 *A fine grid generates a higher level of connectivity and permeability, as demonstrated by the number of intersections: the Crossings neighborhood before (left) and after (right) redevelopment*

Source: Adapted from Google Earth by Google, 2016.

Before development of Crossings area:
No. of intersections: **25**
Area under parking: 33.11%
Usable public space: 5.97%

After development of Crossings area:
No. of intersections: **46**
Area under parking: 11.85%
Usable public space (includes the streets in the residential area): 12.03%

Figure 4.16 *Sidewalks, narrow streets, and on-street parking in the Crossings neighborhood*

Source: Adapted from Google Street View by Google, 2016.

| 71

been invaluable in cultivating a sense of community and belonging through the community's control and ownership of the local community infrastructure, while still abiding by the local legislation.

The scale of big-box buildings and large parking spaces is humanized through the distribution of small stores fronting the sidewalk. Compact morphology with zero setbacks and rear parking for buildings has resulted in an engaging pedestrian-centric streetscape. An interactive threshold between the private space of the houses and the public space of the streets is a result of the use of stoops, porches, terraces, and other features, all providing much-needed 'eyes on the streets' (Kaiser, 2010, p. 43).

As communities seek deeper connections to their environments, they are keen to experience multi-use spaces that have libraries, recreational centers, and so on, along with retail stores. The mall as an island, a retail venue surrounded by a sea of parking and set apart from everything except highways, is a single-use development that stands isolated from the everyday spaces of the community. The non-human scale and blank architectural façades turn away from surrounding neighborhoods. The mall is failing to meet the expectations of twenty-first-century shoppers (Beyard et al., 2006) and is in need of retrofit.

Edge City Retrofitting: Tysons Corner, Fairfax County, Virginia

Tysons, a small rural community located at the intersection of Route 7 and Route 123 in Fairfax County, Virginia (Mullins, 2015), transformed into a suburban office destination during the 1980s, and came to be known as the 'edge city' owing to the booming office and retail real estate market (Rathbone, 2011). Tysons grew into a tangle of office parks and commercial suburban centers and became a destination where people came to work and shop, but not stay (Davis, 2009; Mullins, 2015). The limited supply of public transport within the region required visitors and residents to use cars as their main source of transport. Tysons' location in close proximity to the highways also facilitated automobile dependence (DeGood, 2014). Around 2008, more than 50 percent of the 1,700 acres of the urban fabric was dominated by traffic-jammed highways, large residential blocks, large shopping malls, and oceans of parking lots (Davis, 2009; Figure 4.17). Civic and business leaders began to worry about roadway congestion.

The Washington D.C. Metrorail proposal to the airport gave Fairfax County the opportunity to reconfigure the existing land use at

Figure 4.17 The car-centric city with car yards (left); residential use being introduced (right)

Source: Pictures by K. Yadav (2016).

Tysons to promote mixed-use, walkable, and transit-oriented development (PB Placemaking & Cervero, 2008). The county put together a 40-year vision while working with the community in 2008 through a Land Use Task Force. TOD, green infrastructure, mobility enhancement, and community engagement were the key guiding principles for Tysons' transformation.

The plan assigns 95 percent of its developed land to be within half a mile of a train station or 600 feet of shuttle routes that provide public transport options with efficient mode transferability. Despite enhanced public transport accessibility and mobility, it is feared that the increased density will generate more vehicles and congestion. However, it can be argued that higher density will encourage a larger share of short trips that would have been driven in individual cars to shift to foot or public transport. The use of information technology (signal timing, congestion avoidance information) and congestion pricing mechanisms can help in alleviating congestion issues (Schipper et al., 2000; Tiwari et al., 2011). A decline in greenhouse gas emissions of 1.2 million tonnes, a reduction of 16 percent per capita, is envisaged (Tiwari et al., 2011).

Socioeconomic diversity has been targeted at Tysons through the proposed placement of affordable row houses on former surface parking lots. Furthermore, 20 acres of car yards with low-rise buildings near a proposed train station are being replaced by mixed-use development (Davis, 2009). These two initiatives will help stimulate diversity.

The large-scale and dispersed grid of roads with emphasis on highway infrastructure is planned to transform into a fine mesh of local and collector streets that are relatable to human scale. The intersections are being analyzed in order to mitigate the impacts of land uses and accommodate multiple modes (Fairfax County, 2015). The redevelopment plan will allow for regular inner-courtyard-type city blocks that have high density, reduced setbacks, and maximized street frontage. The maximum perimeter length for a block is 600 meters, while any block longer than 180 meters is required to have a mid-block pedestrian connection (Rathbone, 2011).

With the metro rail line from Washington opening in 2014 with four connecting stations within Tysons, property values have surged and new businesses have been established. To spur a massive increase in housing, Fairfax County is allowing developers to erect taller buildings in Tysons (Mullins, 2015).

The Tysons Park System Concept Plan proposes recreational green connectors along the majority of street networks, connecting stream valleys, urban parks, plazas, and on-road bike lanes. The greens also provide buffers from the adjacent traffic. The placement of different park types and civic spaces, as well as an emphasis on cultural and natural resource preservation and interpretation, has been given due consideration in the Park System (Fairfax County, 2015).

Public places that have been developed range from signature plazas to pop-up parks and temporary-use spaces. The needs of inhabitants and contextual response have been given due importance. Uses in these places are allocated based on recreational, cultural, and (natural) heritage perspective (Fairfax County, 2014).

MAPPING THE CONTEXT

Figure 4.18 (a) Tysons Corner Center Plaza; (b) pop-up park at Greensboro Green

Source: Reproduced from https://www.google.com.au/maps/uv?hl=en&pb=!1s0x89b64ae68411197e7%3A0x406bce9f886ea9af!2m5!2m2!1i80!2i80!3m1!2i20!3m1!7e115!4zaHR0cDovL3RpbWVsaW5lZGMuY29tL2JsbC3BsYXphLw!5sthe%20plaza%20at%20tysons%20corner%20-%20Google%20Search&imagekey=!1e1!2shttp%3A%2F%2Faccesstysons.com%2Fw%2Fwp-content%2Fuploads%2F2015%2F06%2FTysons-Plaza-Grand-Opening-macerich.jpg&sa=X&ved=0ahUKEwjmv667913PAhVCx2MKHd-_Cd4QoiolczAK. & Julie McCool, http://www.funinfairfaxva.com/wp-content/uploads/2015/07/Greensboro-Pop-up-Park-Tysons.jpg.

Tysons Corner Center Plaza, opened adjacent to the Tysons Corner Metro Station in the summer of 2014, offers at-grade connectivity between the mall and metro station while providing outdoor amenity space (Figure 4.18a). Pop-up parks are emerging; an example is Greensboro Green, which is the result of repurposing excess surface parking near a popular food truck gathering area (Figure 4.18b). The park is privately owned but offers opportunities for everyday optional activites like picnics, lunches, and musical performances (Fairfax County, 2015).

The transformation of edge city to suburban TOD is in progress. Tysons could even be carbon neutral by 2030 (Mullins, 2015). In the long term, it plans to achieve a more balanced jobs-to-households ratio of 4:1 (from the current figure of 13:1) and to include 20 percent moderate-income households in the proposed housing (Planetizen, 2016).

Close

The inner cores of many cities have unrealized potential for growth due to unused or redundant areas. Developments in such areas attract people, investments, and businesses, and present opportunities for recreating or strengthening the identity of the city. On the other hand, compactness becomes important for addressing livability in suburbs and edge cities. Urban density and form can be dramatically impacted and can lead to improvements in the overall sustainability of the city.

As discussed in this chapter, the key to sustainable redevelopment is to avoid a 'cookie-cutter' approach, and instead to apply context-specific design. High-density development principles based on the New Urbanist and transit-oriented approaches cannot be simply replicated in inner-city land, parcels in the existing suburban areas, or in the development of greenfield sites. Every development needs to be in sympathy with the local context, heritage, and culture so that the sense of place is retained.

Each site has to overcome its particular set of sociocultural, political, and economic issues. This chapter has offered many innovative examples of how to overcome the challenges:

- the leadership and sustainability vision implemented by the private developer by reusing the industrial structure in Mockingbird Station;

- the connectivity between Jersey and Hoboken areas proposed through the upgrading of infrastructure and provision of jobs and housing in the unused railway yards of Hoboken;
- the continual attempt to develop a high-quality place in the once-abandoned Melbourne Docklands through greater participation of diverse groups of stakeholders in the decision-making process;
- the conversion of the mono-use institutional Curtin campus into an education city by blurring physical, functional, visual, and psychological boundaries;
- the breaking of the big box-mall at the Crossings in Mountain View through an innovative mechanism of communal ownership of local infrastructure; and
- the edge city retrofit proposal to reduce greenhouse gas emissions by transforming Tysons from a destination to a place to live, work, and play.

All these urban and suburban transformations offer unique lessons in making connected places by utilizing forgotten, abandoned, wasted, and underutilized areas.

Community participation and private-sector involvement in these urban and suburban transformations take the concept of connecting places a step closer to sustainable development, with an enhanced sense of community and the much-needed economic returns.

The concept of connecting places, connecting people is brought to fruition when people are connected to other people and to places through a place-based urban development with reduced carbon emissions on underutilized land, which also meets modern needs and offers different building typologies and mixed use, while still accommodating different income groups. By providing many of the social services that link individuals with each other, such places become vital anchors for individuals and give rise to a sense of communal ownership of the place.

Note

1 A 'node-place' has attributes of being a destination and a high-quality urban space (Bertolini & Spit, 1998).

References

All online references retrieved August 17, 2016.

Ansett, D., & Singline, P. (2012). *Docklands needs more than marketing*. Retrieved from www.trulydeeply.com.au/brand-identity/docklands-place-branding-agency/.

Bailin, D. (2014, January). *Hoboken's post-Sandy resilience: Learning from the past, rebuilding for the future*. Retrieved from http://citeseerx.ist.psu.edu/viewdoc/download?doi=10.1.1.692.3479&rep=rep1&type=pdf.

Bertolini, L., & Spit, T. (1998). *Cities on rails: The redevelopment of railway station areas*. London: E & FN Spon.

Beyard, M. D., Corrigan, M. B., Kramer, A., Pawlukiewicz, M., & Bach, A. (2006). *Ten principles for rethinking the mall*. Urban Land Institute. Retrieved from www.uli.org/wp-content/uploads/ULI-Documents/Tp_MAll.ashx_.pdf.

Bird, J. H. (1971). *Seaports and seaport terminals.* London: Hutchison.
Boroski, J., & Arrington, G. B. (2002). *ULI development case studies: Mockingbird Station.* Retrieved from http://casestudies.uli.org/wp-content/uploads/sites/98/2015/12/C032019.pdf.
Boyer, M. C. (1994). *The city of collective memory: Its historical imagery and architectural entertainments.* Cambridge, MA: The MIT Press.
City of Hoboken. (2012). *Hoboken Yard Redevelopment Plan.* Retrieved from www.hobokennj.org/docs/communitydev/Hoboken-Yard-Redevelopment-Plan-Sept-2012-Draft.pdf.
City of Hoboken. (2014a). *Hoboken Terminal & Yard Redevelopment Plan.* Retrieved from www.hobokennj.org/departments/community-development/redevelopment-areas-and-studies/hoboken-rail-yards-redevelopment-plan/.
City of Hoboken. (2014b). *Hoboken Yard Redevelopment Plan.* Retrieved from www.hobokennj.org/docs/communitydev/Hoboken-Yard-Redevelopment-Plan-October-2014.pdf.
City of Mountain View. (2012, July 10). *Mountain View 2030 General Plan.* Retrieved from www.mountainview.gov/civicax/filebank/blobdload.aspx?blobid=10702.
Congress for the New Urbanism. (2015). *What is New Urbanism?* Retrieved from www.cnu.org/resources/what-new-urbanism.
Council of Europe. (1986). *European Campaign for Urban Renaissance.* Retrieved from https://rm.coe.int/CoERMPublicCommonSearchServices/DisplayDCTMContent?documentId=09000016805101ab.
Creed, J., Giant, J., Thorpe, D., & White, D. (2013). *Transit-oriented development in Minnetonka: Cases and policy recommendations for TOD Implementation in Minnetonka, MN.* Retrieved from http://hdl.handle.net/11299/149018.
Curtin University. (2014). *Greater Curtin Master Plan.* Retrieved from https://properties.curtin.edu.au/local/docs/CurtinMasterPlan_PartB.pdf.
Dalkmann, H., & Brannigan, C. (2007). *Transport and climate change: A sourcebook for policy-makers in developing cities: Module 5e.* Eschborn: Gesellschaft für Technische Zusammenarbeit–GTZ. Retrieved from http://lib.icimod.org/record/13155/files/5302.pdf.
Davis, C. (2015). What to build at Hoboken rail yards? Retrieved from http://hudsonreporter.com/view/full_story/26794881/article-What-to-build-at-Hoboken-rail-yards----Waterfront-activist-group-has-alternate-plan-for-the-area-?instance=search_results.
Davis, L. S. (2009). A (radical) way to fix suburban sprawl. Retrieved from http://content.time.com/time/magazine/article/0,9171,1904150,00.html.
DeGood, K. (2014). *Public transportation and the path dependency of highway investments.* Retrieved from www.americanprogress.org/issues/economy/report/2014/12/18/103509/public-transportation-and-the-path-dependency-of-highway-investments/.
Dittmar, H., & Ohland, G. (2004). *The new transit town: Best practices in transit-oriented development.* Washington, D.C.: Island Press.
Docklands Authority. (2000). *Melbourne Docklands 2000+.* Melbourne, VIC: Victorian Government.
Docklands Community Association. (2016). *News.* Retrieved from www.docklandscommunityassociation.com/news.html.
Docklands News. (2015). NewQuay tower approved. Retrieved from www.docklandsnews.com.au/editions/article/newquay-tower-approved_10811/.
Dodson, J., Sipe, N., & Gavin, N. (2006). *Shocking the suburbs: Urban location, housing debt and oil vulnerability in the Australian city.* Griffith University: Urban Research Program. Retrieved from www.mrra.asn.au/archive1/arc1-planning/Publications/URP_RP8_MortgageVulnerability_Final.pdf.
Duany Plater-Zyberk. (2016). *DPZ profile.* Retrieved from www.dpz.com/About/Profile.
Fairfax County. (2014). *Fairfax County Comprehensive Plan: Tysons Corner urban center.* Retrieved from www.fairfaxcounty.gov/dpz/comprehensive-plan/area2/tysons1.pdf.
Fairfax County. (2015). *Tysons annual report.* Retrieved from www.fairfaxcounty.gov/tysons/implementation/download/2015_tysonsannualreport.pdf.

Global Commission on the Economy and Climate. (2014). *Better growth better climate: The New Climate Economy report* . Retrieved from http://newclimateeconomy.report/2014/wp-content/uploads/2014/08/BetterGrowth-BetterClimate_NCE_Synthesis-Report_web.pdf.

Global Commission on the Economy and Climate. (2015). *The 2015 New Climate Economy report.* Retrieved from http://newclimateeconomy.report/2015/wp-content/uploads/2014/08/NCE-2015_Seizing-the-Global-Opportunity_web.pdf.

Government of Western Australia. (2015). *Liveable neighbourhoods*. Retrieved from www.planning.wa.gov.au/dop_pub_pdf/LiveableNeighbourhoods_2015.pdf.

Hackworth, J., & Moriah, A. (2006). Neoliberalism, contingency and urban policy: The case of social housing in Ontario. *International Journal of Urban and Regional Research 30*(3), 510–527.

Hassell Studio. (2014). *Urban futures: Imagining the cities of tomorrow.* Retrieved from www.hassellstudio.com/en/cms-news/urban-futures--the-urban-housing-challenge.

Jacobs, J. (1961). *The death and life of great American cities.* New York: Random House.

Kaiser, S. H. (2010). *The North Broadway Redevelopment District Plan.* San Luis Obispo: California Polytechnic State University.

Kotharkar, R., Bahadure, P., & Vyas, A. (2012). Compact city concept: Its relevance and applicability for planning of Indian cities. Paper presented at PLEA 2012, the 28th Conference for Opportunities, Limits, and Needs towards an Environmentally Responsible Architecture, Lima, Peru. Retrieved from www.researchgate.net/publication/265915492_Compact_City_Concept_It's_Relevance_and_Applicability_for_Planning_of_Indian_Cities.

Lucas, G. (2014). 5 Docklands property myths busted. Retrieved from http://www.smartpropertyinvestment.com.au/opinion/13848-5-docklands-property-myths-busted.

Mullins, L. (2015). The audacious plan to turn a sprawling DC suburb into a big city. Retrieved from www.washingtonian.com/2015/03/29/the-audacious-plan-to-turn-a-sprawling-dc-suburb-into-a-big-city/.

Newman, P. (2014). The top 10 myths about high density. Retrieved from www.thefifthestate.com.au/spinifex/peter-newman-the-top-10-myths-about-high-density/64481.

NSW Parliamentary Library. (2014). *Population issues for Sydney and NSW: Policy frameworks and responses.* Retrieved from www.parliament.nsw.gov.au/researchpapers/Documents/population-issues-for-sydney-and-nsw--policy-fra/Population%20Issues%20Briefing%20Paper%205-2011.pdf.

Nyström, L. (2001). Urban quality of life in Europe: Reflections on the relationship between urban life and urban form. *Nordisk Arkitekturforskning 4*, 73–85. Retrieved from https://arkitekturforskning.net/na/article/download/332/290.pdf.

OECD. (2012). *Strategic transport infrastructure needs to 2030.* Retrieved from www.oecd.org/futures/infrastructureto2030/49094448.pdf.

Pappas, L. (2016, November 28). The Hudson River Gold Coast. *New Jersey Business: A Publication of the New Jersey Business and Industry Association.* Retrieved from https://njbmagazine.com/monthly_articles/hudson-river-gold-coast/.

Parolek, D. G., Parolek, K., & Crawford, P. C. (2008). *Form based codes: A guide for planners, urban designers, municipalities, and developers.* Hoboken, NJ: John Wiley & Sons.

PB Placemaking & Cervero, R. (2008). *Transforming Tysons*. Retrieved from www.fairfaxcounty.gov/dpz/tysonscorner/finalreports/transforming-tysons.pdf.

Pearson, C. (2012). New labour: New renaissance. *City 16*(5), 576–594.

Phillips Preiss Shapiro Associates. (2006, November). *Redevelopment study for the Hoboken Terminal & Yard.* Retrieved from www.hobokennj.org/pdf/mplan/Redevelopment_Plans/Hoboken_Rail_Yards/HobokenRailYards.pdf.

Pitts, G. (2008) Landmarks: Mockingbird Station in Dallas. Retrieved from www.multifamilyexecutive.com/design-development/landmarks-mockingbird-station-in-dallas_o.

Places Victoria & City of Melbourne. (2012, June). *Victoria Harbour Docklands Conservation Management Plan.* Retrieved from http://participate.melbourne.vic.gov.au/application/files/8614/1221/3715/Victoria_Harbour_Conservation_Management_Plan_CMP.pdf.

Places Victoria & City of Melbourne. (2013, March). *Access Docklands: A strategy for the Docklands transport network.* Retrieved from www.places.vic.gov.au/__data/assets/file/0007/9178/Access_Docklands_Final_April2013,0.pdf.

Planetizen. (2016). Comprehensive plan for Tysons Corner. Retrieved from www.planetizen.com/plan/comprehensive-plan-tysons-corner.

Rathbone, D. B. (2011). Transforming Tysons Corner: Achieving sustainability by adding density in the most congested area in the USA. Paper presented at the European Transport Conference 2011, Glasgow, UK. Retrieved from http://abstracts.aetransport.org/paper/download/id/3798.

Schiller, P. L., Brunn, E. C., & Kenworthy, J. R. (2010). *An introduction to sustainable transportation: Policy planning and implementation.* London: Earthscan.

Schipper, L., Marie-Lilliu, C., & Gorham, R. (2000, June). *Flexing the link between transport and greenhouse gas emissions: A path for the World Bank.* Retrieved from www.ocs.polito.it/biblioteca/mobilita/FlexingLink1.pdf.

SGS Economics & Planning. (2003). Costs of urban form. Unpublished research report. Melbourne, VIC: Western Australian Planning Commission.

Shaw, K. (2013). Docklands dreamings: Illusions of sustainability in the Melbourne Docks redevelopment. *Urban Studies 50*(11), 2158–2177.

Slack, B. (1975). *Harbour redevelopment in Canada.* Ottawa: Department of State for Urban Affairs.

Slack, B. (1980). Technology and seaports in the 1980s. *Tijdschrift voor Economische en Sociale Geografie 71*(2), 108–113.

Smith, G. (2008). Contributions of brownfield development to urban internal expansion and urban renewal in practice. Paper presented at the 44th ISOCARP Congress, Dalian, China. Retrieved from www.isocarp.net/Data/case_studies/1202.pdf.

State Government of Victoria. (2016). *Docklands revitalised.* Retrieved from www.places.vic.gov.au/precincts-and-development/docklands/about.

Tachieva, G. (2010). *Sprawl repair manual.* Washington, D.C.: Island Press.

Talen, E. (2013). Zoning for and against sprawl: The case for form-based codes. *Journal of Urban Design 18*(2), 175–200.

Tiwari, R., Cervero, R., & Schipper, L. (2011). Driving CO_2 reduction by integrating transport and urban design strategies. *Cities 28*(5), 394–405.

Trubka, R., Newman, P., & Bilsborough, D. (2010). The costs of urban sprawl–infrastructure and transportation. *Environment Design Guide 83*, 1–6. Retrieved from www.crcsi.com.au/assets/Resources/b6e1625f-d90b-433d-945a-6afeff2e42f6.pdf.

US Environmental Protection Agency. (2016, March 29). *Provide transportation choices: The Crossings, Mountain View, California.* Retrieved from www.epa.gov/smartgrowth/provide-transportation-choices-crossings-mountain-view-california.

Wood, S. (2009). Desiring docklands: Deleuze and urban planning discourse. *Planning Theory 8*(2), 191–216.

Zetter, J. (1982). European Campaign for Urban Renaissance. *Landscape Research 7*(2), 28–29.

Zukin, S. (1998). Urban lifestyles: Diversity and standardisation in spaces of consumption. *Urban Studies 35*(5–6), 825–839.

PART III

Connecting Places, Connecting People: Making It Happen!

Our principal impediments at present are neither lack of energy or material resources nor of essential physical or biological knowledge. Our principal constraints are cultural.

(Marion King Hubbert, 1976)

Hubbert made the above comment while theorizing about 'peak oil' and its challenges. The core message remains valid for any discussion about *making* connections happen between places and people through urban reconfiguration. Urban reconfiguration is rendered ineffective unless there is a strong cultural shift, and the community embraces the interventions. A democratic decision-making and implementation process can assist in meeting the challenge of building broad-based support for and market acceptance of new urban forms, and green alternative modes of travel among an increasingly diverse group of stakeholders.

Bringing the people and place connections to fruition also depends on an accurate diagnosis of the connectivity attributes and a precise prognosis of the required actions.

This part of the book focuses on the two areas mentioned above. Together, these represent important methodological approaches and a connectivity audit framework that urban planning and related professions need to embrace in the quest to improve the quality and livability of places and the connectivity between them. It is thus centrally about implementation—putting the ideals of connecting places into practice over the coming decades and beyond.

Reference

Hubbert, M. K. (1976). Exponential growth as a transient phenomenon in human history. Paper presented at 4th International Congress, World Wildlife Fund, San Francisco, CA. Retrieved from www.hubbertpeak.com/hubbert/wwf1976/print.htm on August 17, 2016.

CHAPTER 5

REMODELING APPROACHES
Empowering Place Making and Connectivity

The importance of engaging citizens meaningfully in policy development has been deliberated in previous chapters. Appropriate engagement of citizens engenders a sense of ownership in the quest for place making and connecting places. Disengaged local residents are prone to adopt a NIMBY (not-in-my-back-yard) attitude to improved accessibility proposals, thus hampering the developments meant to be of benefit for all. More inclusive community interaction brings several advantages, including balanced perspectives and smoother implementation.

The need to shift to more sustainable patterns of urban transport and urban development while contending with the interconnected issues of climate change, urban sprawl, economic development, and social equity is recognized as a 'wicked problem'[1] (Rittel & Webber, 1973). The difficulties of developing strategies to address these issues are compounded by other factors, including a lack of consensus, uncertainty of information, and high levels of ambiguity in the values or causal relations underlying the problem. Addressing these problems requires flexible, deliberative, participatory approaches.

This chapter suggests an approach to connecting people with people and citizens with government agencies. The approach allows different meanings and values to be expressed, fresh solutions to emerge, and new institutional resources to develop (Healey, 1997; Innes & Booher, 2010), leading to connected places.

Contextualizing Public Involvement

Current debates on sustainable transport and urban development reflect a move away from a narrow 'line-oriented' focus prioritizing the automobile to 'area-oriented' solutions integrating transport planning with land use planning, together with diversification of travel modes (Heeres et al., 2012). Because funding is distributed to a larger number of projects in the area-oriented approach, greater collaboration between stakeholders and authorities is required. The actors involved in the collaboration include designers, operators, authorities, residents, commuters, academicians, developers, and environmentalists. Together, the stakeholders possess technical, political, institutional, and tacit knowledge (Healey, 1997; Lash, 1976).

Besides the increase in number and types of stakeholders in a transport project, the emphasis in transport planning has now shifted from being based on traffic demand to demand management. Simply building more roads to meet the demand is no longer a sustainable solution. This was evident in the UK of the 1960s and 1970s, when there was a reactionary resistance to road building and to the public's lack of opportunity to challenge the decisions being made (Innes & Booher, 2010). The way in which policies are developed sets the stage for collaborative planning. The policy framework since the 1980s has evolved from being 'demand responsive' to achieving 'sustainable development'. The policy framework is now seen as the instrument to achieve sustainable development by uniting stakeholders in a common cause. This requires that the stakeholders are well informed about the issues and possess the power to tackle them.

As Bray et al. (2011) observe, the mode of policy formulation has also changed, shifting from policy by master plans to policies that allow the rationale for a decision to evolve through extensive stakeholder engagement and communication. Planning that was previously focused on providing infrastructure in an inflexible way now focuses on the behavioral aspects of the people concerned, thus influencing their attitudes towards transportation.

However, unfortunately, many of the attempts to foster participation have been ineffective. This can be attributed to the constrained and partial nature of public involvement and a lack of inclusiveness during the decision-making stages (Booth & Richardson, 2001). 'Strategic communication' has also been used by government and other interest groups to conceal the absence of sincere and meaningful public participation (Sunter & Wigan, 2011). This has led to a questioning of the legitimacy of transport planning.

In Curitiba in Brazil, transport and urban land use planning have been integrating and, at the same time, promoting development of both business and the local community (Adler, 2016). The success stems from the way in which the issues are managed, as discussed in Chapter 3. The policy framework, infrastructure, innovative technologies, and effective leadership must all pass a critical test: the community's acceptance or rejection of the system. A project succeeds when the community for which it is intended is involved in the planning process. Planning without public legitimation can be blocked and ultimately prevented.

The sections below review methods of understanding, engaging with, and influencing residents and other stakeholders. The value of deliberative and ethnographic approaches for connected places is discussed, and the chapter concludes by identifying the strengths and weaknesses of the various methods.

Soft Policy Measures and Behavioral Change

Soft policy measures have been seen as an effective tool to bring about a shift in communities from car dependency to using sustainable transport means (Cobiac et al., 2009; Marsden et al., 2011; Scheepers et al., 2014). The traditional hard policy measures provide physical infrastructure and facilities with strict regulation and pricing structures, whereas soft policy measures are education and advertising programs that provide information to change individuals' perceptions, motivations, habits, and routines (Cools et al., 2012).

Individuals could choose to change their travel behavior if the infrastructure is already in place, but they need to change their attitude or need further information to do so (Brog et al., 2009). The soft policies used to alter travel behavior have been either 'stick' approaches, which discourage the use of personal cars through mechanisms like congestion pricing,[2] or 'carrot' approaches, which encourage alternative travel behavior (Brog et al., 2009).

Information dissemination and persuasion tactics have been used to alter individuals' travel behavior. The former includes marketing public transport, travel awareness campaigns, and destination travel plans (Bamberg et al., 2012).

The Personalised Travel Planning (PTP) Program was adopted in the UK as a small-scale trial. Here, a helper presented a menu of options for participants, a personal advisor informed participants of the best travel alternative, or a pamphlet detailed the best options (Chatterjee, 2009). Careful media planning was required to prevent potential participants gaining a negative perception of the program (Chatterjee, 2009). To achieve higher participation rates, potential participants were contacted throughout the day and the week. Written invitations were left where direct contact could not be made. The review finding from the trial was that there was a reduction in car-driven trips of 7–15 percent for the targeted population in urban areas, with better impact in residential-based projects compared to those in schools and workplaces (Department for Transport, 2005). To achieve more reliable evaluation, data from larger programs in PTP in the UK were analyzed and the results were found to be consistent with the trial, with an average reduction in car-driven trips of 11 percent (Chatterjee, 2009).

Based on the broader concept of personalized travel planning, in Germany an initiative called IndiMark (short for Individualized Marketing) was used to encourage alternative travel behavior (Brog et al., 2009). Travel plans in IndiMark include one-on-one buddy systems, mentors, and self-help groups to encourage and maintain change. The program was introduced to Perth, Western Australia, in 1997, with modifications to align with hard policy system improvements. In a sample of 400 individuals, the combination of hard policy infrastructure with soft policy initiatives saw a reduction in 'car trips by 10% and increased use of other modes (walking, cycling and public transport) without constraining mobility' (Brog et al., 2009, p. 284). Following the success of the initial IndiMark Program, this combination of soft policy with hard policy infrastructure was extended to over 400,000 residents in Perth under the TravelSmart Program. The destination travel plans, using mass social marketing of alternative transport options, encourage individuals to be responsible for the externalities of their travel. By demonizing the use of automobiles and promoting alternative transport options through guilt and social pressure, citizens are persuaded to change their travel behavior. TravelSmart has now been used across Australia, Europe, and North America, with over a million participants. Besides reducing car use, it has encouraged organizations to set challenging but feasible, rather than easy, targets to effect greater modifications in travel behavior (Brog et al., 2009).

PTP, TravelSmart, and other information dissemination programs are found to be more effective when used in conjunction with persuasion tactics. The latter could include 'sticks', like congestion charging and road tolls, or 'carrots', like pool loan bikes and employers paying public transport costs, to name a few (Bamberg et al., 2011). One study compared workplace travel plans for two areas with common denominators (Petrunoff et al., 2015). The first PTP included strategies of encouraging transit and active modes of travel. This was complemented with a parking management plan that reduced parking by 50 percent over three years and introduced parking prioritization and a permit system. TravelSmart induction was conducted for new staff, and employees were provided with e-bikes to be used within the campus and discounted parking for those who pooled their cars. The second PTP did not do any of the above; it relied solely on information dissemination. A difference of 37 percent in driving reduction was found between the two areas: while the first plan was able to achieve a 42 percent reduction in car use, the second plan achieved only a 5 percent reduction (Petrunoff et al., 2015).

Some research suggests that incentives and deterrents are effective in changing travel behavior. Policies to alter the travel behavior of individuals and reduce their use of automobiles could be an effective government initiative, emphasizing the need to reduce automobile dependence as a response to the resultant state of car-disconnect and the environmental impact of automobiles.

Collaborative Stakeholder Engagement Approaches

Education and awareness-raising play an important role in modifying a community's behavior towards connected places. Although changes might be beneficial to one section of the community, other sections might feel marginalized. Conflicts between stakeholder groups may arise. In Jayanagar, a suburb in Bangalore, India, for example, bicycle paths and footpaths were built and promoted through soft policy measures. After one week of operation, these pathways were converted to on-street parking facilities for vehicles (Francis, 2012), and bicycle riders took to the roads as usual with the mixed traffic. This outcome could be a result of the incomplete consensus achieved before the bike lanes were designed. Stakeholders did not have an opportunity to be heard. People and stakeholders must be involved at every stage of planning, from policy formulation to implementation.

Using several case studies, the advantages and drawbacks of various approaches using collaborative stakeholder dialogue (CSD) that have been adopted in different parts of the world are elaborated below.

The Deliberative Approach at the City Scale

The Network City metropolitan planning strategy to enable more sustainable travel in Perth, conceived in 2003, included extensive community consultation (Curtis, 2008, p. 105). The 25-year framework began with a one-day dialogue with the community, from whom working groups were created to produce the strategy over a one-year process of collaboration (Curtis, 2008). The Network City framework relied on integrating land use and transport planning to create multiple centers linked by public transport across the Perth metropolitan region.

A challenge for the Network City plan was the high target for infill development and the capability of local governments to enforce such targets and concepts. The strategy used, Dialogue with the City, a deliberative democracy tool, had two objectives: first, make the community aware of the impending challenges; and, second, invite community views and suggestions for the future. Community surveys (mailed to 8,000 residents), a range of media advertisements, papers, and digital publications were used to achieve the first objective of raising community awareness. This generated an informed dialogue, a key aspect of deliberations. These deliberations continued for around eight months, with a good representation of participants from the local communities, professions, and government. Small-group dialogue with representation of diverse participants was used to encourage free discussion, increase access to information, and move towards consensus (Curtis, 2008, p. 105).

There were a few limitations in the process. Measurement of the participant demographic profile could have ensured a more equitable participation and diversity of views. The comprehensiveness of the information disseminated prior to the dialogue was another issue (Hartz-Karp, 2005). However, the process did lead to a positive outcome. One important compromise between the community stakeholders and the development industry was the need to limit urban sprawl. The community stakeholders modified their position of an urban growth boundary to managing growth through sustainability criteria. This was a first step towards achieving a connected city. A lesson learned was that the success of collaboration in city-scale projects is not necessarily to reach consensus, but to unveil all of the issues and different points of views relating to those issues (Legacy et al., 2012, p. 15).

The Deliberative Approach at the Neighborhood Scale

While the Network City plan was at a broader, strategic level of decision making, in Pune, India, the deliberative process of stakeholder engagement to create a walkable neighborhood as a key aspect of connected place took place at a micro level; that is, in a neighborhood (Curtin University, 2013). This pioneering exercise, which included Open Space Technology and Enquiry by Design workshops, was conducted in 2012 and called for representation from authorities, politicians, academicians, residents, and street users, among others, to sit together and discuss their issues and design a pedestrian-friendly neighborhood: Dattawadi in Pune. The process was inclusive and achieved good representation from all residents, including the elderly, women, and children.

The Pune project began with the aim of answering the following questions:

1. Do streets in Indian cities have the design capacity to include sustainable transport modes and prioritize pedestrians?
2. Does deliberative democracy help to achieve this goal?

The answer to both questions was 'yes'. Events were very well attended. Participant comments (Curtin University, 2013, p. 16) included:

- [The deliberation was] the first time I spoke as a citizen of India.
- [G]ive people a little chance and they deeply respond. It is a spiritual matter.
- It is very important to see how much people understand.
- It made me very excited when we first heard about it and then it came true.
- A unique way for getting things done.
- A very different experience. Don't usually involve people like this.
- Training that reaches into every class.

The Municipal Corporator for Pune Municipal Corporation announced the implementation and funding of detailed designs resulting from the deliberative workshops. She cited the significance of the deliberative process in helping to reach a quick decision on funding. Implementation of the street designs was scheduled to be an ongoing project over the next two to three years (Curtin University, 2013, p. 16).

Unless such deliberative forums are sustained and the community informed, little success can be achieved in our quest for creating connected places. Informing people at regular intervals of a project's progress keeps interest high and develops community trust in the government and a sense of ownership towards the place.

Engagement Tools

This section explores various tools that can be used in public engagement exercises. Engagement tools should be selected according to the aim and level of engagement. Printed material, media advertisements, and digital information are important when the aim is to provide information prior to deliberations. Face-to-face interviews and telephone and digital communication are essential during information collection and stakeholder management stages. Workshops/deliberative forums, enquiry by design exercises, and round-table discussions are effective during consultation and participation stages.

It is not easy to engage the wider demographics and canvass diverse opinions using common public participation tools. Communication skills and time management are critical to encourage the public and to include all opinions, but such resources may be limited (Zhong et al., 2008). Online deliberation has been used effectively to achieve wider representation, since individuals' involvement is in their own time and at their own pace. Information is quickly provided and fewer resources are required. The internet is a useful distribution tool, as individuals can participate in their own homes and time schedules. The Public Participation Geographic Information System (PPGIS), for example, is a form of public participation through digital mapping (Brown & Weber, 2011). The PPGIS method, when used in the Victorian Greater Alpine region, achieved acceptable participation rates from contacted individuals, with a robust communication medium and descriptive answers to the questions posed. Limitations included a small sample size, a low participation rate of managerial staff, a grouping of mapping activity around the locations where the majority of participants were engaged, and a limited scope (breadth and depth) of questions asked (Brown & Weber, 2011).

Even with a public participation process, a lack of public transparency and explanation can cause a perception of unmerited decisions (Zhong et al., 2008, p. 126). Online processes tend to delay responses by email from officials, which means that participants can lose interest in the project during a lengthy deliberation process. This delay can take the emotion out of discussions and make them analytical (Zhong et al., 2008, p. 127). This can be resolved through an ethnographic engagement process, where urban professionals become change agents by positioning themselves within the local community, either as active members or as participant observers (Tiwari & Pandya, 2014). The following sections elaborate on some tools that can be used by these urban ethnographers.

Software Programs

Computer programs have allowed a high level of participant engagement, an exploration of issues by participants, and a quick response rate from them. An Optimization Tool achieves community involvement during the planning stages of projects (Lowry, 2010b, p. 95). A participant is able to input scores that reflect his/her weightage and value of project goals and issues and his/her preference for possible outcomes. Solution determination takes into account the participant input scores to meet the participant's expectations in the best possible way.

There are a few drawbacks. The tool is limited to those who have access to computers and are computer literate. The goals, issues, and values made available to participants are limited to those that do not require a technical understanding on the participant's part, resulting in possible inaccuracies in results (Lowry, 2010a). A study of the process and success of online public deliberation for a project on regional transportation found that the participants were optimistic about the future use of the technology, but public preference for participation methods was different for different participants. The general consensus was that face-to-face methods should continue to be used (Lowry, 2010a).

Photo-simulations

A study was conducted in Stockton, California, by Cervero and Guerra (2010) on public perceptions towards required density increases to attain cost-effective, expanded BRT services. With a population of 290,000, Stockton has a citizen advisory committee whose members are politically well positioned to influence decisions on density increases along the BRT corridors. Photo-simulations for parts of Stockton that currently have low-end BRT services were created. The scenarios ranged from low to medium and high densities and were presented against proportionately increased amenities like landscaping, street furniture, bike lanes, improved building façades, and so on. The aim was to soften people's negative perceptions of high densities by making them understand how the area would 'feel' and how its image would be improved by increased amenities and place-making initiatives.

The building envelope, resultant sense of enclosure for the pedestrian, and level of transit amenities increased from Scenario 1 to Scenario 3. The low-density scenario had a one–two-story built form and separated BRT, while the high-density scenario had a five–six-story mixed-use built form with high-end BRT, wider sidewalks, and protected bike lanes. There was general public agreement on Scenario 2, with three–four-story mixed-use built form. The public rejected Scenario 3 as they felt the densities were too high, both for the present and in the future, and the traffic congestion was not serious enough for high-end BRT.

Photo-simulation worked to a certain extent as a public engagement tool. However, the researchers felt that single-image photo-simulations of improvements to the quality and image of the place ('carrots') should be accompanied with simulations of congestion pricing and higher parking and motoring costs ('sticks') to achieve a more informed response from the community and offset the opposition to higher densities in traditional auto-centric areas.

Ethnographic Engagements

A lack of sufficient knowledge of the local culture (structure, processes, practices, relations, and agents) of the neighborhoods and communities (Maginn, 2007) presents a major challenge. A lack of reflective understanding of planners' and policy makers' own practices adds to this challenge. As Maginn (2007) notes, applied ethnography, when thrown into the mix of collaborative planning theory, shows policy makers a way forward to achieve valuable community participation. The two together provide a

> governance and methodological framework that has the potential to promote inclusionary argumentation and consensus building, and give partnership stakeholders an opportunity to become more

aware of and critically reflective about their cultural relations, practices and processes, thus paving the way forward for more effective community participation.

(Maginn, 2007, p. 1)

Using the method of experimental ethnography to study the bike infrastructure in Los Angeles during CicLAvia (an open streets event), researcher Adonia Lugo (2013) considered inanimate infrastructure and living practices to analyze urban mobility. Lugo's project was based on the belief that academic enquiry, conducted by living and working alongside the cultural group, can bring to social movements the possible use of human infrastructure that could alleviate the concerns around physical infrastructure. As an ethnographer, Lugo spent time listening to the cyclists, biking with people, and observing the way in which they rode. This revealed the diverse nature of cycling in Los Angeles. For example, the decision to use sidewalk, street, or cycle lane depended on each cyclist's sociocultural and economic background. This meant that safety and other concerns were specific to different groups of cyclists. A blanket approach targeting the improvement of bike infrastructure was not necessarily going to resolve all concerns. Instead, a focus on human infrastructure that included knowledge-sharing online platforms, group rides that helped in appropriating the street space (if only for a short time), bike repair cooperatives, and the like was better able to respond to the specific problems faced by different user groups.

In a similar vein, in order to distinguish and define the multiple issues faced by pedestrians in Nehru Place, a busy commercial area housing a major metro rail station in New Delhi, India, a research team from Curtin University, Australia, conducted interviews and field observation surveys (Creedon et al., 2012). Through combining the methods of experimental ethnography and performativity, the researchers were able to 'live' and 'perform' the place along with the local community and stakeholders. As ethnographers, the researchers lived the space, talked to people, walked with them, and acted as catalysts in conversations related to walking. As researchers, they engaged with stakeholders and the local authorities to sensitize them to the issues related to the area. Talking to people and observing their actions within the space was useful in recognizing major hotspots where many people converge and where serious pedestrian issues arise. While the traditional model rests on a conceptual divide between the researcher and the object of study, this approach was for researchers to interact with the object and situate themselves as part of the human infrastructure. The researchers were thus part of the everyday shared urban space.

With the help of a local theater group, a performance was choreographed to simulate issues faced by pedestrians in the streets of Nehru Place. The objective was to make people more aware of the issues that they face while walking (Figure 5.1). The performance was the most critical aspect of this project, because it incorporated the researchers' understandings and communication of their survey findings. The initial ethnographic study showed that people in spaces where walkability was an issue learned to adjust to the constraints of

MAKING IT HAPPEN

Figure 5.1 Educational engagement through performance
Source: Pictures by R. Tiwari (2012).

the space. Challenging users of public space through exposing them to the issues that they had taken for granted helped to engage them in reconnecting with their local environment.

An initiative of this kind can be deemed successful if it communicates to the users and alerts the decision makers at various levels. The groups of people who gathered to discuss the performances interpreted the acts in different ways. They engaged in fruitful conversations with each other and with the researchers. They also came up with new ideas. The performance encouraged people to talk about their issues and raise their voices to demand their rights. At the same time, the information generated through this performance was spread through media to a wider community and to decision makers (*Times of India*, 2012). Soon after the success of this study, Clean Air Asia adopted the methods developed in this research to increase awareness among people as part of their walkability studies called Steer to Safety (Clean Air Asia, n.d.).

While ethnographic engagement enables stakeholders to reach common understandings by connecting with each other, it also increases the pool of knowledge used by decision makers to design places for the users of the space. This becomes a prerequisite in stimulating the sense of belonging and identity that are essential to the healthy development of a living environment, as well as to its preservation.

The Ingredients of Successful Collaboration

So far we have looked at different forms of collaborative engagement, the policy context, and various tools and methods used, with their pros and cons. Successful collaboration for a connected place must possess a few ingredients, which I term the three Es: education, engagement, and empowerment.

Educating the public about the issues is important. Soft policies become useful in making people aware of their responsibility to society. When all stakeholders are aware of the issues, the second E—engagement—may commence. Knowledge is shared and issues deliberated on a common engagement platform. The deliberations then empower the stakeholders by giving them an integral role in decision making. Empowered citizens are responsible for their actions, trust the system of governance, and develop a sense of ownership with respect to the decisions made.

The use of ethnographic methods and the creation of platforms for deliberation using various tools and techniques, as discussed in this chapter, help educate, engage, and empower the community.

Close

The public's actions and behavior strongly shape their urban habitat, and are often responsible for the degradation of that habitat. The constraints, while connecting places and connecting people, are not necessarily around subject knowledge and resources, but are around bringing a cultural shift or change. Soft and hard policy measures and the use of 'carrots' and 'sticks' can work simultaneously and be complementary while facilitating this shift. However, the way in which this shift is made is as important as the shift itself. If the aim is to create a connected place through place making, it becomes important to be inclusive and to involve the people of that place effectively, so they can acknowledge the challenges and work together to find solutions.

Community engagement in decision making goes a long way to reinforcing the feeling of belonging and ownership and leads to a connected community. A sense of belonging to a place can strongly affect people's perceptions and strengthens their realization that they are responsible for the urban habitat.

Ethnographic engagements can provide a closer socio-scape to develop, try, and test policies through opportunities for direct communication and action between professionals and the public, thus producing the most effective collaborative framework. This facilitates a proper appreciation of the wide range of inputs and results in concurrent solutions to address the diverse needs, increasing project efficiency.

It is not always easy to bring a diverse community together and keep it interested and involved through the decision-making process. Selecting the appropriate public participation tools for the size and diversity of the community becomes important and must be done carefully to avoid making unmerited decisions and undermining the accountability of governance. For instance, the higher cost of printed participation tools can be a hindrance to some communities, for whom an invitation to a collaborative software workshop platform could be more affordable and attractive. It becomes critical to select the correct engagement tools to maintain the public's interest and keep the faith between organizers and the community alive. Loss of interest can be restored with the continual evaluation and auditing of the process; however, the subject demands further exploration.

A society with different values, attitudes, social standings, and perceptions can shape political directions affecting policy. Despite the time needed to bring different groups into the decision-making process, and cases of citizen resistance and cash-poor governing bodies, public outreach and engagement have the advantage of smooth implementation with improved efficiency, savings in time and funds, greater citizen satisfaction, and an increased sense of ownership. Such collaborative approaches constitute deliberative democracy and bring the providers and users together, which increases accountability and trust in these processes over the long term.

Notes

1. A 'wicked problem' is one that is very complex and therefore difficult or impossible to solve. Rittel and Webber (1973) observe that solutions for these problems cannot be idealized; they can only be good or bad and hence they should be assessed continually for improvement.
2. The economic principle behind congestion pricing suggests that the road should not be treated as a 'free good' and that its use should be charged to limit build-up of congestion and encourage wider use of an efficient transport system instead (Litman, 2006). London's congestion charge obliges motorists driving in central London between 7 a.m. and 6 p.m. on weekdays to pay a toll (£5 in 2003, which increased to £8 in 2005 and £11.50 in 2014), with a 90 percent discount for residents who live within the boundary.

References

All online references retrieved August 17, 2016.

Adler, D. (2016, May 6). How radical ideas turned Curitiba into Brazil's green capital. Retrieved from www.theguardian.com/cities/2016/may/06/story-of-cities-37-mayor-jaime-lerner-curitiba-brazil-green-capital-global-icon.

Bamberg, S., Fujii, S., Friman, M., & Garling, T. (2011). Behaviour theory and soft transport policy measures. *Transport Policy 18*(1), 228–235.

Ben-Elia, E., & Ettema, D. (2009). Carrot versus sticks: Rewarding commuters for avoiding the rush-hour: A study of willingness to participate. *Transport Policy 16*(2), 68–76.

Booth, C., & Richardson, T. (2001). Placing the public in integrated transport planning. *Transport Policy 8*(2), 141–149.

Bray, D. J., Taylor, M. A. P., & Scrafton, D. (2011). Transport policy in Australia: Evolution, learning and policy transfer. *Transport Policy 18*(3), 522–532.

Brog, W., Erl, E., Ker, I., Ryle, J., & Wall, R. (2009). Evaluation of voluntary travel behaviour change: Experiences from three continents. *Transport Policy 16*(6), 281–292.

Brown, G., & Weber, D. (2011). Public Participation GIS: A new method for national park planning. *Landscape and Urban Planning 102*(1), 1–15.

Cervero, R., & Guerra, E. (2010). *Urban densities and transit*. Retrieved from www.its.berkeley.edu/sites/default/files/publications/UCB/2011/VWP/UCB-ITS-VWP-2011-6.pdf.

Chatterjee, K. (2009). A comparative evaluation of large-scale personal travel planning projects in England. *Transport Policy 16*(6), 293–305.

Clean Air Asia. (n.d.). Citizens of India demand for livable cities. Retrieved from http://cleanairasia.org/node12192/.

Cobiac, L. J., Vos, T., & Barendregt, J. J. (2009). Cost-effectiveness of interventions to promote physical activity: A modelling study. *PLoS Med 6*(7). Retrieved from http://dx.doi.org/10.1371/journal.pmed.1000110.

Cools, M., Brijs, K., Tormans, H., Laender, J. D., & Wets, G. (2012). Optimizing the implementation of policy measures through social acceptance segmentation. *Transport Policy 22*(1), 80–87.

Creedon, J., McCagh, K., Chan, D., & Tiwari, R. (2012). To walk or not to walk? A walkability survey. Working paper submitted to Clean Air Asia. Perth, WA: Curtin University.

Curtin University. (2013). Stemming car dependency in Indian cities. Unpublished research report. Perth, WA: Curtin University.

Curtis, C. (2008). Planning for sustainable accessibility: The implementation challenge. *Transport Policy 15*(2), 104–112.

Department for Transport. (2005). *Personalised Travel Planning: Evaluation of 14 pilots part funded by the DfT*. London: Department for Transport. Retrieved from http://webarchive.nationalarchives.gov.uk/20101124142120/http:/www.dft.gov.uk/pgr/sustainable/travelplans/ptp/personalisedtravelplanningev5774.

Francis, M. (2012, 19 October). Jayanagar cycle track, a flop till now. *Daily News* Analysis. Retrieved from www.dnaindia.com/bangalore/report-jayanagar-cycle-track-a-flop-till-now-1753953.

Hartz-Karp, J. (2005). A case study in deliberative democracy: Dialogue with the City. *Journal of Public Deliberation 1*(1). Retrieved from http://search.proquest.com/openview/8cd756f4e2db9ad2311fb9c1ab67eeb7/1?pq-origsite=gscholar.

Healey, P. (1997). *Collaborative planning: Shaping places in fragmented societies*. Vancouver: University of British Columbia.

Heeres, N., Tillema, T., & Arts, J. (2012). Integration in Dutch planning of motorways: From 'line' towards 'area-oriented' approaches. *Transport Policy 24*(0), 148–158.

Innes, J. E., & Booher, D. E. (2010). *Planning with complexity: An introduction to collaborative rationality for public policy*. London: Routledge.

James, B. (2003) TravelSmart/individualised marking in Perth, Western Australia. In R. Tolley (Ed.) *Sustainable transport planning for walking and cycling in urban environments* (pp. 384–402). London: Woodhead.

Lash, H. (1976), *Planning in a human way: Personal reflections on the regional planning experience in Greater Vancouver*. Vancouver, BC: Ministry of State for Urban Affairs.

Legacy, C., Curtis, C., & Sturup, S. (2012). Is there a good governance model for the delivery of contemporary transport policy and practice? An examination of Melbourne and Perth. *Transport Policy 19*(1), 9.

Litman, T. (2006). *London congestion pricing: Implications for other cities*. Retrieved from www.vtpi.org/london.pdf.

Lowry, M. B. (2010a). Online public deliberation for a regional transportation improvement decision. *Transportation 37*(1), 39–58.

Lowry, M. B. (2010b). Using optimization to program projects in the era of communicative rationality. *Transport Policy 17*(2), 94–101.

Lugo, A. E. (2013). CicLAvia and human infrastructure in Los Angeles: Ethnographic experiments in equitable bike planning. *Journal of Transport Geography 30*, 202–207.

Maginn, P. J. (2007). Towards more effective community participation in urban regeneration: The potential of collaborative planning and applied ethnography. *Qualitative Research 7*(1), 25–43.

Marsden, A., & Tunny, G., & Fitzgibbons, A. (2011). Evaluation of the TravelSmart local government and workplace programs. Perth, WA: Marsden Jacob Associates. Retrieved from www.transport.wa.gov.au/mediaFiles/active-transport/AT_TS_P_Evaluation_LocalGov_Workplace.pdf.

Petrunoff, N., Rissel, C., Wen, L. M., & Martin, J. (2015). Carrots and sticks vs carrots: Comparing approaches to workplace travel plans using disincentives for driving and incentives for active travel. *Journal of Transport and Health 2*(4), 563–567.

Rittel, H. W., & Webber, M. M. (1973). Dilemmas in a general theory of planning. *Policy Sciences 4*(2), 155–169.

Scheepers, C. E., Wendel-Vos, G. C. W., den Broeder, J. M., van Kempen, E. E. M. M., van Wesemael, P. J. V., & Schuit, A. J. (2014). Shifting from car to active transport: A systematic review of the effectiveness of interventions. *Transport Research Part A: Policy and Practice 70*(0), 264–280. Retrieved from www.sciencedirect.com/science/article/pii/S0965856414002493.

Sunter, P., & Wigan, M. (2011). Enhancing community participation in metropolitan strategic transport planning through shared analysis. *Road and Transport Research: A Journal of Australian and New Zealand Research and Practice 20*(1), 20–31. Retrieved from https://search.informit.com.au/documentSummary;dn=988032915085672;res=IELENG.

Times of India. (2012, October 30). Nehru Place pedestrian paths score low on quality, accessibility. Retrieved from http://timesofindia.indiatimes.

com/city/delhi/Nehru-Place-pedestrian-paths-score-low-on-quality-accessibility/articleshow/17013919.cms.

Tiwari, R., & Pandya, Y. (2014). An ethnographic and collaborative model of inquiry: Activity centre project in India. In R. Tiwari, M. Lommerse, & D. Smith (Eds.) *M² models and methodologies for community engagement* (pp. 25–41). London: Springer.

Zhong, T., Young, R. K., Lowry, M., & Rutherford, G. S. (2008). A model for public involvement in transportation improvement programming using participatory Geographic Information Systems. *Computers, Environment and Urban Systems 32*(2), 123–133.

CHAPTER 6

EVALUATING PEOPLE, PLACE, AND TRANSPORT CONNECTIVITY

Based on the practices and strategies that have the potential to provide the required connectivity, as identified in Part II, this chapter develops actionable knowledge[1] for *Connecting Places, Connecting People*. Key research findings from the previous chapters are converted into audit measures to benefit practice settings.

The audit framework is the principal tool used to evaluate effective connected places. An area is audited using five key dimensions of connected places. These are the dimensions that impact on people, place, and transport connectivity. Qualitative and quantitative metrics are illustrated for each dimension with examples.

A connected place is a pedestrian-friendly environment that encourages the use of sustainable transport and is well connected and in close proximity to other connected places. These places can be mixed use, medium to high density, with fine urban grain. Importantly, a connected place allows people to connect to an efficient and well-integrated transport network with easy access to destinations. By involving users and residents in the process of place making, a connected place reinforces the community's positive identity and a sense of ownership. Thus, people can connect and relate to the places that they occupy. Connected places reduce travel time and improve social interactions: they connect people to people. This solution-based approach is an answer to the prevalent state of car-disconnect and contributes to sustainable cities by providing a range of social and economic benefits and reducing the city's carbon footprint.

There are three key connectivity attributes of connected places:

1 *People connectivity*—provided by environments that promote social interaction and community engagement, and offer a sense of place identity, community attachment, and social diversity, where people from all walks of life come into everyday contact with each other. This attribute builds social capital and empathy for others across the sociocultural spectrum.

2 *Place connectivity*—land use programs with a mix of activities enabling short-distance travel and ease of access to everyday neighborhood activities. This attribute brings Place A and Place B closer together.
3 *Transport connectivity*—low-impact modes of travel and sustainable mobility that enhance or at least do not detract from the quality and livability of places, including the origins and destinations of trips as well as places along the way. This attribute makes getting between Place A and Place B safe, efficient, and enjoyable.

In the form versus function dichotomy, place and people connectivity pertains mostly to the urban *form*, fostering place making and creating vibrant, livable, and aesthetically pleasing urban places. Place and transport connectivity, on the other hand, speaks mostly to urban *function* and primarily represents the accessibility dimension of urban places. High place and transport connectivity–bringing Place A and Place B closer together, or making it faster and easier to travel between them–translates into high access.

Audit Tool

There are five key dimensions of connected places. These are:

1 city and neighborhood structure
2 diversity
3 walkability and cyclability
4 place making
5 transport.

These are listed in the first column of the Audit Tool (Table 6.1). The qualitative and quantitative design variables for each dimension are listed in the next column. It is hard to categorize a design variable under a single dimension. Many of the listed variables are a measure for more than one dimension. However, their placement in the table is under the dimension that they measure directly. The final three columns refer to the people, place, and transport connectivity attributes that are directly impacted by each variable.[2]

Audit Metrics

People/better communities are central to the idea of connecting places, connecting people. This is evident in Figure 6.1, which shows that the majority of design variables influence people connectivity, followed by place and transport connectivity.

A well-connected place scores highly on many, but not all, of the variables. Indeed, the place identity of different settings depends partly on uniqueness and departure from the norm. However, all well-connected places score highly enough on the five physical dimensions so that the three key attributes—people connectivity, place connectivity, and transport connectivity—are achieved. A rating scale can be developed in the future based on an audit of a range of connected places.

PEOPLE, PLACE, AND TRANSPORT CONNECTIVITY

Table 6.1 Audit Tool showing dimensions of connected places and the variables affecting people, place and transport connectivity

Dimensions	Design Variables	People Connectivity	Place Connectivity	Transport Connectivity
1. City and neighborhood structure	a. Network type (gridded/non-gridded)		✓	✓
	b. Density (low/medium/high; residential/gross/employment)		✓	✓
	c. Block size (smallest area that is surrounded by streets)		✓	✓
2. Diversity	a. Lot size (size range of land parcels within a block)		✓	
	b. Activities (mixed use and range of necessary and optional activities)	✓	✓	
	c. Housing typologies and price (apartment/townhouse/condominium/row house/detached dwelling; low/high cost)		✓	
	d. Building types (horizontal/vertical layering of uses)		✓	
3. Walkability and cyclability	a. Street typology (multi-modal activity corridor/freight/environmental corridor*)	✓		✓
	b. Ped-shed accessibility (5-minute walk circles around main uses, 10-minute walk to transport nodes, or 2-minute walk to neighborhood parks)		✓	✓
	c. Space syntax (connectivity and permeability)		✓	✓
	d. Footpath width	✓		
	e. Vehicle speed	✓		
	f. Street façade continuity	✓		
	g. Building setbacks	✓		
	h. Façade solid:void ratio (openings on the façade)	✓		
	i. Mechanical/formal surveillance (CCTVs/patrol)	✓		
	j. Tree-lined streets	✓	✓	
	k. Lighting	✓		
4. Place making (quality of architecture and urban design)	a. Active edge	✓		
	b. Human scale (urban massing)	✓		
	c. Aesthetically pleasing/green architecture/water-sensitive urban design	✓		
	d. Public art	✓		
	e. Street furniture (seats, bins, etc.)	✓		
	f. Landmarks/heritage/landscape (identity and sense of place)	✓		
	g. Personalization/interactive built form	✓	✓	
	h. Building state; abandoned sites; isolated places		✓	
	i. Social width (psychological dimension dependent on street width and barriers between the two sides)	✓		
5. Transport	a. Access to train network		✓	✓
	b. Access to and frequency of bus services		✓	✓
	c. Pedestrian and cycle network and end-of-trip facilities	✓	✓	✓
	d. Shared transport/smart cars/smart technology			✓
	e. On-street parking			✓
	f. Freight/loading			✓

Note: * Refer to Chapter 3.

MAKING IT HAPPEN

Figure 6.1 Audit metrics: number of dimensions responding to the three attributes of people, place, and transport connectivity

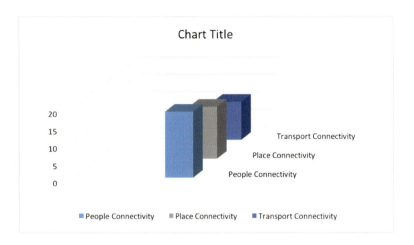

The metrics for some variables are illustrated below. It is important that metrics are appropriate for the area to be audited. The density metric applicable to TODs in the US, for example, will not be applicable to places in South Asia. The interplay between different dimensions or dimensional relationships must also be considered. For example, the impact of block sizes on walkability when considered in isolation will be different from the combined impact of block size and street width (Price, 2013).

Density (Dimension 1, Variable b)

Density impacts directly on place and transport connectivity by shortening trips and bringing activities together, and making transit viable by increasing vehicle occupancy (Ewing, 1995). The rule of thumb for auditing or planning incorporates four types of density:

1. *Residential density*: there is a direct correlation between transit ridership and the density of people living in an area.
2. *Average gross residential density within a station area*: this is an indication of the levels of activity needed to support types of transit services.
3. *Employment density*: the number of jobs per acre translates into the number of jobs within a half-mile radius of a station.
4. *Desirable density* (Nematollahi et al., 2015): the community associates an increase in density with overcrowded public housing developments and social problems (Lozano-Gracia et al., 2013). A desirable density recognizes the sociocultural aspects of the area and the community needs for privacy, available views, ease of access to the ground floor, and so on.

Table 6.2 quantifies the different types of densities that support different transit services.

Table 6.2 Types of densities for transit systems

Types of densities	Residential density	Average gross density within a station area	Employment density	Desirable density
(Types of transit services supported)	(The below are applicable to the US TODs)			
Basic bus service	7 units per gross acre (Ewing, 1999, p. 3)	18 dwelling units per acre (Calthorpe, 1993) with a 'wedding cake' density gradient required to maximize transit ridership (Cervero, 1993, p. 101)		<20 dwellings per acre—direct access to grounds, unit identity maintained, no need of common parking 20 dwellings per acre—direct access to the ground cannot be provided to each unit 35–50 dwellings per acre—low-rise apartment 3 stories walk-ups 45–50 dwellings per acre—visual intimacy is lost
Premium bus service	15 units per gross acre (Ewing, 1999)		25 jobs per acre, translating into 15,000 jobs within a half-mile radius of a station (Ewing, 1999; Puget Sound Regional Council, 1999)	65–75 dwellings per acre—mid-rise apartment 6 stories high
Rail service	20 to 30 units per acre (Ewing, 1997)		50 jobs per acre (Puget Sound Regional Council, 1999)	>80 dwellings per acre—wide variety of facilities to each dwelling (provision of parking and open space becomes an issue) (Lynch, cited in Eduardo, 2013, p. 404)

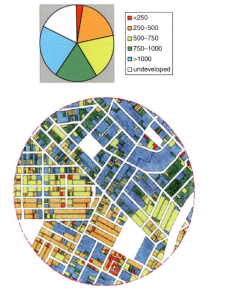 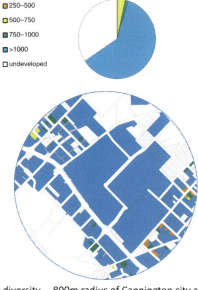

Block size diversity – 800m radius of Mount Lawley   Block size diversity – 800m radius of Cannington city center

Figure 6.2 *Land use efficiency and block size*

6.2a Source: Reprinted from Which suburbs work? A comparison between traditionally planned suburbs and conventional suburban development *(p. 16), by M. Mackay, 2001, Perth, WA: Department for Planning.*

Diversity of Block/Lot Sizes (Dimension 2, Variable a)

The diversity of block sizes is directly proportional to the land use efficiency.[3] For example, a high diversity of block sizes, essential for connected places, is a feature of Mount Lawley, Perth, 2.7 kilometers from the CBD (shown on the left of Figure 6.2); this results in a high land use efficiency of 64 percent. This is compared with a lower block size diversity that yields a lower land use efficiency of 33 percent, as shown on the right of Figure 6.2 for Cannington, Perth, 11 kilometers from the CBD (Tiwari, 2011). Cannington is impermeable for active transport as 60.89 percent of the lots are above 1,000 square meters.

Connectivity (Dimension 3, Variable c)

Connectivity is measured as the number of intersections per square kilometer. A comparison of conventional non-gridded and traditional gridded suburbs in Perth, shows that the street pattern of Nedlands, a traditional older suburb, offers a variety of reasonably direct routes from one part to another. On the other hand, the non-gridded streets of Ballajura, a conventional suburb, constitutes a big-box development with restricted connectivity and increased travel distance. Residents are obliged to use the car as the main mode of travel (Mackay, 2001). In terms of connectivity, there are 28 intersections per square kilometer in Ballajura and 78 intersections per square kilometer in Nedlands, as shown in Figure 6.3.

PEOPLE, PLACE, AND TRANSPORT CONNECTIVITY

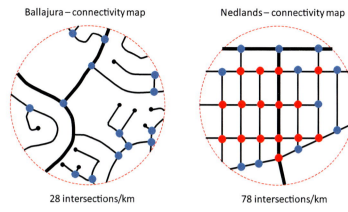

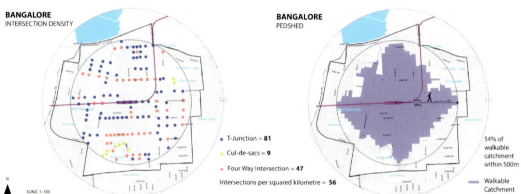

Figure 6.3 Connectivity maps of a conventional and a traditional suburb—28 intersections/km in Ballajura and 78 intersections/km in Nedlands

Source: Reprinted from Which suburbs work? A comparison between traditionally planned suburbs and conventional suburban development (p. 8), by M. Mackay, 2001, Perth, WA: Department for Planning.

Figure 6.4 (a) Permeability index (left); and (b) ped-shed accessibility (right) in Indira Nagar, Bangalore, India

Source: Reprinted from Designing a safe walkable city, by R. Tiwari, 2014, Urban Design International 20(1) pp. 16, 17.

Ped-shed[4] Accessibility and Permeability (Dimension 3, Variables b and c)

The permeability index[5] measures the ease of making a trip. Figure 6.4a shows that, with 56 intersections per square kilometer, Indira Nagar, Bangalore, not only has a very high connectivity but is highly permeable, due to a large number of four-way intersections and T-junctions. The areas in the south and north-east, highlighted in yellow, become impermeable due to a large number of cul-de-sacs. These areas also do not lie within 54 percent of the walkable catchment within a 500-meter radius of the metro station (Figure 6.4b).

Physical permeability depends on block width. A block of less than 240 feet serves as a traffic-calming device (Sucher, 2010). Pedestrian accessways and courtyards between buildings can provide permeability for pedestrians while retaining larger block sizes for speedier traffic (Figure 6.5).

Solid:void ratio (Dimension 3, Variable h)

A low solid:void ratio enhances people-to-place interaction. Buildings with glazing instead of structural components encourage more visual and physical exchanges (Figure 6.6). This can be

| 103

MAKING IT HAPPEN

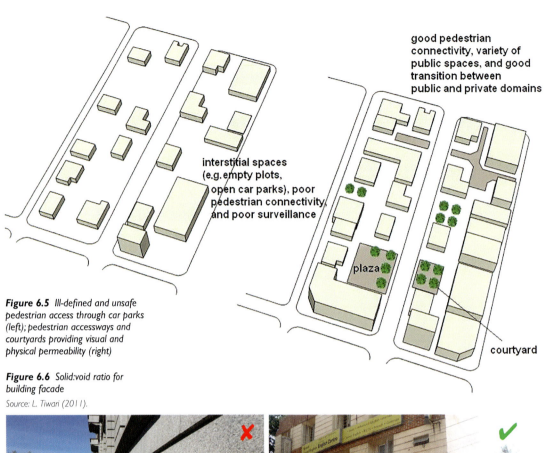

Figure 6.5 Ill-defined and unsafe pedestrian access through car parks (left); pedestrian accessways and courtyards providing visual and physical permeability (right)

Figure 6.6 Solid:void ratio for building facade
Source: L. Tiwari (2011).

104

comforting and convenient even if only perceived subconsciously. Positive interactions between pedestrians boost business and create a pleasant streetscape. Melbourne has a regulation of providing at least 5 meters or 80 percent of the street frontage (whichever is the greater) as entry or display window to a shop or a food premises, which has helped in encouraging a high level of pedestrian interaction (City of Melbourne, 2015, p. 27). Regulations to ensure appropriate design control can promote the aesthetic and functional components of retail streets. Important elements to consider include frontage:access ratio, parking locations, loading/unloading spaces, setbacks, definition of edges, and other design details (Tiwari, 2012).

Urban massing (Dimension 4, Variable b)

To achieve a sense of enclosure and comfort for users, the generally recommended ratios of height to width are 1:1 for urban scale, 1:2 for medium scale, and 1:3 for suburban scale (Abbate, 2007; Figure 6.7).

In suburban settings, street trees play a more important role in defining a sense of enclosure than buildings do. Walls and fences, either low or over six feet tall, as Kevin Lynch points out, can also provide spatial definition (Lynch, quoted in Ewing & Clemente, 2013, p. 8). Focal points at street ends and irregular grids can help close vistas.

Public art (Dimension 4, Variable d)

Public art is not simply artworks that are not in a gallery or studio. Public art aims to engage audiences and to create spaces. These spaces with which people can identify can be material, virtual, or imagined. They hold a mirror to the community, reflecting the uses of public spaces or our behavior within them. Public art contributes to the visual attractiveness of the city and to aesthetically rich urban spaces, and creates connection with place. In addition, it allows public authorities to signal their awareness of social and environmental problems (Sharp et al., 2005).

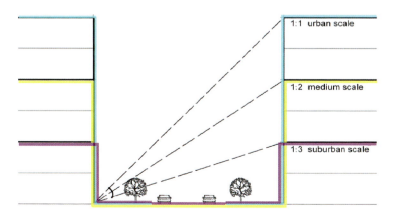

Figure 6.7 The impact of height:street-width ratio on 'sense of enclosure'

MAKING IT HAPPEN

Figure 6.8 Public art and graffiti, Melbourne

Source: Pictures by L. Tiwari (2016).

Introduced in 2003 in Victoria, Australia, the Victorian State Government's Grappling with Graffiti strategy obliges municipalities to develop graffiti management strategies conforming to a particular regulatory template (Crime Prevention Victoria, 2003). The core components are eradication, education, and enforcement. The strategy emphasizes engagement with the communities of graffiti writers and street artists through a partnership model. The stakeholders that are invited to participate are defined broadly, and include residents, traders, community groups, galleries, transport companies, utilities providers, the Victorian Police, construction companies, and hoarding manufacturers as well as the graffiti writers and artists (Tiwari, 2012; Figure 6.8).

Audit Demonstration: King Street, San Francisco

To measure their impact on people, place, and transport connectivity, some attributes of connected places have been audited (Table 6.3). Embarcadero Boulevard in San Francisco (which becomes King Street) replaced the elevated Embarcadero Freeway after the 7.1-magnitude Loma Prieta earthquake in 1989.

Converting the freeway into a boulevard attracted private investment to the vicinity. Other benefits were jobs, residential growth, and increased land prices (Cervero et al., 2009). After the construction of the Embarcadero in the 1990s, there was a 75 percent increase in public transit commute trips and a 1.6 percent increase in walking to work trips measured in the influence zone of the streetcar-served Embarcadero Boulevard (Cervero et al., 2009, p. 40). The attributes audited are for King Street (Figure 6.9).

King Street provides a direct east–west connection between the Embarcadero and the I-280 on and off ramps at Fifth Street. Fourth Street Station is a stub-end terminal with six platforms located at King

PEOPLE, PLACE, AND TRANSPORT CONNECTIVITY

Street–Fourth Street. The street section explored is from the San Francisco Bay Bridge to Fourth Street (highlighted in red in Figure 6.9). Data from a study conducted by Kott (2011) is used to illustrate the impact of the five key connectivity dimensions on people, place, and transport connectivity (Table 6.3).

Figure 6.9 Geographical setting of King Street and Mission Bay
Source: Image adapted from Google Earth by Google, 2016.

Table 6.3 Audit Tool application on King Street, San Francisco

Dimension 1: City and Neighborhood Structure	
Design Variables	**King Street, Mission Bay, San Francisco**
a. Network type	Grid.
b. Density (400m corridor)	38 people and 91 jobs per hectare/37.12 jobs per acre (Kott, 2011, p. 192).
c. Block sizes*	Average 107×183m.
Impact on People, Place, and Transport	
Mixed-use development has enabled smaller lots suited to the immediate vicinity, but concentrated along the boulevard (Kott, 2011). It has generated an average daily traffic volume of 21,580 east of Third Street, which makes the area vibrant.	
A job density of 12–50 jobs per acre, as per Table 6.2, makes the tram and train services viable. With 37.12 jobs per acre, there are around 4,839 transit boardings per day, demonstrating a good transit service. The area has been able to serve technology companies, allied services, and multi-unit buildings.	
The geographical boundary of the shoreline, the presence of mass transit (multi-modal), and the proximity to the CBD, the University of California, and recreational activity (AT&T Park) provide unique locational value to the neighborhood. This has generated a good market for housing, resulting in a high density of residents and jobs.	

Dimension 2: Diversity	
Design Variables	**King Street, Mission Bay, San Francisco**
a. Diversity of block sizes and residential lot[†] sizes	190×162m; 80×80m; 245×76m; 243×50m (Figure 6.10).
b. Mixed-use and range of necessary and optional activities	Dedicated blocks with commercial and retail activity.
c. Range of housing typologies and prices	Apartments and condominiums, single-bedroom apartments to three-bedroom apartments.
d. Building types (horizontal/vertical layering of uses)	Typical city block with courtyards, ground-floor activity is commercial and retail in most buildings.

MAKING IT HAPPEN

Impact on People, Place, and Transport

Figure 6.10 Diverse block and lot sizes[a]

Source: Drawn on maps from Google Earth by Google, 2016.

Figure 6.11 Diverse rental values reflecting diverse residential quality and typology[b]

Source: Adapted from Trulia by Trulia, 2016, Drawn on map from Google Earth by Google, 2016.

The diversity of block sizes has resulted in a neighborhood housing a number of information technology companies, media houses, financial institutions, a car rental company, pharmacy, Fire Department, retail stores, a bowling alley, art stores, design studios, dry cleaners, cafeterias, and restaurants. This has provided an opportunity for a diverse demographic mix. Students from the Mission Bay campus of the University of California, San Francisco, and the Center for Health Research and Education and the mix of office workers add to the diversity and result in a demand for number of demographically specific functions/services.

The presence of plazas, parks, and AT&T Park, home of the Giants, San Francisco's major league baseball team, add to the place's recreational character (Kott, 2011). This diverse mix of functions attracts people to visit, run businesses, work, shop, and live, resulting in a vibrant neighborhood character and economy.

Various medium- and high-rise residential condominium projects have been built on King Street. There are also multi-family residential buildings. The diverse typology of apartments acts as a pull factor for all age groups and family sizes. The rents, shown in Figure 6.11, illustrate this diversity.

PEOPLE, PLACE, AND TRANSPORT CONNECTIVITY

Dimension 3: Walkability and Cyclability	
Design Variables	**King Street, Mission Bay, San Francisco**
a. Street typology	Designated as a major arterial, primary transit streets, a neighborhood connection street, and a bicycle route (US Department of Transportation Federal Transit Administration, 2007, pp. 3–18).
b. Ped-shed accessibility (5-minute walk circles around main uses or 10-minute walk to transport nodes)	47 percent of lots accessible within 400m (5-minute walk).
c. Space syntax (connectivity and permeability)	87 intersections per square kilometer. There are 24.9 pedestrian connections per kilometer[‡] with 10.7 crossing signals per kilometer (Kott, 2011). There are 10.7 along crosswalks and 17.9 across crosswalks per kilometer (Kott, 2011).
d. Wide footpaths	Around 6m wide in the vicinity of Third and Fourth Streets; 4.1m along the rest of the section; 3m along light rail.
e. Vehicle speeds	30mph between the Embarcadero and Fifth Street.
f. Street façade continuity	Shortest to longest: 39.62m, 48.76m, 51.8m, 109.7m, 121.9m, 124.9m (Kott, 2011).
g. Setbacks	1.5–11.2m.
h. Façade solid:void ratio	50–70 percent openings on ground floor; 30–50 percent openings on first floor and upwards (Figure 6.12). There are 732.1 linear street front windows per mile and 128.6 street front doors per mile (Kott, 2011). The 38.4 percent frontage gaps[§] are made up for by aesthetic views of the bay and improved pedestrian connections. Lesser commercial driveways on streets. These are at 10.7 driveways per mile (Kott, 2011).
i. Mechanical/formal surveillance	Yes.
j. Tree-lined streets	Yes; tree canopy covers 4.3 percent of ROW at King Street, which may be increased for a big city arterial (Kott, 2011).
k. Lighting	Yes.

MAKING IT HAPPEN

Impact on People, Place, and Transport

Figure 6.12 Solid:void ratio on building façade[d]
Source: Pictures by R. Tiwari (2008).

Figure 6.13 Pedestrian amenity and permeability[e]
Source: Pictures by R. Tiwari (2008).

King Street has sidewalks, bicycle lanes, light rail lines, platforms, and strollers. The inner streets (i.e. Second, Third, and Fourth) have clear signage, such as of speed limits. Legibility, safety, pedestrian path connectivity, and permeability (Figure 6.13) have led to the use of the street by people walking dogs, on bikes, sitting on the benches, and walking to shops and offices (Kott, 2011).

80 percent of respondents report the street environs as comfortable, safe, attractive, convenient, and active, as per the survey conducted by Kott (2011).

Smaller lots within a traditional grid network have allowed connectivity, permeability, and better accessibility to transit (Kott, 2011). The connectivity index of 87 intersections per square kilometer exceeds the connectivity index of 78 intersections per square kilometer for Nedlands (Figure 6.3). Hence, Kings Street precinct rates higher than Nedlands for the connectivity dimension. One sees good movement of pedestrians and cyclists.

King Street has 29.4 percent buffer[||] for pedestrians, with continuous bicycle lanes in each direction, sidewalk, and markings for on-street parking, resulting in an area that is safe for users. The pedestrian safety index is comparatively high despite high vehicle speeds and volume on the boulevard (the 85th percentile speed[¶] is at 35 miles per hour; Kott, 2011).

A low solid:void ratio, with 732.1 linear street front windows per mile and 128.6 street front doors per mile, attracts people and increases activity and interaction on the streets, making the streets safe.

PEOPLE, PLACE, AND TRANSPORT CONNECTIVITY

Dimension 4: Place Making (Quality of Architecture and Urban Design)	
Design Variables	**King Street, Mission Bay, San Francisco**
a. Social width	The four-lane two-way street with Muni metro tracks in the central median creates a barrier between the two sides and acts as a psychological barrier that results in a reduced social width (Figure 6.14).
b. Active edge	40–50 percent (approx. façade coverage of commercial activity based on observation).
c. Human scale (urban massing)	1:2 (medium scale) and 1:1 (urban scale) (Figure 6.15).
d. Aesthetically pleasing/ green architecture/water-sensitive urban design	South Beach Park, South Beach Yacht Club, Willie Mays Plaza.
e. Public art	Yes.
f. Street furniture (seats, bins, etc.)	There are 14.3 public transit benches per mile and 35.6 café chairs per mile.
g. Landmarks/heritage/ landscape (identity and sense of place)	AT&T Park (baseball stadium); Caltrain (commuter rail transit system); remembrance of the past (Figure 6.16).
h. Personalization/ interactive built form	Fair interaction at the ground floor due to commercial/retail/business use. Less interaction at higher levels.
i. Building state; abandoned sites; isolated places; incompatible uses (territoriality)	All buildings are functional with active use.
**Impact on People, Place, and Transport**	

Figure 6.14 Reduced social width on King Street[e]
Source: Pictures by R. Tiwari (2008).

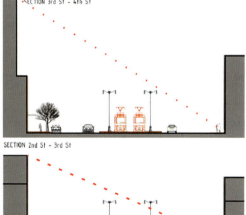

Figure 6.15 Building height:street-width ratio changes along King Street, approximately 1:1–1:2[f]
Source: Drawn by T. Seangsong (2010).

| 111

Although the social width can be improved across the street, the street edges are well activated: 1,132 feet per mile and 624 feet per mile, respectively, are occupied by restaurant and retail use at the street façade. This provides active edge, character, and eyes on the street (Kott, 2011).

The building height to street:width ratio along King Street changes as per the change in adjacent uses. This adds variety to the street character (Figure 6.15).

As one respondent noted, 'The scale of buildings seems appropriate. The street is interesting and lively' (Kott, 2011, p. 289).

Respondents appreciated the streetscape details and/or the architectural scale of buildings on the street, the views from the street, and its cleanliness and landscaping (Kott, 2011).

AT&T Park is a landmark and attracts large crowds on game days, resulting in crowded sidewalks. Users reported that the place is a good attractor for travel, commerce, recreation, and aesthetic enjoyment. This is facilitated by the 392.1 feet per mile of vacant street frontage (Kott, 2011).

15.4 percent 'green gaps' in street frontage complement the busy boulevard. The park lawn, which opens a vista to the bay, complements the urban design and sense of place, mostly on the east or bay side of the street (Kott, 2011).

Past events are remembered throughout the landscape, adding depth and character to the area (Figure 6.16).

Figure 6.16 Past remembrance[g]

Source: Pictures by R. Tiwari (2008).

Dimension 5: Transport	
Design Variables	**King Street, Mission Bay, San Francisco**
a. Access to train network	King Street & 2nd Street and King Street & 4th Street; frequency 5–20 minutes.
b. Access to and frequency of bus services	King Street & 2nd Street and King Street & 4th Street; frequency 10–30 minutes.
c. Pedestrian and cycle network and end-of-trip facilities	4.1m wide footpaths for convenient soft mobility. There are 11 bike racks per mile.
d. Shared transport/smart cars/smart technology	Bike-sharing station at Caltrain; taxis.
e. On-street parking	Parking is permitted between the Embarcadero and Third Street; 2.2m lanes on both sides of the street.
f. Freight and loading	Trucks are allowed; loading bays on side streets.

PEOPLE, PLACE, AND TRANSPORT CONNECTIVITY

Impact on People, Place, and Transport
An inter-city train station, a light rail station, and a ferry provide accessibility for both intra- and inter-city travel. There are 98 regional trains per weekday, 7.1 transit stops per mile, and 1,918 buses or trains per weekday (Kott, 2011). The land use mix attracts a large number of trips, resulting in place connectivity. There are about 4,839 transit boardings per day, representing good transport connectivity. 18.6 percent of right of way (ROW) at King Street is allocated to transit and 25 percent is allocated to pedestrians and bikes, with 11 bike racks per mile (Kott, 2011). Kott (2011) notes there are 436 pedestrians and 74 bikes per hour on the street. These numbers demonstrate the priority given to active transport modes.

Notes:
[*] A block is the smallest area that is surrounded by streets.
[†] A lot is a land parcel within a block. There could be number of lots under different ownerships within a block.
[‡] Pedestrian lateral connections in their respective street segments cohorts. Lateral connections are sidewalks, outdoor passageways between buildings, or other spaces dedicated to travel by pedestrians from a street section to parallel streets and other locations.
[§] Amount of discontinuity in building line (Kott, 2011, p. 233).
[||] The buffer is the area separating the pedestrian walkway from moving motor vehicle traffic (Kott, 2011, p. 243).
[¶] The 85th percentile is the speed at or below which 85 percent of motor vehicles are traveling (Kott, 2011, p. 254).

Sources:
[a] Drawn on maps from Google Earth by Google, 2016. Retrieved from www.google.com.au/maps/place/Bayside+Village/@37.7849278,-122.3899455,321m/data=!3m1!1e3!4m13!1m7!3m6!1s0x808f7fd6a6099611:0x78cfc20ff4aa87fd!2sKing+St,+San+Francisco,+CA,+USA!3b1!8m2!3d37.7758156!4d-122.3949376!3m4!1s0x0:0x25374fff35068ae6!8m2!3d37.7848811!4d-122.3897217www.google.com.au/maps/place/King+St,+San+Francisco,+CA,+USA/@37.780765,-122.38957,320m/data=!3m1!1e3!4m5!3m4!1s0x808f7fd6a6099611:0x78cfc20ff4aa87fd!8m2!3d37.7758156!4d-122.3949376; www.google.com.au/maps/place/King+St,+San+Francisco,+CA,+USA/@37.7772515,-122.3928112,321m/data=!3m1!1e3!4m5!3m4!1s0x808f7fd6a6099611:0x78cfc20ff4aa87fd!8m2!3d37.7758156!4d-122.3949376. Copyright 2016 by Google Inc. Adapted with permission.
[b] Adapted from Trulia, 2016, drawn on map from Google Earth by Google, 2016. Retrieved from www.trulia.com/for_rent/San_Francisco,CA/15_zm/37.7697243750465,37.785056283321836,-122.41607371087741,-122.37616244073581_xy/map_v. Copyright 2016 by Trulia.
[c] Pictures by R. Tiwari.
[d] Picture by R. Tiwari.
[e] Pictures by R. Tiwari.
[f] Drawn by T. Seangsong.
[g] Picture by R. Tiwari.

Community Engagement for Assessing a Pedestrian-Friendly Environment and Place-Making Aspects

Since many audit dimensions are qualitative in nature, the methods of data collection should rely on obtaining perspectives from community members along with observational surveys. This section describes an example of involving the community in measuring 'walkability'. A toolkit developed by Clean Air Asia and the author was used to assess the pedestrian-friendly environment and place-making aspects at Nehru Place in New Delhi (Tiwari & Rapur, forthcoming). Some rating sheets that recorded the community's perceptions are illustrated in Tables 6.4 to 6.9. The degree of difficulty is highest at 0 and lowest at 5.

MAKING IT HAPPEN

(A) Walking Path Modal Conflict Score

This variable measures the conflict between transport modes and pedestrians walking along the walkway/roadway or crossing the road. (While pedestrians' conflict with other non-motorized transport (NMT) modes at higher speeds may be injurious, it has not been considered here.)

Table 6.4 Walking path modal conflict score

Score	Condition
0	Significant conflict with heavy and fast vehicles which prevent walking.
1	Significant conflict with vehicles with high risk of accident, but walking is possible.
2	Walking is possible, but with great inconvenience.
3	Walking is possible, with some inconvenience.
4	Conflict with other slow-moving NMT modes.
5	No conflict with other modes.

Source: Adapted from Walkability Tool-kit, Clean Air Asia Initiative, 2016.

PEOPLE, PLACE, AND TRANSPORT CONNECTIVITY

(B) Quality of Crossing Points Score

This variable determines the quality of space, time, and grade in a crossing.

Table 6.5 *Quality of crossing points score*

Score	Condition
0	Crossing point is not manned or signalized. No road marking/sign board warns motorists, vehicle speed is greater than 50km/h, waiting time is greater than one minute, and the place is poorly lit.
1	Crossing point is grade separated without escalator/elevator.
2	Space for waiting at signal is insufficient, waiting time is greater than 45 seconds, and median/refuge island width is insufficient. Time for crossing the road is less than 10 seconds for two-lane roads and 20 seconds for four-lane roads.
3	Space for waiting is just sufficient and at times congested. Time for crossing the road is 10 to 15 seconds for a two-lane road and 20 to 30 seconds for a four-lane road.
4	A safe grade separates crossing with escalator, with adequate lighting, or at-grade crossing with pedestrian pelican signal facility providing more than 15 seconds for crossing a two-lane road and 30 seconds for crossing a four-lane road.
5	Pedestrians can safely cross the road anywhere.

Source: Adapted from Walkability Tool-kit, Clean Air Asia Initiative, 2016.

MAKING IT HAPPEN

(C) Amenities Score

This variable reflects the quality of the walk. Various amenities such as lighting, shade, and information signs are measured.

Table 6.6 Amenities score

Score	Condition
0	No amenities available.
1	Trees spaced far apart, shade for pedestrians is inadequate, benches in poor condition.
2	Signboards, benches, and shade available but these obstruct pedestrian movement.
3	A few signboards, shade, and lights available but they are insufficient.
4	Signs, lights, rubbish bins, and shade available but could be improved with better placement and alignment.
5	All amenities available. Benches available every 100m with tree cover, efficient lighting, and wayfinders. A public toilet is available within 500m of the metro station.

Source: Adapted from Walkability Tool-kit, Clean Air Asia Initiative, 2016.

PEOPLE, PLACE, AND TRANSPORT CONNECTIVITY

(D) Special Needs Infrastructure Score

This variable measures the infrastructure for people with special needs. This includes ramps, handrails, tactile paving, auditory pelican signals, and so on.

Table 6.7 Special needs infrastructure score

Score	Condition
0	No amenities available, giving no access for pedestrians with special needs.
1	Disability infrastructure insufficient.
2	Some disability infrastructure present but not up to appropriate standards.
3	Disability infrastructure requires maintenance.
4	Disability infrastructure is in good, clean condition but could be better placed.
5	Disability infrastructure well placed and in excellent condition. Auditory pelican crossing/elevator situated at height accessible to a wheelchair, etc.

Source: Adapted from Walkability Tool-kit, Clean Air Asia Initiative, 2016.

MAKING IT HAPPEN

(E) Safety from Crime Score

This variable should be assessed by a woman who understands the vulnerability of women on the streets. Elements such as setback, lighting, building frontage, speed of vehicles, vendors, and so on can make a street safe or unsafe.

Table 6.8 Safety from crime score

Score	Condition
0	Pedestrians are extremely vulnerable to crime: uninhabited streets, no lighting, lack of activity, very high vehicle speeds.
1	Pedestrians are vulnerable to crime: high setback of buildings, tinted windows of commercial spaces, high compound walls, inactive edges, and overcrowded.
2	Pedestrians do not feel psychologically safe: few pedestrians on the street after dark, not much activity, poor lighting, few entrances or exits to buildings.
3	Pedestrians feel marginally safe: slow traffic speed, buildings facing away from the street with few entrances or exits, but not many active edges.
4	Pedestrians feel safe but with few vendors present, other pedestrians, houses with compound walls of 1m or less, active edges, more entrances and exits.
5	Pedestrians feel very safe with more eyes on the street, open building frontage, vendor zones, etc., active street with reduced vehicle speeds.

Source: Adapted from Walkability Tool-kit, Clean Air Asia Initiative, 2016.

PEOPLE, PLACE, AND TRANSPORT CONNECTIVITY

(F) Motorists' Behavior Score

Motorists' behavior towards pedestrians on the road can demonstrate how pedestrian friendly a city is.

Table 6.9 *Motorists' behavior score*

Score	Condition
0	Motorists encroach on pedestrian space.
1	Motorists do not slow down for pedestrians at all.
2	Motorists rarely yield to pedestrians.
3	Motorists yield, but only if pedestrians are in large numbers and in a group.
4	Motorists often yield to pedestrians.
5	Motorists do not encroach on pedestrian space and always yield, or there are pedestrian priority areas.

Source: Adapted from Walkability Tool-kit, Clean Air Asia Initiative, 2016.

The above examples offer important insights into the attributes, dimensions, and variables that constitute a connected place.

Close

Connecting a place becomes the precursor to connecting people. People live in places and move between places. Besides the tangible aspects of a place, there are intangible aspects of imageability, identity, and sense of belonging shaped by a community's values, memories, behaviors, and interactions. The Audit Tool presented in this chapter includes both the tangible and intangible dimensions that impact the place, people, and transport connectivity directly or indirectly. It can be used in a variety of ways:

- *Research:* Researchers can objectively and consistently develop metrics for different dimensions based on the context of the area under review. A rating scale for connected places can be developed using the metrics for places with similar contexts.
- *Planning and urban design:* Planners and urban designers can take an inventory of the physical characteristics to assess the quality of an area, identify problems, and recommend improvements. A before-and-after evaluation using the Audit Tool can measure the success of the strategies.
- *Community input:* A number of dimensions in the Audit Tool incorporate the community's perceptions and feedback. Community rating sheets can be developed for each dimension based on the context of the area under review.

Notes

1. 'Actionable knowledge' is the creative intersection between what we know and putting what we know into everyday practice (Blood, 2006).
2. Nearly all variables impact all attributes; however, the attributes being directly impacted are highlighted.
3. Land use efficiency is expressed as the land occupied by buildings and other private purposes as a percentage of the study area.
4. A 'ped-shed' is defined as a five-minute walk circle around the main uses, a ten-minute walk to transport nodes, or a two-minute walk to neighborhood parks'
5. The permeability index is defined as the 'number of intersections per square kilometer weighted according to the ability to keep moving forwards' (Mackay, 2001, p. 9). The ability to keep moving forward is proportional to the number of ways (or arms) at an intersection; a four-way intersection is more permeable than a three-way intersection. To calculate permeability, a four-arm intersection is generally assigned a positive number (+1), a three-arm intersection is zero (0) and dead-ends are assigned a negative number (–1) to reflect the need to turn around and go back (Mackay, 2001).

References

All online references retrieved August 17, 2016.

Abbate, A. (2007). *Broward County county-wide community design guidebook.* Retrieved from www.broward.org/PlanningAndRedevelopment/DemographicsAndEconomics/Pages/UrbanDesign.aspx.

Blood, M. R. (2006). Only you can create actionable knowledge. *Academy of Management Learning and Education 5*, 209–212.

Broward County. (2008, May 22). *Final report on alternative roadway design guidelines*. Retrieved from http://urbanhs.com/wp-content/uploads/2012/06/BC-Design-Guidelines.pdf.

Calthorpe, P. (1993). *The next American metropolis: Ecology, community, and the American dream*. New York: Princeton Architectural Press.

Cervero, R. (1993). *Transit-supportive development in the United States: Experiences and prospects* (DOT-T-94-08). Washington, D.C.: Federal Transit Administration.

Cervero, R., Kang, J., & Shively, K. (2009). From elevated freeways to surface boulevards: Neighbourhood and housing price impacts in San Francisco. *Journal of Urbanism: International Research on Placemaking and Urban Sustainability 2*(1), 31–50.

City of Melbourne. (2015). Last kilometer freight. Retrieved from http://participate.melbourne.vic.gov.au/application/files/8414/2525/0768/Last_Kilometre_Freight_-_Background_Report_27_02_15.pdf.

Crime Prevention Victoria (2003). *Grappling with Graffiti: A management strategy for Victoria*. Melbourne, VIC: Victorian State Government.

Ewing, R. (1995). Measuring transportation performance. *Transportation Quarterly 49*(1), 91–104. Retrieved from http://worldcat.org/oclc/7938948.

Ewing, R. (1997). *Transportation and land use innovations*. Chicago, IL: Planners Press.

Ewing, R. (1999). *Pedestrian and transit friendly design: A primer for smart growth*. Retrieved from www.epa.gov/sites/production/files/documents/ptfd_primer.pdf.

Ewing, R., & Clemente, O. (2013). *Measuring urban design: Metrics for livable places*. Washington, D.C.: Island Press.

Kott, J. (2011). Streets of clay: Design and assessment of sustainable urban and suburban streets. Doctoral dissertation. Retrieved from www.academia.edu/2775099/Streets_of_Clay_Design_and_Assessment_of_Sustainable_Urban_and_Suburban_Streets.

Lozano, E. E. (2013) Density in communities, or the most important factor in building urbanity. In M. Larice & E. Macdonand (Eds.) *The urban design reader* (pp. 399–414). New York: Routledge.

Lozano Eduardo. 2013. Density in communities, or the most important factor in building urbanity in Larice, M. and Macdonald, E. edited The Urban Design Reader, New York. P. 399 - 414

Lozano-Gracia, N., Young, C., Lall, S. V., & Vishwanath, T. (2013, January). *Leveraging land to enable urban transformation: Lessons from global experience* (Paper No. 6312). Retrieved from http://dx.doi.org/10.1596/1813-9450-6312.

Mackay, M. (2001). *Which suburbs work? A comparison between traditionally planned suburbs and conventional suburban development*. Perth, WA: Western Australian Planning Commission. Retrieved from www.planning.wa.gov.au/dop_pub_pdf/whichsubshow.pdf.

Nematollahi, S., Tiwari, R., & Hedgecock, D. (2015). Desirable dense neighbourhoods: An environmental psychological approach for understanding community resistance to densification. *Urban Policy and Research 36*(2), 132–151.

Price, A. (2013). Optimizing the street grid. *Strong Towns*. Retrieved from www.strongtowns.org/journal/2013/11/27/optimizing-the-street-grid.html.

Puget Sound Regional Council. (1999, June). *Creating transit station communities in the Central Puget Sound Region: A transit-oriented development workbook*. Retrieved from www.psrc.org/assets/3463/_99-09_todreport.pdf.

Sharp, J., Pollock, V., & Paddison, R. (2005). Just art for a just city: Public art and social inclusion in urban regeneration. *Urban Studies 42*(5/6), 1001–1023.

Sucher, D. M. (2010). *City comforts: How to build an urban village*. Seattle, WA: City Comforts Inc.

Tiwari, R. (2011). *Land use performance study for Cannington activity centre*. Unpublished research report. Perth, WA: Curtin University.

Tiwari, R. (2012, June 22). Walk the talk on 'walkability'. Paper presented at the Walkability Forum: Better Air Quality and Liveable Indian Cities, New Delhi.

Tiwari, R. (2014). Designing a safe walkable city. *Urban Design International 20*(1), 12–27.

Tiwari, R., & Rapur, S. (Forthcoming). Walkable streets for the people, by the people. *Journal of Planning Theory and Practice.*

US Department of Transportation Federal Transit Administration. (2007, October). *Central Subway: Third Street Light Rail Phase 2.* Retrieved from www.transit.dot.gov/funding/grant-programs/capital-investments/third-street-light-rail-phase-2-central-subway-capital

Source: Adapted from Transitioning activity corridors: Place making and traffic management, by R. Tiwari, 2008, Working Paper for Department of Planning and Infrastructure, Western Australia. (Unpublished report).

PART IV

The Future

How does the concept of connecting places, connecting people meet the dual challenges of the swing in the global economy, opportunity, and wealth towards the Global South[1] and the mega-trends of shifting demographic and technological changes? As the twenty-first century continues to unfold, the challenges of place making and improving connectivity increase in scope and complexity.

A significant proportion of future population growth is projected to occur in the cities of the Global South—cities where the numbers of residents are growing more rapidly than in advanced economies, and which are increasingly motorizing, modernizing, and industrializing. The built, social, political, and cultural environments of rapidly developing cities are quite different from those in advanced economies, and therefore connecting places, connecting people will take on different complexions in different settings.

The other challenge for the connecting places, connecting people framework is an emerging era of hyper-connectedness. The fast pace of technological advances, including social media, app-based forms of mobility, and the emergence of autonomous vehicles, will have a significant impact on mobility and sociability. Furthermore, increased life expectancy and a reduction in the proportion of young people will add new and unexpected demands and aspirations for mobility, housing, and overall well-being.

What will the nature of connected places be in the future?

Note

1 All developing countries are classified in a category called the 'Global South', and all developed nations are classified in a catagory called the 'Global North', based on gross national income per capita. China, Hong Kong, India, Indonesia, Malaysia, the Republic of Korea, Singapore, Thailand, Argentina, Brazil, Mexico, and South Africa are all countries of the Global South that have demonstrated a fast pace and magnitude of growth (Damerow, 2007).

Reference

Damerow, H. (2007). *Global South: International politics*. Retrieved from http://faculty.ucc.edu/egh-damerow/global_south.htm on August 17, 2016.

CHAPTER 7

EMERGING CHALLENGES
Connected Places in the Global South

Is the concept of connecting places, connecting people relevant to the cities of the Global South? By the 'Global South', I mean countries of the developing world, mostly in the Southern Hemisphere. These countries share many common characteristics, including a low human development index and low gross national income per capita compared with developed countries, termed the 'Global North'.[1]

Most future global population growth is projected to occur in developing cities, where the number of residents is growing more rapidly than in advanced economies, alongside more rapid motorization, modernization, and industrialization. With some 70 million new residents added to these cities each year, the challenges of creating livable, sustainable communities while providing basic but critically important services such as shelter, education, and affordable transport are immense. Given that poverty-linked problems are most pronounced in parts of the world where there is vast urban growth—that is, the Global South—special attention must be given to the social, environmental, and physical challenges of connecting places in these very different environments.

Most of the cities of the Global South are characterized by high densities and organically evolved land use mixes. Compared to developed cities, this tends to produce short trip distances and a high proportion of walking, cycling, and informal carriers. Public transport is also prevalent in these cities. Often lacking, however, are rationally designed and well-connected road networks, safe walking and cycling corridors, civic gathering places, and safe zones for kids.

According to the World Health Organization's global status report on road safety (WHO, 2009), more than 1.2 million people die in road accidents each year. An alarming 90 percent of these fatalities occur in the low- and middle-income countries of the Global South, while 75 percent of the deaths involve pedestrians, cyclists, and other vulnerable road users (WHO, 2009). This is a consequence of an environment that does not promote walkability and is not adapted for cyclists and other users of non-motorized transport (NMT).

Although there are no basic street amenities for an NMT user in many mega-cities of the Global South, the infrastructure for motor vehicles is doubling every seven years. The result is more accidents and congestion, escalating air pollution, and constraints on economic development. These negative externalities cost about 6–7 percent of GDP per year (Cervero et al., 1998). Giving higher priority to road infrastructure than to public transport exacerbates the situation. Being able to access services and public spaces is a major challenge for most urban residents, who cannot afford to drive or own a personal vehicle. A lack of access is a particular issue for the urban poor, the physically challenged, and women and children (Cohen, 2006).

With the creation of hubs at scattered locations in the populous cities, the problem of locating people near their work or services is yet to be resolved. Rising incomes in the Global South mean more trips with more goods to be transported. When the residents of the Global South reach the income levels of Europe or the US, only one-third of travel will be to or from work, which means the number of trips in the future will be multiplied and associated problems exacerbated. Hence, planning for accessible, interactive places is critically important for the social and economic well-being of these populations.

Despite all these issues in the cities of the Global South, a strong sense of identity is visible in their streets and squares, which have retained their role as social hubs. What, then, are the issues that constrain but also provide opportunities for the cities of the Global South to create viable urban places, as well as safer, greener transport connectivity between them? The following section addresses this core question.

Formal and Informal Peri-urban Developments in the Cities of the Global South

Responding to ever-increasing population numbers, many new cities are being planned in the Global South. Even though the transport characteristics of these cities are different from those of cities in Global North, many are still reliant on conventional auto-centric, Western city planning (Dimitriou, 2010; Feng et al., 2010).

An example of applying Western-style planning in developing countries is the edge city concept emerging in China, India, and the United Arab Emirates. City outskirts brim with gated and boxed mid-rise glass office towers surrounded by gardens and parking lots. Shopping malls, wholesale supermarkets, and high-tech industry hubs have located to city peripheries and add to congestion. A study of the travel impacts of 900 households that shifted from organically evolved, mixed-use areas in Shanghai's urban core to isolated superblocks on the peripheries revealed a 50 percent increase in vehicle kilometers traveled by the households and an alarming shift from non-motorized to motorized travel (UN-Habitat, 2013).

These developments not only relinquish the advantages of traditional place-based, pedestrian-oriented morphology and pattern of the old city cores, but also hinder future economic growth based on knowledge and innovation. Human-to-human interaction increases knowledge, innovation, and economic opportunity. This happens only when cities are more connected and provide the time and places for human interactions.

Although outward city expansion to cope with population growth is unavoidable, is this the only solution? The assumption that the dense inner-city areas cannot support further infill is not necessarily true. In most cases, applying a uniform floor area ratio (FAR) fails to capitalize on premium locations. Cities such as Singapore, Seoul, Tokyo, and Hong Kong have developed living environments with efficient, high-quality services by adopting different density ranges for different areas and taking into consideration the varied socio-economic features (Suzuki et al., 2013). A responsive urban form achieved through articulated densities instead of average density opens up the possibility of vertical expansion in place of peri-urban sprawl.

While some residents choose to live in planned peri-urban developments, others are forced to live in unplanned, informal peri-urban locations. The cities of the Global South are characterized by increasing numbers of people forcibly evicted from city centers, and living in informal settlements on the urban periphery. The urban poor who occupy the city sub-urban rail/road rights of way must be resettled to accommodate major roadworks. Squatters on land in the city core that was previously considered undevelopable have also been forcibly shifted. This has an adverse effect on the urban poor in several ways. First, the relocation decreases the average income of the relocated families by 30–50 percent, which must now be spent on transport. Second, a resettlement 10–15 kilometers away from job locations results in a shift from walking to motorized transport (Suzuki et al., 2013; Tiwari, 2007). Inadequate access to public transport compounds the transport issues. Flexible transportation and a housing model that is well connected to public transport are essential to respond to the woes of the peri-urban slum dwellers.

A good example of connectivity for peri-urban lower-income communities and slum settlements can be found in Cape Town. Here, the objective of the arterial road design was to link the pockets of disadvantaged communities to the city centre (Watson, 2002). Responding to the fractured internal spatial structure after the collapse of Apartheid, the vision for Cape Town was to achieve a higher density and a spatially integrated city. The resulting plan identified arterial roads, with a concentration of middle-class residents, and the roads that connected the city core with the south-east section of Cape Town, where there was an over-representation of disadvantaged people. These were the Tygerberg Arm, the Southern Arm, and the Klipfontein Road (Curtis & Tiwari, 2008; Figure 7.1).

A square grid with nodes and corridors aimed to promote equity, access, and integration (Watson, 2002) by linking the CBD to three centers on the three corners of the square with the three identified arterial arms. The diagonal arm known as the Klipfontein Corridor was begun in 2003 and provided connectivity to the relatively undeveloped land in close proximity to poor residential areas identified as industrial (Figure 7.2).

The corridor design principles integrate people, space, activity, and movement through interrelated spatial layers. In this example,

THE FUTURE

Figure 7.1 The corridor system in Cape Town

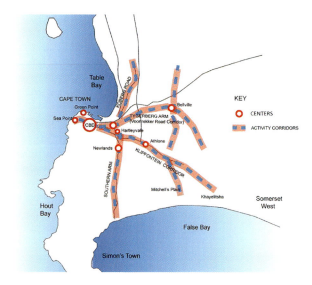

Figure 7.2 The conceptual diagram for the corridor system

Source: Based on Watson, 2002, and adapted from Transitioning activity corridors: Place making and traffic management, by R. Tiwari, 2008, Working Paper for Department of Planning and Infrastructure, Western Australia. (Unpublished report).

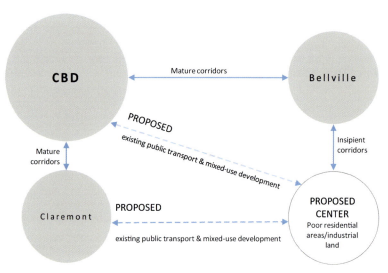

Conceptual Diagram for Nodes & Corridors

the NMT layer provided local area access and integration; a layer of socio-spatial generators encouraged economic activity and investment; and a public transport layer with a new BRT system connected the impoverished township of Khayelitsha and the middle-class suburbs of Rondebosch and Mowbray to the city center. The plan was completed with a strategic land use distribution layer (NM Associates, 2005). The calculation of the width of the corridor was based on a maximum of 10–15 minutes' walking distance (Figure 7.3). A high-density strip of 100 dwelling units per hectare (or more mixed use) was planned adjacent to the activity spine. Further out, densities of 40 dwelling units per hectare or more were allowed up to 1 kilometer on either side of the corridor (Watson, 2002).

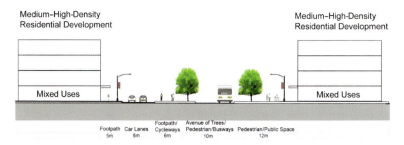

Figure 7.3 *Cross-section of the Klipfontein Corridor*

Source: Based on Klipfontein-Capetown Brochure available on NM & Associates. Adapted from Transitioning activity corridors: Place making and traffic management, by R. Tiwari, 2008. Working Paper for Department of Planning and Infrastructure, Western Australia. (Unpublished report).

Economic, social, and demographic concerns were pivotal for the corridor design, which aimed to maximize proximity and connectivity while improving the quality of transport and providing a safe urban space (Curtis & Tiwari, 2008).

Another consideration for projects providing connectivity is the affordability of the public transport system. A study of the use of transit in Delhi's slums revealed that only 2 percent of the respondents used the metro to go to work occasionally, while 87 percent had never used the metro because of the high fares (Arora & Tiwari, 2007). Providing affordable housing next to unaffordable public transport does not necessarily improve accessibility or promote equity (Chava et al., forthcoming). Through promoting connectivity, the city of Bogotá in Colombia has successfully reduced the cost of both housing and transportation (Cervero, 2011). The Metrovivienda initiative, an innovative land-banking program introduced in 1999, integrated TransMilenio (BRT) with affordable housing projects (Suzuki et al., 2013). TransMilenio operates 200 kilometers of feeder systems in low-income neighborhoods and peripheral areas. After acquisition, open agricultural land in these areas was sold to developers. The government provided the infrastructure on condition that the average unit price was capped at US$8,500. This ensured the availability of affordable housing. A uniform ticket price avoided penalizing the poorer peri-urban communities with higher transport costs (Chava et al., forthcoming).

While connectivity to peri-urban communities through improved public transport and affordable housing strategies is critical, another unique feature of the cities of the Global South is their reliance on informal public transport and two-wheelers to achieve this connectivity.

Role of Informal Collective Transport and Private Two-Wheelers

While car ownership may be on the rise in the cities of the Global South, informal collective modes, sometimes referred to as 'paratransit' or low-cost transport (for example, jitneys and tempos), and private two-wheelers are leading the way in mass motorization (Feng et al., 2010; Johnston, 2004; Khisty & Arslan, 2005; Samberg et al., 2011; Zheng et al., 2011).

Informal transit coexists with formal public transport, such as buses, metro systems, and trams, and survives by filling service gaps.

In Nairobi, Kenya, 33 percent of total public transport trips are provided by *matututs*, consisting of a range of vehicles from minibuses and vans to pickups (Cervero & Golub, 2007). Mini- and micro-buses provide 5–10 percent of trips in India and Thailand, and about half of all trips in the Philippines (Cervero, 2000). Thirty percent of all trips in Mexico City are in 30,000 *collectivos* (minibuses and vans; Sperling & Kurani, 2003). Although tolerated by the authorities, these *collectivos* are uninsured and unsafe, but serve as a popular form of transit for low-income earners and have strong political backing (Cervero, 2000). Informal transport vehicles can respond quickly and cheaply to changing markets and passenger demands. They can also ferry goods in and around neighborhoods. They do, however, contribute significantly to air and noise pollution, traffic congestion, and accidents. There is little incentive to introduce clean and efficient vehicles. Estimates suggest that the *collectivos* in Mexico City consume more gasoline than the entire bus fleet operated by the two major bus companies (PCFV, 2010). A lack of regulations and enforcement leads to competition and conflict for customers among unlicensed operators. In South Africa, rival cartels fight over the most profitable routes, resulting in paratransit-related violence (Cervero & Golub, 2007). Public health and safety are threatened.

The positives and negatives of informal transport pose difficult questions for future planning. In Jamaica, the longstanding regulations for informal transport have merely served to increase illicit operations. What is needed is monitoring and enforcement. Each city and circumstance needs careful assessment. A balanced response would lie somewhere between the extremes of acceptance and outright banning of informal transport (Cervero & Golub, 2007). In Rio de Janeiro, Brazil, for example, the circumstances require regulation of informal transport, and investment in and concessions for formal modes of transport.

There is fierce competition between collective informal transit and individual two-wheelers in many cities of the Global South. Currently, 84 percent of all households in Hanoi, Vietnam, own a motorcycle, and 40 percent of households have more than two. The use of the once important *cyclo* (bicycle rickshaw) has declined with the introduction of taxis and the informal *xe om* (motorcycle taxi; Schipper et al., 2008). Similar shifts to two-wheelers have occurred in the cities of China, India, Indonesia, and Thailand. In China, Thailand, and Malaysia, the percentage of two-wheelers exceeds 50 percent of the total motor vehicle fleet (GIZ SUTP, 2010), while in Vietnam the number of two-wheelers is more than six times the country's car population (World Bank, 2011).

Two-wheeler transport is not without risk. Two-wheeler users are more prone to road accidents and deaths than other motorized vehicle users (WHO, 2009), and riders suffer from high levels of air pollution exposure (PCFV, 2010).

In traffic, two- and three-wheelers dominate when measured in terms of vehicle kilometers and emissions. In Hanoi, motor vehicular activity is a major source of emissions, causing both primary and secondary pollution. Ninety percent of the 1.6 million registered private vehicles are motorcycles, making these the major contributor to emissions (Urban Emissions, 2016). In some cities, 40 percent of particulate matter and carbon dioxide, 50 percent of carbon monoxide, and 70 percent (or more) of volatile organic compounds are due to motorcycles (Manufacturers of Emission Controls Association, 2008). In metropolitan Manila, the Philippines, and Colombo, Sri Lanka, significant pollution is caused by unmaintained two-stroke engines (PCFV, 2010).

While many cities rely on tailpipe policies and regulations based on fiscal benefits to increase e-bike purchases and promote clean engines, non-tailpipe solutions are also being adopted. In Hanoi, for example, formal public transport systems incorporate two-wheelers assigned as feeders to the systems (PCFV, 2010). With the establishment of new bus routes, the expansion of vehicle fleets, the introduction of bus shelters, and passenger information systems, bus ridership in Hanoi reached 350 million trips by 2005 (ALMEC Corporation et al., 2007). Transportation in Hanoi now consists of two systems: formal public transport based on a bus fleet on fixed routes, and an area-oriented system based on smaller vehicles. The individual vehicle system consists of informal motorcycle taxis, traditional bicycle rickshaws, and car taxis (Schipper et al., 2008).

While investing in formal public transport might be a solution in some cases, it can only work when citizens accept the new system and change their behavior. It is therefore critical to make the system attractive and easy to use. In the absence of a clear strategy, the business-as-usual scenario results in an undesirable shift of current public transport users to two-wheelers and old cars (Figure 7.4). The challenge is to effect a shift towards public transport, particularly targeting users of motorized two-wheelers and old cars (Agarwal, 2009). The limitations that public transport presents to these users are:

- unacceptable door-to-door time (owing to inadequate public transport and a lack of network integration);
- marginal costs of informal/two-wheeler modes (which are often lower than bus fares); and
- poor social image of public transport.

Apart from affordability and the quality of public transport, serious consideration needs to be given to the amenities for 'feet and

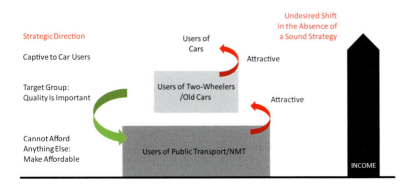

Figure 7.4 Factors affecting mode shift

pedal', as every public transport user is first a pedestrian or an NMT user.

Inadequate Amenities for Pedestrians and Cyclists

Heavy reliance on NMT is a distinguishing feature of Global South nations. In Tianjin, China, for example, 80 percent of all commuter trips are by non-motorized modes, mainly bicycles (UN-Habitat, 2013, p. 110). The bicycle is also an important mode of transportation in Vietnam. In Indian cities, cycling and walking account for 50–75 percent of community trips in the informal sector, while the remainder are dependent on public transport (Tiwari, 2007). Providing adequate facilities for this significant user group is often neglected, making them feel vulnerable and isolated.

Owing to inadequate amenities for the NMT-dependent majority of the Global South, safe travel cannot be assumed. Interviews conducted by Clean Air Asia in 15 cities in nine Asian countries (India, China, Pakistan, Sri Lanka, Indonesia, Vietnam, Mongolia, Nepal, and the Philippines) revealed that 81 percent of respondents would prefer motorized transport to walking, since the walking environments were considered unsuitable (Gota et al., 2010). Better planning and use of a scale more sympathetic to the needs of pedestrians and cyclists would address this issue.

The fundamentals of walkability—high density and mixed use—identified as the key ingredients of TOD for cities in developed countries are already present in the cities of the Global South. But this does not mean that it is easy to walk in these cities. Barriers to walkability include:

- absent or discontinuous pedestrian pathways;
- narrow, uneven, or unmaintained pathways;
- constant obstacles on pathways, such as encroachments by vendors/shops, trees, and temples; and
- a lack of shade, concerns about personal safety, and erratic motorists' behavior.

Even where there are good footpaths with designated pedestrian- and cycle-ways, thoughtless motorists often use these spaces to escape traffic congestion (Figures 7.5a and 7.5b). It is common to see two-wheelers take to the footpaths and cycle paths in Indian cities. Cars and two-wheelers also use footpaths as parking spaces. The weaker NMT user can be pushed out of the pedestrian space, the footpaths deteriorate, and pedestrians feel unsafe.

In some cities, footpaths can support many street activities, including vending, extension of shop frontages, and display places. They may be thronged by kiosks selling food, beverages, clothes, shoes, accessories, and so on (Figure 7.5c). The customers attracted by these activities restrict the space for pedestrians, forcing them to take to the roads. Unplanned built interventions, such as small temples and unadorned shrines, sprout up under shady

Figure 7.5 *Appropriation of pedestrians' and cyclists' space*
Source: Pictures by R. Tiwari (2012).

trees, along country roads, at bus terminals, and along footpaths on countless streets in Indian cities (Figure 7.5d). These should not be treated as encroachments that need to be removed. In fact, for residents going to work, they are places for everyday rituals. They do, however, disrupt the flow of pedestrians. Footpaths also serve as homes for the homeless, and as places of work (Figure 7.5e). Another consideration is the accumulation of litter on footpaths. The bad odor and unsightly appearance make walking or cycling very difficult (Figure 7.5f). These issues have a strong sociocultural dimension and they are not simply caused by a lack of a pedestrian-friendly infrastructure.

Some footpath activities do create a vibrant environment and promote interaction between different communities. Place-making strategies can enhance these spaces and encourage people to connect, provided the needs of pedestrians are met. A community-centered approach can raise awareness of the problems faced by pedestrians. An example is the Space Reclamation movement, introduced in a number of Indian cities (Bhatt, 2014).

In 2014, a group named Raahgiri started reclaiming the streets and petitioning the public authorities to plan for accessible public spaces for all sections of society. The idea is similar to Ciclovia, an initiative that began in Bogotá, Colombia, in 1976 and later spread to other countries. Raahgiri is a collaboration between civil society, the media, NGOs, and local government, which aims to create public awareness of sustainable transport, safe streets and inclusive development. Every Sunday, from 7 a.m. to 12 p.m., a section of road is closed to vehicles and opened for people to use. The citizens enjoy recreational and leisure activities, including street dancing, yoga, and live music. The outcomes in the city of Gurgaon, where the movement began, have been overwhelmingly positive.

A survey conducted by Embarq India in Gurgaon found that:

- 350,000 people participated in Raahgiri in its first six months;
- 28 percent of participants bought bicycles post-Raahgiri;
- 87 percent started walking/cycling for short trips;
- there was a 29 percent increase in sales for local businesses;
- noise levels reduced by 18 percent—from 90db to 74 db; and
- exposure particulate matter 2.5 reduced by 49 percent.

(Bhatt, 2014, pp. 32–34, 38–40)

Raahgiri has started contributing indirectly towards equitable access to public places, services, and infrastructure. Local government is now obliged to make infrastructure improvements that are accessible to all, and is planning for sustainable transport infrastructure, such as widening footpaths and cycle tracks instead of widening road carriageways. The movement had spread to at least seven Indian cities within a year, and others have similar plans. People are becoming sensitized to the importance of public spaces and issues of accessibility. This space reclamation movement is gaining acceptability among the citizenry.

There is growing recognition that citizens must be engaged in the planning process to ensure that changes are accepted. This is a major shift for the cities of the Global South, where citizens have not previously been involved in any stage of the project life-cycle, even though the project may influence their lives and livelihoods. However, bringing citizens into the conversation poses significant challenges, especially when there is a history of distrust, inadequate and conflicting knowledge, and lack of agreement over the nature of problems between the authorities themselves (Cox, 1997; Vigar, 2000).

Bogotá: Striving to Become a Connected Place in the Global South

The city of Bogotá is actively working to find the right balance between formal and informal public transport and creating an environment that meets the needs of pedestrians and NMT users. An integrated approach has been used to establish a strong intermodal network, transit-linked social housing, and public places with innovative finance schemes (Cervero et al., 2009; Suzuki et al., 2013). Home to some 8.7 million people in 2014 (Kraul, 2015), half of Bogotá has grown spontaneously and illegally, often on hard-to-access mountain slopes (David & Peñalosa, 2005). Social inclusivity, the primary aim of the approach, has been addressed by connecting the geographies of the dispersed social housing sites and promoting equal opportunity for all citizens. The divide between rich and poor in Bogotá had long been embedded and reflected in the city's fabric, resulting in economic and social isolation in many parts of the city. The TransMilenio system has been successful in reducing this isolation. Within the first year of its operation, there was a 32 percent reduction in average bus travel times, a 93 percent drop in bus accidents, and a 98 percent passenger approval rating. Property values along the busway corridor rose owing to improved access and reductions in crime rates and noise levels. Public buses, previously stuck in traffic, now enjoyed dedicated lanes to avoid the jams (Cervero, 2005).

TransMilenio comprises a trunk- and feeder-route grid network. With a fleet of 1,400 buses, the trunk line operates on dedicated bus lanes covering 112 kilometers. There are 12 lines and 144 dedicated, self-contained stations, some with wi-fi (Global Mass Transit, 2011; World Public Library, 2015). An additional 410 feeder buses transport commuters from important stations to many locations not covered by the trunk line. Feeder buses operate without dedicated lanes and charge no additional fare (World Public Library, 2015). The trunk and feeder buses operate using an integrated intelligent transport system (ITS) for operation optimization, fare integration, and smooth interchanges (Bocarejo, 2012). TransMilenio serves up to 2.2 million people daily (World Public Library, 2015). All of the major work centers in the city are within the catchment area of the network (Tufts University, 2005).

When building TransMilenio, the Mayor of Bogotá, Enrique Peñalosa, incorporated some 350 kilometers of bicycle paths into the system (ITDP, 2004). From 1990 to 2002, US$180 million was invested in bikeways, approximately half the amount spent annually in the US on cycling infrastructure (Hook, 2004). There are huge bicycle facilities at the end of each TransMilenio line to encourage cyclists to use the system (World Public Library, 2015). To promote cycling and walking, 127 kilometers of the city's main streets and roads are closed to automotive traffic every Sunday and on holidays throughout the year. On these days, over a million users take to the streets on their bicycles (Invest in Bogotá, 2015). With 12,000 persons per square kilometer, Bogotá is one of the most densely populated cities in the Western Hemisphere, and the mixed land use patterns make it very attractive for cycling. Three-quarters of daily trips in the city are less than 10 kilometers, and bicycles can often cover journeys through the city's traffic-snarled streets faster than cars (Cervero, 2005).

Using 'green connectors', Bogotá has focused planning on pedestrian and bicycle accessibility. Perpendicular and grade-separated pedways and bikeways connect some of the poorest barrios and informal housing settlements (with highly transit-dependent populations) to the busway. As a result, 45 percent of TransMilenio users travel to stations by foot or bicycle (Cervero, 2006). The TransMilenio busway has encouraged more walking per day, even controlling for socioeconomic factors such as age and car ownership (Cervero et al., 2009).

Place making has been carried out in Bogotá in an interesting manner. The use of symbols and performance art to demonstrate the need for a behavioral shift to achieve safe pedestrian spaces was encouraged by the mayor. The initiative has educated motorists while providing public spaces that stimulate community interaction. Ciclovia (see above) has reactivated public spaces by transforming vacant lots into parks. It has also improved safety, encouraged active living, and created a stronger sense of community. The bike routes traveling through the rich and poor areas of the city have provided connectivity and have attempted to merge the divide between these areas (Project for Public Spaces, 2012).

Bogotá's city-wide model, which is environmentally sustainable, has now been adopted by more than 50 cities worldwide. The success of the model is demonstrated by the fact that public transport is used for 69 percent of all trips within the city (Invest in Bogotá, 2015). However, in spite of its progressive and innovative policies and measures, Bogotá faces significant challenges concerning land use and transport integration, ineffectual density policies and inadequate physical design detailing, institutional inefficiencies, and a lack of coordination.

The increase in building density across the city has been lower for areas closer to the BRT stations than along the surface bus corridors feeding the stations. There was a 7 percent increase in the mean FAR throughout the city between 2004 and 2010 as compared to a 5 percent increase within 1 kilometer of stations along the initial 42-kilometer system (Suzuki et al., 2013). The lack of station area plans encouraging private investment through incentive zoning mechanisms has hampered growth and reduced the ability to capitalize on the added value created by the new transit. The placement of stations at the medians of busy roads has created a poor pedestrian environment, and thus discouraged commercial development around stations.

Bogotá is now developing a new integrated transit project based on the concept of a public transportation integrated system, which will allow the city to work in close collaboration with private developers to sell or lease air rights or underground use rights. The revenue generated could fund a range of social housing, infrastructure provision, and place-making initiatives (Suzuki et al., 2013).

Institutional support is needed to implement these plans, but this can be problematic within the current planning and administrative structure. Bogotá has a decentralized administrative system. Although it is vertically aligned to allow harmonious sectoral planning and development, a weak horizontal relationship across sectors makes it almost impossible to manage both planning and implementation. Barter (2001) argues that the way to overcome this is through dialogue, meetings, workshops, and seminars, which will allow everyone to participate, identify problems, and suggest solutions. A conversation in three dimensions is required: between land use and transit investments, between long-range and short-range planning, and between different levels of government (Suzuki et al., 2013; Walker, 2011). On the other hand, Shanghai and Singapore have demonstrated the benefits of coordinated decision making, centralized control over land use, and housing and transit investment by local municipal government (Cervero et al., 1998).

Close

Cities of the Global South need improved access to jobs and amenities, increased economic and social development, and efficient movement of goods. Informal transport and two-wheelers make a positive contribution to these goals. Social and environmental sustainability is, however, a major concern if enhanced mobility relies primarily on conventional modes of transport. The result will be worsening air pollution and traffic congestion (Sperling & Salon, 2002). Reducing the use of individual vehicles and promoting the use of environmentally sustainable collective modes of transport are key challenges.

Although large populations present a significant challenge, cities benefit from high population density. Other useful benefits that are rarely found in developed cities, such as 'eyes on the street', are present in most cities of the Global South. However, many sociocultural issues greatly hamper the use of the available infrastructure. Community engagement movements that empower citizens by bringing them into the conversation are critical. It is important that the cities of the Global South leverage their innate strengths by retaining their sustainable transport modes (walking and biking) and higher densities when planning for future transport and place connectivity.

Reducing negative externalities, such as air pollution and greenhouse gas emissions, while promoting social equity can occur only if automobile-dependent sprawl is avoided. Large increases in urban population add to already compromised transportation systems. The study by Suzuki et al. (2013) reveals that transit in many of the cities of the Global South has so far focused only on relieving congestion. Such a myopic vision may fail to incorporate strategies that would connect places.

The cities of the Global South need to adopt innovative solutions that should be city specific, as even cities within the same country may require a customized approach. Above all, urban professionals need to recognize that applying solutions designed for developed countries will probably prove unworkable and, in some cases, even counterproductive.

Note

1. Today, the World Bank classifies countries by their economic performance as derived by world development indicators, such as gross national income per capita. This classification puts developing countries in a category called the 'Global South' and developed nations in a category called the 'Global North'. Also, as per the United Nations Development Program (UNDP), the 'Global North' refers to the 57 countries that have a Human Development Index (HDI) above 0.8 in the UNDP's 2005 report (including Australia and New Zealand), while the 'Global South' refers to the rest of the countries of the world, most of which are located in the Southern Hemisphere (Damerow, 2007). The term 'Global South' does

not imply that all developing countries are similar and can be grouped together in one category. It highlights that although developing countries range across the spectrum in every economic, social, and political attribute, they all share a set of vulnerabilities, challenges, and opportunities (UNDP, 2004). Considering the diverse backgrounds and histories of the nations of the Global South, it may be rather misleading to discuss the increased share of world output of these countries. China, Hong Kong, India, Indonesia, Malaysia, the Republic of Korea, Singapore, Thailand, Argentina, Brazil, Mexico, and South Africa have all demonstrated their overwhelming importance, but it should be noted that the pace and magnitude of their growth have not been uniform. The nature of development in these countries has been associated with structural change in output and employment, not with improved living standards for the majority of the population (Nayyar, 1978).

References

All online references retrieved August 17, 2016.

Agarwal, O. P. (2009). *Climate change and transport in India: Initiatives and experience.* Retrieved from www.slideshare.net/EMBARQNetwork/climate-change-and-transport-in-india-initiatives-and-experience-presentation.

ALMEC Corporation, Nippon Koei Co. Ltd., & Yachiyo Engineering Co. Ltd. (2007). *The comprehensive urban development programme in Hanoi, capital city of the Socialist Republic of Vietnam (HAIDEP).* Retrieved from http://open_jicareport.jica.go.jp/pdf/11856093_01.pdf.

Arora, A., & Tiwari, G. (2007). *A handbook for socio-economic impact assessment (SEIA) of future urban transport (FUT) projects.* Retrieved from www.rlarrdc.org.in/images/SEIA%20Handbook%20Delhi%20Metro.pdf.

Barter, P. (2001). *Linkages between transport and housing for the urban poor: Policy implications and alternatives.* Retrieved from www.unhabitat.org/pmss/getElectronicVersion.aspx.

Bhatt, A. (2014). Webinar on impact of Raahgiri Day. New Delhi: EMBARQ India. Retrieved from www.slideshare.net/EMBARQNetwork/raahgiri-day-impact-embarq-india-amit-bhatt-may-2014.

Bocarejo, J. (2012). Integrated public transport system SITP-Bogotá. Retrieved from www.slideshare.net/EMBARQNetwork/tt2012-bogotajuanpablobocarejo.

Cervero, R. (2000). *Informal transport in the developing world.* Nairobi: United Nations Commission on Human Settlements.

Cervero, R. (2005). Progressive transport and the poor: Bogotá's bold steps forward. *ACCESS Magazine 1*(27). Retrieved from www.uctc.net/access/27/Access%2027%20-%2005%20-%20Progressive%20Transport%20and%20the%20Poor.pdf.

Cervero, R. (2006). *Public transport and sustainable urbanism: Global lesson.* Retrieved from http://escholarship.org/uc/item/4fp6x44f.

Cervero, R. (2011). *State roles in providing affordable mass transport services for low-income residents.* Retrieved from www.oecd-ilibrary.org/docserver/download/5kg9mq4f4627.pdf?expires=1474399322&id=id&accname=guest&checksum=0F9F1B8D4D47C19FD470EC2CCDFA397A.

Cervero, R., & Golub, A. (2007). Informal transport: A global perspective. *Transport Policy 14*(6), 445–457. Retrieved from www.sciencedirect.com.dbgw.lis.curtin.edu.au/science/article/pii/S0967070X07000546.

Cervero, R., Sperling, D., & Mason, J. (Eds.). (1998). *Proceedings: Conference on Transportation in Developing Countries.* Retrieved from https://escholarship.org/uc/item/0323x465.

Cervero, R., Sarmiento, O. L., Jacoby, E., Gomez, L. F., & Neiman, A. (2009). Influences of built environments on walking and cycling: Lessons from Bogotá. *International Journal of Sustainable Transportation 3*(4), 203–226.

Chava, J., Newman, P., & Tiwari, R. (Forthcoming). Housing affordability and gentrification and transit-oriented developments. *Journal of Housing Studies.*

Cohen, B. (2006). Urbanization in developing countries: Current trends, future projections, and key challenges for sustainability. *Technology in Society 28*(1), 63–80.

Cox, K. R. (Ed.). (1997). *Spaces of globalization: Reasserting the power of the local*. New York: Guilford.

Curtis, C., & Tiwari, R. (2008). Transitioning activity corridors: Place making and traffic management. Unpublished research report for Department of Planning and Infrastructure, Western Australia.

Damerow, H. (2007). *Global South: International politics*. Retrieved from http://faculty.ucc.edu/egh-damerow/global_south.htm.

David, M., & Peñalosa, E. (2005) Interview: Bogotá: A city transformed. Retrieved from https://enriquepenalosa.wordpress.com/page/2/.

Dimitriou, H. T. (2010). *Urban transport planning*. London: Routledge.

Feng, X., Zhang, J., Fujiwara, A., Hayashi, Y., & Kato, H. (2010). Improved feedback modeling of transport in enlarging urban areas of developing countries. *Frontiers of Computer Science in China 4*(1), 112–122.

GIZ SUTP. (2010). *Challenges of urban transport in developing countries – a summary*. Retrieved from www.sutp.org/files/contents/documents/resources/J_Others/GIZ_SUTP_Challenges-of-urban-transport-in-developing-countries_EN.pdf.

Global Mass Transit (2011). TransMilenio in Bogotá: Case-study of PPP in BRT. Retrieved from www.globalmasstransit.net/archive.php?id=7392.

Gota, S., Fabian, H. G., Mejia, A., & Punte, S. (2010). *Walkability surveys in Asian cities*. Philippines: Clean Air Initiative for Asian Cities Center. Retrieved from www.ictct.org/migrated_2014/ictct_document_nr_663_102A%20Sophie%20Sabine%20Punte%20Walkability%20Surveys%20in%20Asian%20Cities.pdf.

Hook, W. (2004). Automobile dependency and the global cultural war: Lessons from Bogotá. *Sustainable Transport 16*, 1–3.

Invest in Bogotá. (2015, June). Transportation in Bogotá. Retrieved from http://en.investinbogota.org/discover-bogota/art-culture-and-tourism-bogota/transportation-bogota#Byclicles.

ITDP (2004) *Institutional and regulatory reform options for Trans-Jakarta BRT system*. Retrieved from www.itdp.org/wp-content/uploads/2014/07/Institutional_Reform_Options_for_TransJakarta_ITDP.pdf.

Johnston, R. A. (2004). The urban transportation planning process. In S. Hanson & G. Giuliano (Eds.) *The geography of urban transportation* (pp. 115–141). New York: Guildford.

Khisty, C. J., & Arslan, T. (2005). Possibilities of steering the transportation planning process in the face of bounded rationality and unbounded uncertainty. *Transportation Research Part C: Emerging Technologies 13*(2), 77–92.

Kraul, C. (2015, March 19). A dynamic Bogotá attracts foreign buyers and businesses. *New York Times*. Retrieved from www.nytimes.com/2015/03/20/greathomesanddestinations/a-dynamic-bogota-attracts-foreign-buyers-and-businesses.html?_r=0.

Manufacturers of Emission Controls Association. (2008). *White paper on emissions control of two and three wheeled vehicles*. Retrieved from www.meca.org/galleries/files/Motorcycle_whitepaper_final_081908.pdf.

Nayyar, D. (1978). Transnational corporations and manufactured exports from poor countries. *Economic Journal 88*(349), 59–84. Retrieved from www.jstor.org/stable/2232014?seq=1#page_scan_tab_contents.

NM Associates (2005). Klipfontein Corridor: Conceptual urban planning and design. Retrieved from www.nmassociates.co.za/projects/selected/klipfontein-corridor-conceptual-urban-planning-and-design.

Partnership for Clean Fuels and Vehicles (PCFV). (2010). *Managing two and three wheelers in Asia*. Nairobi: United Nations Environment Programme and CAI-Asia.

Project for Public Spaces. (2012). Place making and the future of cities. Report for UN-Habitat Sustainable Urban Development Network. Retrieved from www.pps.org/wp-content/uploads/2012/09/PPS-Placemaking-and-the-Future-of-Cities.pdf.

Samberg, S., Bassok, A., & Holman, S. (2011). Method for evaluation of sustainable transportation: Toward a comprehensive approach.

Transportation Research Record: Journal of the Transportation Research Board 2242, 1–8.

Schipper, L., Maria, C., Robyn, L., Le Anh Tuan, O. H., & Weishiuen, N. G. (2008). Measuring the invisible: Quantifying emissions reductions from transport solutions—Ha Noi Case Study. Retrieved from http://pdf.wri.org/measuringtheinvisible_hanoi-508c_eng.pdf.

Sperling, D., & Kurani, K. S. (2003). *Transportation, energy, and environmental policy: Managing transitions*. Washington, D.C.: Transportation Research Board.

Sperling, D., & Salon, D. (2002). Transportation in developing countries: An overview of greenhouse gas reduction strategies. Retrieved from http://escholarship.org/uc/item/0cg1r4nq.

Suarez, J. (2014). New infrastructure approaches to BRT. Retrieved from http://volvobusenvironmentblog.com/2014/05/15/new-infrastructure-approaches-to-brt/.

Suzuki, H., Cervero, R., & Iuchi, K. (2013). *Transforming cities with transit: Transit and land-use integration for sustainable urban development*. Washington, D.C.: World Bank.

Tiwari, G. (2007). Urban transportation planning. Paper presented at seminar in IIT, New Delhi. Retrieved from http://tripp.iitd.ernet.in/publications/paper/planning/579%20Geetam%20Tiwari,%20Urban%20transportation%20planning.htm.

Tufts University. (2005). Bus rapid transit: Equity & efficiency. Retrieved from http://sites.tufts.edu/sustainablebrt/social-equity/.

UN-Habitat. (2008). *State of the world's cities 2008/2009—Harmonious Cities*. Nairobi: United Nations Human Settlements Program.

UN-Habitat. (2013). Equitable access to urban mobility. Retrieved from http://unhabitat.org/wp-content/uploads/2013/06/GRHS.2013.06.pdf.

United Nations Development Program (UNDP). (2004). *Forging a Global South*. Retrieved from www.ctchealth.org.cn/file/2012060807.pdf.

Urban Emissions. (2016). An air quality management plan for Hanoi. Retrieved from http://urbanemissions.info/model-tools/sim-air/hanoi-vietnam.html.

Vigar, G. (2000). Local 'barriers' to environmentally sustainable transport planning. *Local Environment 5*(1), 19–32.

Walker, J. (2011). *Human transit*. Washington, D.C.: Island Press.

Watson, V. (2002). *Change and continuity in spatial planning: Metropolitan planning in Cape Town under political transition*. London: Routledge.

World Bank. (2011). *World development indicators 2011*. Washington, D.C.: World Bank.

World Health Organization (WHO). (2009). *Global status report on road safety: Time for action*. Retrieved from http://apps.who.int/iris/bitstream/10665/44122/1/9789241563840_eng.pdf.

World Public Library. (2015). TransMilenio. Retrieved from www.worldlibrary.org/articles/transmilenio.

Zheng, J., Atkinson-Palombo, C., McCahill, C., O'Hara, R., & Garrick, N. (2011). Quantifying the economic domain of transportation sustainability. *Transportation Research Record: Journal of the Transportation Research Board 2242*, 19–28.

CHAPTER 8

EMERGING CHALLENGES
Technology Mega-trends and Demographic Shifts

In this chapter, I ask whether contemporary technological advances can enhance the concept of connecting places, connecting people. Technological innovations such as app-based mobility, driverless cars, collaborative mobility models, and the shifting of activities in cyberspace have facilitated the creation of a 'hypermobile' society (Sager, 2014, p. 52). As we reach for a future where 'distance is dead and there is no longer any general organizational principle governing the distribution of people and activities' (Couclelis, quoted in Sager, 2014, p. 36), what will be the 'glue' that holds society together?

Modern societies are undergoing major shifts in age and household composition. As the global population is aging, young people are drifting towards urban centers and there is a decline in the number of family households (Rérat, 2012). Can the demographic shifts and technological innovations be harnessed to generate economic and environmental benefits? Can we build better communities by connecting places and people in light of the mega-trends that are changing how urbanites live, communicate, travel, consume, and interact?

Mega-trend 1: Collaborative Consumption

Collaborative consumption,[1] made possible by connectivity between consumers, is on the rise (Hajkowicz et al., 2012). Examples such as AirBnB (a peer-to-peer rental network), GoGet (Australia's largest car-sharing company in 2016), and Vélib (Paris' most popular bike-sharing scheme;[2] Citiesnext, 2013) abound. Shared transportation among multiple users is growing in popularity in various cities. What is the impact of these trends?

The growth of car sharing in Australia, especially in Melbourne and Sydney, where 90 percent of the users and vehicles are based (International Car Sharing Association, 2016), has shifted transport strategies from car ownership to car rental to car sharing. The speed of this trend has seen a doubling of GoGet members every year since its launch in 2003 (Frost & Sullivan, 2012). In 2015, GoGet had 1,500 vehicles Australia-wide, estimated to remove 100,000 cars from the road (University of Wollongong, 2016). The City of Sydney (2014) and other Australian municipalities have reported reductions in car ownership and street congestion. This shift from personal to shared cars is facilitated by a concurrence of factors, including smartphones with access to car-sharing apps, limited and costly parking in Sydney and Melbourne, and the convenience of retaining access to car transport while not using a personal vehicle.

The number of members in car-sharing schemes has also increased in the Americas (Brazil, Canada, Mexico, and the Unitied States)—from 62,348 in 2002 to 1.5 million in January 2015 (Shaheen & Cohen, 2015, p. 2). A study conducted by automotive consulting house AlixPartners suggests that car sharing is a growing threat to car sales. It forecasts that car sharing will replace 1.2 million new vehicles in the US by 2021. Moreover, a single car-sharing fleet vehicle will displace 32 vehicles that otherwise would have been purchased (LeBeau, 2014), leading to less congested roads.

Yet another benefit of car sharing would be reduced parking requirements, as shared vehicles tend to present much fewer parking demands than owned vehicles, as they are on the move for most of the day. Earnings for driver-led services such as Uber depend on the number of rides, to maximize which the cars tend to be in motion all day, and hence demand less parking in comparison to commuters' cars that are parked in the lot (Fulton, 2015).

In acknowledging and responding to shared mobility, the automotive industry is promoting the option of electric vehicles (EV). The Car2go program, launched by Mercedes-Benz, allows users to share the Smart Fortwo EV (LeBeau, 2014). The Bollore Group, based in France, has plans to send 3,000 EVs to London for sharing, with a tentative investment of £100 million. Such heavy backing of funds and brands demonstrates confidence in the prediction that competition will become more intense as more drivers start to opt for sharing rather than owning (Prakash & Kar-gupta, 2014).

This trend towards car sharing is replicated in other transport modes, such as bike sharing, which has grown exponentially in the last decade. The number of cities globally with bike-sharing schemes increased from just four in 2001 to 1,000 in 2016 (DeMaio, 2016; Richter, 2015). Cities such as Amsterdam would be significantly worse off without bicycles. Cycling constitutes 32 percent of all journeys in Amsterdam and 48 percent in the city centre (Cathcart-Keays, 2016; iamsterdam, 2016). Currently, the city boasts 800,000 bikes (both shared and owned) and more than 250,000 public bike-parking spots (iamsterdam, 2016). With an increasing commitment to cycling, the city will invest in 40,000 new bike-parking spaces by 2030. A subaquatic 7,000-bike parking garage is planned under the artificial waterfront, near the Central Station. Another two new islands, each with a capacity for 2,000 bikes, will be constructed by 2030 (Payne, 2015). The imperative for the city is not the scale of the undertaking, but the recognition that space in Amsterdam is at a premium. It may be an exceptional case; however, it does present a promising scenario of the benefits of investment in cycling infrastructure to be considered by other cities where bike-sharing schemes are already growing in popularity and usage (Cripps, 2013).

According to data compiled by Russell Meddin, the global bike-share fleet comprises almost a million bicycles (Richter, 2015). Innovative technological advancements in smart cards and tracking of cycle fleets have made it increasingly feasible for more cities to adopt bike sharing. Information communications technology (ICT) has enabled efficient management of fleets and reduced theft. If bike sharing, with its exposure to the elements, is to compete with climate-controlled cars, it must become more convenient and accessible. Innovation is essential to make the bike-sharing industry a strong mobility contender. Companies such as JCDecaux, operator of Paris' Vélib, are leading the way. It is testing a pedelec (pedal electric) system and automatic gear-change mechanism in Vélib bikes to increase comfort and convenience and attract new users (DeMaio, 2016).

The increase in bike sharing has made a substantial contribution towards making cities more connected. Operating at a human scale (Aldred, 2014), bikes open up opportunities for city managers to encourage interactive places and place making.

Mega-trend 2: Changing Vehicle Technology

As we have seen, the advent of collaborative consumption is reshaping the automotive industry and mobility practices (Hajkowicz et al., 2012). The future will also include autonomous or driverless cars (Corwin et al., 2015). Self-driving vehicles have been widely anticipated and their commercial introduction is becoming a reality (Barr & Ramsey, 2015). Google's driverless cars have already driven more than a million miles in autonomous mode. Ford, BMW, Daimler, and Cadillac are developing plans for vehicles quite distinct from those of the present (Corwin et al., 2015). Toyota expects to introduce its first self-driving car by 2020 (Caddy, 2015). As he stated at the 2015 Frankfurt Auto Show, US Secretary of Transportation Anthony Fox expects self-driving cars to be in use all over the world by 2025 (Hauser, 2015).

Yet another innovation in vehicle technology has been in the area of vehicle-to-vehicle (V2V) and vehicle-to-infrastructure (V2I) communications that can potentially avoid road hazards and accidents (Corwin et al., 2015). A V2V communication warns the driver of an impending collision, provides traffic in view, suggests rerouting, and so on. Data like the car's position, speed, steering-wheel position, and brake status are broadcast to other vehicles within a few hundred meters in order to make them aware of what is unfolding around them (Knight, 2015). BMW's app, called Real Time Traffic Information, uses the same technology to provide precise information on the traffic situation. Movement profiles downloaded from the network, GPS data available from vehicle fleets, smartphone apps, and police reports alert users to a threat and suggest potential alternative routes (BMW Insights, 2013). According to Forbes, automatic emergency braking (AEB) is another safety feature that about ten of the top automakers, representing 57 percent of global vehicle sales in 2014, are developing (Yvkoff, 2015). The Insurance Institute for Highway Safety's dedicated Vehicle Research Center will be incorporating the AEB feature across its vehicle lineup (Yvkoff, 2015). The same institute revealed the technology has been shown to reduce insurance injury claims by as much as 35 percent (Insurance Institute for Highway Safety, 2015).

According to the US Department of Transportation (Sheehan, 2015), which is conducting research on V2I communications, this technology can enable application designs for the avoidance and alleviation of vehicle crashes, particularly for those that are not addressed by V2V communications alone. The technology communicates with vehicles through infrastructure such as traffic signals, dedicated installations, and state vehicles, to convey information to drivers and pedestrians about crosswalk warnings, stop sign gaps, curver speed warnings, and so on. Impacts projected by the Federal Highway Administration include a 20 percent reduction in vehicle emissions, a 50 percent decrease in pedestrian conflicts, and a significant reduction in collisions, injuries, and fatalities at intersections (Arnold & Walker, 2014).

Mega-trend 3: Increased Use of Virtual Spaces

A third global mega-trend is increased use of virtual spaces (Hajkowicz et al., 2012). The use of ICT has altered lifestyles in many ways. An example is e-commerce, which is growing globally at close to 20 percent annually as consumers no longer rely on stores as their sole means of access to products (Stephens, 2014). E-commerce is providing convenience, variety, and personalized shopping experiences that are changing the retail stores' business models (Securepay, 2014). Global online retail sales are projected to reach US $4.3 trillion by 2025, an increase from just US $0.55 trillion in 2011 (Frost & Sullivan, 2014). In the US, the increased trend in e-commerce slowed retail foot traffic from 35 billion visits in 2009 to 17 billion in 2013 (PWC, 2015). The increase in 'clicks' (online modes) has meant a reduced footprint of 'bricks' (offline or physical infrastructure), and an evolution of 'concept' (appealing to specific lifestyles) and 'express' (fast and convenient fill-in and stock-up shopping) stores (Frost & Sullivan, 2014, p. 15). Companies like IKEA that rely on big showrooms (the largest being 59,000 square meters) are planning to launch small urban stores and pick-up points (Mitchell, 2015). Big-box retailers like Best Buy and Staples in the US are moving to smaller spaces to better serve the digitally savvy consumer (Pomerantz, 2014). The average retail store size by 2020 is expected to be reduced by 15–20 percent from the 2013 figures (Singh & Saini, 2013, p. 8).

The growth in internet commerce has been accompanied by a growth in background logistic operations and supporting industries (Productivity Commission, 2011).[3] Online transactions combined with the triggered background operations further enable domestic and international freelancing models and offshoring to grow rapidly. A report from Deloitte describes the emergence of a fluid ecosystem with rapid blurring and dissolving of fundamental boundaries that have historically determined the relationships, interactions, and potential of most businesses (Corwin et al., 2015).

Increased teleworking—where people can work from 'third spaces', including the home, parks, cafés, libraries, or other public spaces—is enabling a life of zero commuting. There is increased interest in these spaces as well as investment from knowledge workers and the office property sector (REGUS, 2011). Such spaces challenge the notion of the traditional office and the associated commute. Hence, the designs of both working spaces and transportation services have been affected (Hajkowicz et al., 2012).

Online retail and teleworking together still represent a relatively minor share of turnover and labour markets. However, the heft of activities taking place in the virtual space is fast paced and so impacts the real world. Cyberspace has accommodated social and recreational activities to an enormous extent. An example is the recent Pokémon Go game, which took over the world soon after its launch in July 2016. The cellphone-based game had about 25 million active players in the US within a week of its launch, setting a new record in the world of smartphone games (Allan, 2016). It creates 'augmented reality' through GPS and cameras, overlaying physical space with digital images (Keogh, 2016). The original 1996 franchise concept of a nomadic hunt for virtual creatures has been retained. Players interact with virtual elements of the game, like Poké-stops and -gyms, while navigating real, physical spaces. The virtual creatures are hidden around landmarks and other well-known public spaces. Hence, the game compels users to walk and reactivates the public spaces and landmarks, popular or unpopular. The key point to be noted is that Pokémon Go has forced people into the public realm and especially to rarely visited areas, such as memorials and local parks (Buffa, 2016). Survey findings note that the game captures a diverse demography (MFour, 2016; Zhao, 2016) by attracting people of different ages, genders, races, and incomes to explore the local environment.

The gaming interactions are redefining activities in the forgotten public realm and make a case for capturing the potential of urban spaces through augmented experience. Dan LaTorre, of the Project for Public Spaces, acknowledges the interweaving of technology and public realm. According to him, 'Gamifying gives people a feeling of new permissions to explore the city' (Project for Public Spaces, 2016).

The appropriation of cyberspace for the everyday activities of shopping, working, recreating, and socializing has led to the development of new relationships and institutions. Increased digital connectivity then has the potential to change (positively or negatively) societal behaviors, labor markets, retail models, city design, and transportation systems (Hajkowicz et al., 2012).

How Do Some of the Technological Mega-trends Align with the Predicted Change in Global Demographic Patterns?

An examination of demographic trends clearly demonstrates an increase in life expectancy and a proportional reduction in the young population (European Environmental Agency, 2011). According to the United Nations (2015), between 2015 and 2050, the proportion of persons aged 80 years or over is projected to rise from 1.7 percent to 4.5 percent. The percentage aged 60 years or over will increase from 12.3 percent in 2015 to 21.5 percent in 2050.

The growth in the aged population presents the vast societal challenge of ensuring that infrastructures can support and enable them to live healthy, independent, and productive lives (Czaja & Sharit, 2009). As technology is being used commonly, and is likely to become more important over the next few decades (Horgas & Abowd, 2004), it becomes critical to determine its potential to cater for the lives of the aging population. Technology has the capacity to improve the quality of life of senior and older adults, but they tend to be reluctant users of technology (Charness & Boot, 2009).

Research by the RAND Corporation (2004) suggests that pension plans and reforms to social security may allow later retirement for older workers, and they would benefit from the existing growth in alternative work arrangements, like distance working, working from home, and flexible work hours. Safety, security, and technological devices to assist cognition may be able to delay or avoid the relocation of seniors from their homes as they age (Horgas & Abowd, 2004). Communication technologies can support connection and frequent interaction with their distant relatives and friends.

The challenge will be in adapting to rapid technological changes. These will require education and training. Home retrofitting to accommodate technological improvements will be required for homecare provision, which further raises concerns around affordability, need-responsiveness, suitability, and availability for all (Maddox, 2001).

Automatic driving would provide greater mobility to older people and those with disabilities. These social groups would appreciate automatic driving because of greater comfort and door-to-door service (Alessandrini et al., 2015).

While the number of aged people is on the rise, there has been another demographic shift of young people moving to city centers to pursue studies, and for jobs and apprenticeships (Hillman, 2007). Markus Moos (2015) suggests that our cities are experiencing not only gentrification but 'youthification'. Driven towards the city by ambition and curiosity, young people tend towards smaller families and shared households. In fact, there has been a growing demographic shift to solo living in the city over the past few decades. In Australia, one-person households have increased from 8 percent in 1946 to 24 percent in 2011 (Vasus & Qu, 2015). Renting studio apartments and refurbished lofts in the US is increasingly favored by a younger age group (Florida, 2016). This trend is most evident in cities and areas with populations with a range and depth of knowledge and well-developed technical economies, such as Boston, Seattle, and Silicon Valley. The surge in the number of residential rents in these cities has been even greater than in superstar cities such as New York and Los Angeles. Florida (2016) terms this 'the Great Reset' of housing from owning to flexible renting, which is taking place in dense urban areas in sync with the knowledge economy.

The expanding influence of electronic communication and social media and the rise in the number of daily activities occurring in cyberspace—including those related to work, shopping, and leisure—make possible new lifestyles and habits for all, but particularly for the young (OPTIMISM, 2013). A survey of 15 countries found that while many young people were internet users, fewer than average had driving licenses. Another survey highlighted that young interviewees felt that the world accessible to them by car could now be accessed through social media (*Economist*, 2012). There was a rise in the share of young households without cars from 20 to 28 percent between 1998 and 2008 in Germany, where cars were increasingly considered as appliances rather than aspirational products (Sessa et al., 2013).

These transformations rely on sophisticated technology embedded in integrated (mostly) smartphone-based urban solutions. As a new breed of city dwellers emerges, the dissolution of traditional boundaries will cause a reassessment of daily practices, ranging from the need to travel to the nature of space required at home.

How Do Digitally Enabled Places of the Future Measure Up against the Connecting Places, Connecting People Attributes Outlined in Chapter 6?

Frost & Sullivan's conclusion is that the cities of the future will have multiple downtowns and TODs (Frost & Sullivan, & Hitachi Ltd, 2014, p. 6). New York, where around 70 percent of the population lives within half a mile of mass transit and 80 percent of the unit housing capacity created since 2000 is transit accessible, sets a pattern for future cities. Developing infrastructure around transit will retain the role of connecting places while being responsive to the shifting paradigm.

The capacity to work from anywhere generates new networks and mobility patterns. If not content with a conventionally fitted workplace, the urban inhabitant could rent an electric car to move to a space offering a productive environment. This productive environment would be a socially and culturally vibrant place with appropriate equipment suited to the new patterns of living and mobility. Possible negative consequences of such a scenario include atypical power consumption, congestion, and an increase in unproductive parking spaces. Breakthrough technology in electricity generation and storage, vehicle and fuel technology, and collaborative consumption models, along with open data[4] and big data,[5] would provide ways of alleviating such negative effects, and new opportunities for sustainable and resilient planning, urban design, and development (Connected Cities, 2015).

Box 8.1 outlines key characteristics of future places, such as the new cities of Masdar in Abu Dhabi and Songdo in South Korea. Masdar was originally planned as a zero-carbon city for 45,000 to 50,000 residents, 1,500 businesses, and 60,000 commuters. Currently, it houses 300 students and employs around 2,000 people (Lau, 2012, p. 77). With the downgrading of Masdar's sustainability goals, it is now branded as 'carbon-neutral' rather than 'zero-carbon' (Bsat, 2010, p. 243). Songdo is being built from scratch on 1,500 acres

THE FUTURE

of reclaimed land on the Yellow Sea coast. With a current population of 22,000, the plan is to have around 65,000 residents and 300,000 daily commuters by 2017 (Frommer, 2012). The city is trying to implement policies at a city level that previously have been tested only at the neighborhood scale. Both of these cities have been dogged by controversy and are not presented here as best-practice models for connecting places, connecting people. They do, however, demonstrate strong innovative strategies that align with key attributes of the paradigm, as summarized in Box 8.1.

Box 8.1 Attributes of Connecting Places, Connecting People Corresponding with Those of Digitally Enabled Future Places

First Attribute of Connecting Places, Connecting People: City and Neighborhood Structure

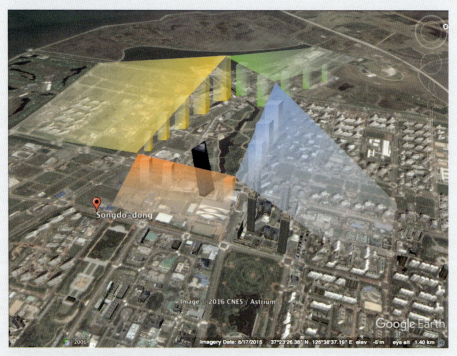

Figure 8.1 A graduated density gradient proposed at Songdo
Source: Image adapted from Google Map by Google, 2016.

Attributes of Digitally Enabled Future Places

Driverless cars require a gridded structure. Arterials will need to house EV-supportive infrastructure. With more retail going online (5 percent of retail sales online in 2011 to 19 percent online in 2025; Frost & Sullivan & Hitachi Ltd, 2014), buildings will be reduced in size. Small block sizes that cater for pop-up commercial/business and concept stores will be in demand.

Examples from Songdo

Songdo's small-sized pedestrian grid of 66×32 meters is aimed towards encouraging active mobility and 15-minute destination accessibility. A graduated density strategy has been proposed, aided by diversity of block sizes with mixed-use neighborhoods surrounding a central hub (Lee, 2012; Whitman et al., 2008; Figure 8.1).

The city and neighborhood structure provides a flexible blueprint for accommodating smart infrastructure in the future. A parallel information technology network linking all services and all residential, business, and government systems with shared data (Halegoua, 2012) has been proposed.

Second Attribute of Connecting Places, Connecting People: Diversity

Attributes of Digitally Enabled Future Places

Most recreation/entertainment/work will be pushed into the digital world on movable/transparent screens requiring zero to minimal space. This will reduce the space requirements within the house and allow more area to be devoted to communal spaces outside individual shelter units. Communal uses—cafés, football fields, community interaction spaces, hospitals, and local stores—will be accommodated within walking distance, ensuring diversity of land use.

Examples from Songdo

Communal spaces have been provided in Songdo by accommodating parking underground. The total green and public spaces constitute about 40 percent of the total area (Lee, 2012). A city-scale public park covering 100 acres is located within the city center and serves as an outdoor community center, hosting flea markets and art exhibits in dedicated exhibition spaces (Kunwon, 2008; Lee, 2012). Smaller pocket parks are scattered throughout the commercial, business, and residential sections.

Hospital units from multinational groups are proposed to be included in the near future and a university district anticipates satellite campuses of US- and Seoul-based universities (Lee, 2012).

Demographic diversity has yet to be achieved (Lichá, 2015).

Third Attribute of Connecting Places, Connecting People: Walkability and Cyclability

Attributes of Digitally Enabled Future Places

With more activities shifting online and freight shifting underground, the environment for active transport will be excellent and will connect people to the places they live in with attendant health benefits.

More people walking and cycling on the streets will result in safer streets. Pop-up infrastructure that is responsive to users (benches, lighting, information screens, bins, kiosks) will make the environment user friendly. User-interactive sensory devices will guide everyday life.

Examples from Songdo and Masdar

With parking shifting underground, Songdo has more space for public greens.

The land uses are well connected through sidewalks and bicycle lanes, ensuring accessibility. The city has defined sidewalks and 25 kilometers of segregated bike lanes supported by bike racks and free bike-rental stations. Active mobility has been encouraged in Songdo (Lee, 2012).

THE FUTURE

However, on the ground, things are rather different. The citizens have reported that distances are too large for them to walk around the city. It has to be kept in mind that Songdo is a work in progress and, with time and an increase in population services, might be available to people at walkable distances (Lichá, 2015).

Masdar's master plan provides green, shaded spaces for residents, workers, and visitors that include walking, jogging, and cycle trails, recreational and other pedestrian amenities. The linear parks connect recreation areas located throughout the city, and their orientation facilitates the movement of cool breezes (Walsh, 2011).

Fourth Attribute of Connecting Places, Connecting People: Place Making (Quality of Architecture and Urban Design)

Attributes of Digitally Enabled Future Places

The experience of the living environment will be mediated through augmented locative media applications (Bilandzic & Foth, 2012), augmented reality (Nischelwitzer et al., 2007), and wearable computing and ambient displays (Veerasawmy & Ludvigsen, 2010). The opportunities for enhancing a global sense of place through technology will be immense (Bilandzic, 2013).

SMART buildings with zero-carbon footprints will create a green environment. 3D and 4D printing will allow users to be architects of their living environments. This will increase a sense of attachment to the living environment and enhance the local sense of place.

Examples from Masdar and Songdo

Masdar has a number of projects that minutely specify everything from the type of electricity meters to the façades, with a view to optimizing and focusing on efficiency (Lau, 2012; Masdar City, 2011). Being built on high ground, tall wind towers and narrow streets signify pre-modern Arabian architecture (Lau, 2012). The buildings have to adhere strictly to efficiency regulations concerning cooling, lighting, water consumption, and even landscaping (Masdar City, 2011). The regulations direct users with the use of sensors, materials, and design to reduce energy consumption and wastage (Lau, 2012). The residential buildings at the Masdar Institute portray traditional alignment with their wavy façades, which shield the interior from direct sunlight and prevent inhabitants from seeing into the windows of buildings across the street.

Lau (2012) notes that Masdar uses the financial potential of new technologies to combat social concerns. The Abu Dhabi government intends to encourage scientific research in renewable energy through Masdar entrepreneurship and shift from an oil-based economy (Lau, 2012).

Songdo aims to incorporate technology in the built form. Besides a SMART built form, the city is trying to emphasize a link with the natural landscape. A canal system highlights the water theme, which is utilized by the waterfront shopping districts, green, and recreational spaces (Lee, 2012).

Songdo has unfortunately not responded to the regional geographic or cultural context (Lee, 2012). The landscape lacks the vibrant streets bustling with activities that are typical of Korean culture. Instead, the city announces itself as a global blend of cities, with its building blocks replicating icons from around the world (Hou, 2012).

Fifth Attribute of Connecting Places, Connecting People: Transport

Attributes of Digitally Enabled Future Places

Transport modes will include EVs, driverless cars, pods, and high-speed rail. Walking and cycling should be adequate for access to local needs.

Freight will increase in response to increased online retailing. Measures for improving the last-mile logistics will be critical. Cross-company collaboration will be essential to improve vehicle utilization and avoid empty trips. Online traffic-routing systems reliant on modular, environmentally friendly vehicles and delivery-on-demand systems that enable coordination with recipients will aid in time optimization, while also contributing positively to the environment. Measures at the macro scale will involve co-modality and alternative delivery modes (metro utilization for freight transport) and high-speed strategic transport corridors (Merten, 2015). Freight could be shifted to underground fast-movement corridors, leaving on-ground corridors for people movement.

Examples from Masdar and Songdo

In Masdar, the initial design banned automobiles and provided mass transit through personal rapid transit (PRT) systems. Under the revised design, PRT was dropped (Walsh, 2011) and the use of electric and other clean-energy vehicles for mass transit inside the city was recommended. A majority of private vehicles will be restricted to parking lots along the city's perimeter. Abu Dhabi's existing light rail and metro lines will connect Masdar's center with the greater metropolitan area (Aktan, 2012; PRT Consulting, 2010).

In Songdo, alternative modes of transportation, bike rentals, and water taxis have been restricted to the central park area. The express bus terminal has been built but has never been used. In summary, insufficient public transport and the slow development of infrastructure services have resulted in spatial stratification (Lichá, 2015).

One important lesson from the Masdar and Songdo case studies is that whatever the nature of the future place might be, it will be successful as long as it emerges from the ground up. For Masdar, place making has not emerged from community values and preferences (Jensen, 2016). Further, Masdar's sustainability standards do not correspond to the values held by the regional and local community. A waning political will has prevented the regime from attempting to curb demands from the local population for an unrestrained lifestyle (Crot, 2013).

If we are to advance the paradigm of connecting places, connecting people, the important challenge is to confront those aspects that do not allow an alignment in benefits for the individuals and for the community. Individuals make choices in ways that return them pleasure or pain. Their preferences are shaped in time depending on these outcomes and do not consider equitable distribution of resources and services. Therefore, an increase in one individual's utility may reduce another individual's utility or utility for the community, considering resources are scarce (Bentham, 1987). In that sense, what works for an individual may not work for the community, and what works for the community may not work for certain individuals. The paradigms of today address issues of sustainability as of utmost importance. It has been established that private vehicles, low-density residential developments, consumerism, sedentary lifestyles, and so on carry costs for humanity and the planet. While 'Individuals are continually sensitized and encouraged towards a sustainable lifestyle, and urban paradigms are simultaneously striving to achieve sustainability goals. However, there are still miles to go.

THE FUTURE

Figure 8.2 Benefits and disadvantages for individuals and communities

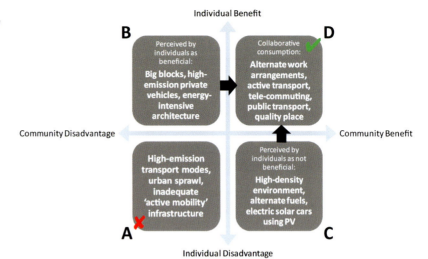

Some examples of design aspects where a mismatch between community and individual benefits is evident are demonstrated in Figure 8.2. Scenario A shows how high-emission transport modes, inadequate infrastructure for active transport modes, and insensitive urban planning and design can have harmful effects for both individuals and community. These practices should be avoided and stopped. Scenario B highlights that big block subdivisions and high-emission private vehicles are perceived by individuals as beneficial, perhaps due to a lack of awareness and lifestyle choices. These individual perceptions need to be changed through information and education programs to effect a cultural and lifestyle shift towards sustainable practices. Individuals also perceive high-density environments as causing traffic jams and leading to poor living environments (Nematollahi et al., 2016). There is hesitation about using electric vehicles due to concerns and reservations about the particular technology, its supporting infrastructure, and a fear of obsolescence caused by rapid changes in technology. These are, on the other hand, beneficial to the community, as shown in Scenario C. By resolving individual concerns, a way forward is possible where these aspects, along with those enabled by mega-trends and technological transformations (Scenario D), become the determining factors for a connected place that unites individual needs and choices with those of the community.

For a successful accommodation of community values towards sustainability and individual preferences for lifestyle in future cities, an approach that is simultaneously top down and bottom up will be required (Figure 8.3). Cities can and should intelligently harness the potential released by ICT and instil positive transformation in manufacturing, infrastructure, services, and the digital economy. Given the scarcity of resources and pressure on competitive economies across the world, it is imperative to adopt sustainable models for production and consumption. ICT applications can be conditioned as sensors to be placed amidst civic life to understand demands, and as enablers

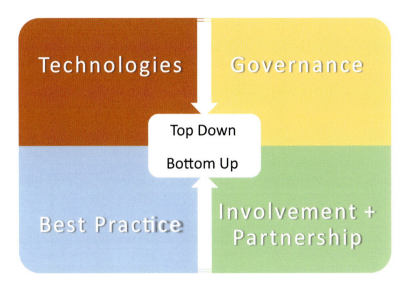

Figure 8.3 Using a top-down and a bottom-up approach

to support efficiency on the supply side. This leads to the creation of bottom-up and top-down models that use ICT to reap benefits from what is present in civil society. While a greater top-down approach could enable more investment in and regulation of infrastructure, as well as innovate business models and applications (Mega, 2013), the bottom-up approach could increase convenience, health, safety, and informed choices in daily life, thereby leading to a sustainable future.

Close

Working patterns and enterprises mobilized through social networks, and cities with e-governance, smart cards for multi-modal transport, connected vehicles, e-learning, and mobile banking are all projected to have a captive market of around US$730 billion by 2020 (Jawad, 2014). ICT applications will have their place in fully automated homes and workplaces with unified communications. Many such ICT applications are already in operation today, and governments are investing heavily to create smart cities, digital cities, future cities, and/or intelligent cities (Hollands, 2008). This mega-trend has the potential to generate connected living in the world and will be evidenced in our home, work, and city environments.

Parallel to virtual connectivity will be connectivity in the real realm. The increasing investment in transit and growing numbers of TODs and place-making projects will create future cities that are connected and active urban places accessible by sustainable and integrated transport. ICT-enabled e-governance will provide avenues for e-citizens to participate in decisions about their living environments. A key measure of the attractivemess of a place is the degree to which people feel connected with each other through formal and informal networks. Through ICT-enabled connections, residents can leverage each other's skills. Residents, local organizations, and local businessess can connect to find jobs, services, or products that build individual and community capacity. Care will be needed to bridge the gap between digitally rich and poor residents.

Will machine-to-machine communication, cloud computing, networks of data, virtual connections—the Internet of Things[6]—be the movers and shakers for the connecting place, connecting people paradigm? Will the resultant improved efficiency, optimizations, convenience, safety, and predictability lead to a place that is valued by its citizens (Haque, 2014)? Will the connected virtual place overshadow the connected 'real' place? Will becoming a digital citizen become more important than being a 'real' citizen?

The answers to these questions can be glimpsed in the work done at Medellín in Colombia, which was nominated as one of the 'smartest' cities at the Future Cities Summit of 2013. Medellín, a city that was struggling a few decades ago with its problem *favelas* and high crime rates, was able to reconnect its *favelas* not through smartphones but with publicly funded cable cars. A record drop in homicide rates from more than 200 deaths for every 100,000 inhabitants to around 62 was achieved by linking slum areas to the public transport network. Increased accessibility to new public place infrastructure, including libraries, schools, and sports facilities, allowed the 'communities [to interact] in a way they had never done before' (Poole, 2014, p. 1).

The success of Medellín demonstrates that real connected places will continue to matter and people will continue to value the in-person experiences that proximity affords. There is no doubt that the infusion of ICT makes life easier by making one informed and connected. What is crucial for transformative technologies is to have the sensors in the right places in the city. As society becomes more intelligent by making its citizenry more mindful of the facts, people will do the right thing and strive to avert any predicted disasters.

The plurality of actors involved or associated with the 'digital skin of the cities', including technologists, engineers, civic activists, urban planners, designers, and policy makers, results in plural narratives (Rabari & Storper, 2015, p. 27). These actors work together pragmatically or normatively for the agendas in the real space consisting of real people. Thus, while the internet has taken over our lives, face-to-face communication remains and will remain vital for humans.

Notes

1 'Collaborative consumption' is a phenomenon born of the internet age and driven by information communications technology (ICT). It is defined as 'the peer-to-peer-based activity of obtaining, giving, or sharing the access to goods and services, coordinated through community-based online services' (Hamari et al., 2015, p. 2047).
2 Vélib has the highest market penetration, with one bike for every 97 inhabitants, as of July 2013.
3 The number of inbound parcels in Australia increased by 56 percent in 2010–2011, almost twice the growth rate in 2009–2010 (Productivity Commission, 2011). The logistics industry, including road, rail, and shipping freight, experienced revenue growth of 6.5 percent between 2006 and 2011 (IBISWorld, 2012).
4 'Open data' are data that are available freely without issues of patent and copyright (Open Knowledge International, n.d.).

5 'Big Data is characterized by volume, velocity and variety of data types' (Deloitte, 2015, p. 2).
6 The 'Internet of Things' is visualized as a hyper-connected urban environment—a super-smart city. Sensors provide connectivity to everything from cars to road infrastructure to rubbish bins (Perera et al., 2015).

References

All online references retrieved August 17, 2016.

Aktan, E. O. A. (2012). Toward zero carbon with environmentally friendly transport modes. *WIT Transactions on the Built Environment 128*. Retrieved from www.witpress.com/Secure/elibrary/papers/UT12/UT12009FU1.pdf.

Aldred, R. (2014). The bicycle is human scale. Retrieved from http://rachelaldred.org/writing/the-bicycle-is-human-scale/.

Alessandrini, A., Campagna, A., Site, P. D., Filippi, F., & Persia, L. (2015). Automated vehicles and the rethinking of mobility and cities. *Transportation Research Procedia 5*, 145–160.

Allan, R. (2016, July 21). Has Pokémon Go peaked? The data say 'yes'. Retrieved from www.surveymonkey.com/business/intelligence/peak-pokemon-go/.

Arnold, R., & Walker, J. (2014). Vehicle to infrastructure deployments and guidance. Retrieved from www.tn.gov/assets/entities/tdot/attachments/WalkerV2I_DeploymentsAndGuidance_PresentationRev.pdf.

Barr, A., & Ramsey, M. (2015). Google brings in chief for self-driving cars. Retrieved from www.wsj.com/articles/google-brings-in-chief-for-self-driving-cars-1442199840.

Bentham, J. (1987). *An introduction to the principles of morals and legislations.* Harmondsworth: Penguin.

Bilandzic, M. (2013). The embodied hybrid space: Designing social and digital interventions to facilitate connected learning in coworking spaces. Doctoral dissertation. Retrieved from https://kavasmlikon.files.wordpress.com/2013/09/markbilandzic_phdthesis.pdf.

Bilandzic, M., & Foth, M. (2012). A review of locative media, mobile and embodied spatial interaction. *International Journal of Human–Computer Studies 70*(1), 66–71.

BMW Insights. (2013). Make progress instead of standing still. Retrieved from www.bmw.com/com/en/insights/technology/connecteddrive/2013/services_apps/rtti.html.

Bsat, S. (2010). Masdar 2009 headlines. In T. Reisz (Ed.) *Al Manakh Continued* (p. 243). Amsterdam: Stichting Archis.

Buffa, K. (2016, July 13). Controversy brewing over memorials marked as Pokémon Go stops. NBC News. Retrieved from www.nbcconnecticut.com/news/local/Controversy-Brewing-Over-Memorials-Marked-as-Pokemon-GO-Stops-386690041.html.

Caddy, B. (2015). Toyota to launch first driverless car in 2020. Retrieved from www.wired.co.uk/news/archive/2015-10/08/toyota-highway-teammate-driverless-car-tokyo.

Cathcart-Keays, A. (2016). Where is the most cycle-friendly city in the world? *Guardian*. Retrieved from www.theguardian.com/cities/2016/jan/05/where-world-most-cycle-friendly-city-amsterdam-copenhagen.

Charness, N., & Boot, W. R. (2009). Aging and information technology use potential and barriers. *Association for Psychological Science 18*(5), 253–258.

Citiesnext. (2013). Project: Vélib bikes. Retrieved from http://citiesnext.com/project/velib-bikes/.

City of Sydney. (2014). News and updates. Retrieved from www.cityofsydney.nsw.gov.au/council/news-and-updates/the-facts-of-the-matter/car-share-parking-spaces.

Connected Cities. (2015). Connected Cities. Retrieved from www.citiesconvention.com/connected/.

Corwin, S., Vitale, J., Kelly, E., & Cathles, E. (2015). The future of mobility. Retrieved from http://dupress.com/articles/future-of-mobility-transportation-technology/#sup-2.

Cripps, K. (2013). Bike share boom: 7 cities doing it right. Retrieved from http://edition.cnn.com/2013/12/05/travel/bike-share-boom-global-report/.

Crot, L. (2013). Planning for sustainability in non-democratic polities: The case of Masdar City. *Urban Studies 50*(13), 2809–2825.

Czaja, A. S., & Sharit, J. (2009). The aging of the population: Opportunities and challenges for human factors engineering. *The Bridge: National Academy of Sciences 39*(1), 34–41. Retrieved from www.nae.edu/File.aspx?id=12500.

Deloitte. (2015). Smart cities: Big data. Retrieved from www2.deloitte.com/content/dam/Deloitte/fpc/Documents/services/systemes-dinformation-et-technologie/deloitte_smart-cities-big-data_en_0115.pdf.

DeMaio, P. (2016). The need for innovation. Retrieved from http://bike-sharing.blogspot.com.au/2016_02_01_archive.html.

Economist, The. (2012). Seeing the back of the car. In the rich world, people seem to be driving less than they used to. Retrieved from www.economist.com/node/21563280.

European Environmental Agency. (2011). The European environment: State and outlook 2010: Assessment of global megatrends. Retrieved from www.eea.europa.eu/soer/europe-and-the-world/megatrends/download.

Florida, R. (2005). *Cities and the creative class.* New York: Routledge.

Florida, R. (2015). Where millennials are moving now. Retrieved from www.citylab.com/housing/2015/03/where-millennials-are-moving-now/388748/.

Florida, R. (2016). The study: Rise of renting. Retrieved from www.citylab.com/housing/2016/02/the-rise-of-renting-in-the-us/462948/.

Frommer, D. (2012). Sim city: Inside South Korea's $35 billion plan to build a city from scratch. Retrieved from http://readwrite.com/2012/07/31/sim-city-inside-south-koreas-35-billion-plan-to-build-a-city-from-scratch/.

Frost & Sullivan. (2012). *Executive analysis of carsharing market in APAC.* Retrieved from https://store.frost.com/executive-analysis-of-the-carsharing-market-in-apac.html.

Frost & Sullivan. (2014). Fast-forward to 2025: New mega trends transforming the world as we know it. Retrieved from http://docplayer.net/3165778-Fast-forward-to-2025-new-mega-trends-transforming-the-world-as-we-know-it-macro-to-micro-opportunities-on-future-design-businesses-and-our-personal.html.

Frost & Sullivan, & Hitachi Ltd. (2014). Social innovation whitepaper. Retrieved from www.hds.com/en-us/pdf/white-paper/social-innovation-mega-trends-to-answer-society-challenges-whitepaper.pdf.

Fulton, W. (2015). Future of parking in an era of carsharing. Retrieved from www.governing.com/columns/urban-notebook/gov-drive-less-park-less.html.

GoGet. (2016). About us: GoGet. Retrieved from www.goget.com.au/about-us/.

Hajkowicz, S., Cook, H., & Littleboy, A. (2012). *Our future world: Global megatrends.* Retrieved from https://fial.com.au/system/files/knowledge_repository/Our%20Future%20World%20-%20Mega%20trends%20that%20will%20shape%20the%20way%20we%20live.pdf.

Halegoua, G. R. (2012). *New Mediated Spaces and the Urban Environment.* Doctoral dissertation. Retrieved from http://gradworks.umi.com/35/12/3512069.html.

Hamari, J., Sjöklint, M., & Ukkonen, A. (2015). The sharing economy: Why people participate in collaborative consumption. *Journal of the Association for Information Science and Technology 67*(9): 2047–2059.

Haque, U. (2014, January 29). Usman Haque on the 'internet of everything'. *Guardian* Tech Weekly Podcast. Retrieved from www.theguardian.com/technology/audio/2014/jan/29/tech-weekly-podcast-usman-haque-audio.

Hauser, J. (2015). Amerika schaltet auf autopilot. Retrieved from www.faz.net/aktuell/wirtschaft/unternehmen/verkehrsminister-foxx-selbstfahrende-autos-in-10-jahren-standard-13811022.html.

Hillman, K. (2007). *The migration of non-metropolitan youth towards the cities.* Retrieved from http://research.acer.edu.au/cgi/viewcontent.cgi?article=1042&context=resdev.

Hollands, R. G. (2008). Will the real smart city please stand up? Intelligent, progressive or entrepreneurial? *City 12*(3), 303–321.

Horgas, A., & Abowd, G. (2004). *Technology for adaptive aging*. Retrieved from www.ncbi.nlm.nih.gov/books/NBK97346/.

Hou, J. (2012). Vertical urbanism, horizontal urbanity: Notes from East Asian cities. In B. Vinayak (Ed.) *The emerging Asian city: Concomitant urbanities and urbanisms* (pp. 234–243). Hoboken, NJ: Taylor & Francis.

iamsterdam. (2016). Dossier cycling: Cycling facts & figures. Retrieved from www.iamsterdam.com/en/media-centre/city-hall/dossier-cycling/cycling-facts-and-figures.

IBISWorld. (2012). *Integrated logistics in Australia.* Melbourne, VIC: IBISWorld Industry.

Insurance Institute for Highway Safety. (2015). US DOT and IIHS announce historic commitment from 10 automakers to include automatic emergency braking on all new vehicles. Retrieved from www.iihs.org/iihs/news/desktopnews/u-s-dot-and-iihs-announce-historic-commitment-from-10-automakers-to-include-automatic-emergency-braking-on-all-new-vehicles.

International Car Sharing Association. (2016, January 7). *Uploads: Carsharing*. Retrieved from http://carsharing.org/wp-content/uploads/2016/01/The-Impact-of-Car-Share-Services-in-Australia.pdf.

Jawad, I. (2014). World's top global mega trends to 2025 and implications to business, society and cultures. Retrieved from www.investinbsr.com/ipaforum/wp-content/uploads/Iain-Jawad-IPA-Forum-2014-Presentation.pdf.

Jensen, B. B. (2016). Masdar City: A critical retrospection. In S. Wippel, K. Bomber, & B. Krawietz (Eds.) *Under construction: Logics of urbanism in the Gulf region* (pp. 45–54). New York: Routledge.

Keogh, B. (2016, July 14). Pokémon Go and the politics of digital gaming in public. Retrieved from https://overland.org.au/2016/07/pokemon-go-and-the-politics-of-digital-gaming-in-public/.

Knight, W. (2015). Car-to-car communication: A simple wireless technology promises to make driving much safer. Retrieved from www.technologyreview.com/s/534981/car-to-car-communication/.

Koolhaas, R., Reisz, T., Gergawi, M., Mendis, B., & Decker, T. (2010). *Al Manakh Gulf continued* (Vol. 23). Amsterdam: Stichting Archis.

Kunwon. (2008). New Songdo City: Songdo international business district. Retrieved from www.kpf.com/projects/new-songdo-city.

Lau, A. (2012). Masdar City: A model of urban environmental sustainability. Retrieved from http://web.stanford.edu/group/journal/cgi-bin/wordpress/wp-content/uploads/2012/09/Lau_SocSci_2012.pdf.

LeBeau, P. (2014). Car sharing a growing threat to auto sales: Study. Retrieved from www.cnbc.com/2014/02/04/car-sharing-a-growing-threat-to-auto-sales-study.html.

Lee, E. (2012). Songdo international business district: The reality of sustainable cities. Retrieved from www.academia.edu/10272323/Songdo_International_Business_District_The_Reality_of_Sustainable_Cities.

Lichá, A. (2015). Songdo and Sejong: Master-planned cities in South Korea. Retrieved from https://halshs.archives-ouvertes.fr/halshs-01216229/document.

Maddox, G. (2001). Housing and living arrangements: A transactional perspective. In R. H. Binstock & L. K. George (Eds.) *Handbook of aging and the social sciences* (5th edn) (pp. 426–443). San Diego, CA: Academic Press.

Masdar City. (2011). Exploring Masdar City. Retrieved from www.thefuturebuild.com/assets/images/uploads/static/1745/masdar_city_exploring1.pdf.

Mega, V. (2013). *Quintessential cities, accountable to the future*. New York: Springer.

Merten, T. (2015). Solutions to overcome the challenges faced by urban freight transportation. Retrieved from www.move-forward.com/news/details/solutions-to-overcome-the-challenges-faced-by-urban-freight-transportation/.

MFour. (2016, July 14). Survey gives first systematic study of Pokémon Go players. Retrieved from https://mfour.com/survey-gives-first-systematic-study-of-pokemon-go-players/.

Mitchell, S. (2015). IKEA Australia plans small stores ahead of online push. Retrieved from www.smh.com.au/business/ikea-australia-plans-small format-stores-ahead-of-online-push-20150630-gi1e2c.html.
Moos, M. (2015). From gentrification to youthification? The increasing importance of young age in delineating high-density living. *Urban Studies 53*(14). Retrieved from http://journals.sagepub.com/doi/pdf/10.1177/0042 098015603292.
Nematollahi, S., Tiwari, R., & Hedgecock, D. (2016). Desirable dense neighbourhoods: An environmental psychological approach for understanding community resistance to densification. *Urban Policy and Research 32*(2), 132–151.
Nischelwitzer, A., Lenz, F.-J., Searle, G., & Holzinger, A. (2007). Some aspects of the development of low-cost augmented reality learning environments as examples for future interfaces in technology enhanced learning. Paper presented at the International Conference on Universal Access in Human–Computer Interaction, Berlin. Retrieved from http://link.springer.com/chapter/10.1007/978-3-540-73283-9_79.
Open Knowledge International. (n.d.). *Open data handbook*. Retrieved from http://opendatahandbook.org/.
OPTIMISM. (2013). Deliverable 5.1: Definition of strategies for integrating and optimising transport systems. Retrieved from www.tmleuven.be/project/optimism/Deliverable-4.1-Identification-of-ICT-options-enhancing-co-modality.pdf.
Payne, C. (2015). Inhabitat. Retrieved from http://inhabitat.com/amsterdam-is-out-of-bicycle-parking-spaces-so-its-building-40000-more/.
Perera, C., Liu, C. H., & Jayawardena, S. (2015). The emerging Internet of Things marketplace from an industrial perspective: A survey. Retrieved from https://arxiv.org/pdf/1502.00134.pdf.
Pomerantz, L. (2014). Time for retailers to re-evaluate their store footprint: One size does not fit all. Retrieved from www.forbes.com/sites/laurapomerantz/2014/05/06/time-for-retailers-to-re-evaluate-their-store-footprint-one-size-does-not-fit-all/#30039a0f6d1b.
Poole, S. (2014, December 17). The truth about smart cities: In the end, they will destroy democracy. *Guardian*. Retrieved from www.theguardian.com/cities/2014/dec/17/truth-smart-city-destroy-democracy-urban-thinkers-buzzphrase.
Prakash, A., & Kar-gupta, S. (2014). Rise of the car sharing apps poses threat to auto sector. Retrieved from www.reuters.com/article/us-autos-apps-id USKBN0JW1TX20141218.
Productivity Commission. (2011). *Economic structure and the performance of Australian retail industry*. Retrieved from www.pc.gov.au/inquiries/comp leted/retail-industry/report/retail-industry.pdf.
Project for Public Spaces. (2016, July 27). Go Pokémon Go! The social life of virtual urban spaces. Retrieved from www.pps.org/blog/go-pokemon-go-the-social-life-of-virtual-urban-spaces/.
PRT Consulting. (2010). Why has Masdar personal rapid transit (PRT) been scaled back? Retrieved from www.prtconsulting.com/blog/index.php/2010/10/16/why-has-masdar-personal-rapid-transit-prt-been-scaled-back/.
PWC. (2015). Total retail 2015: Retailers and the age of disruption. Retrieved from www.pwc.ie/media-centre/assets/publications/2015-pwc-ireland-total-retail-february.pdf.
Rabari, C., & Storper, M. (2015). The digital skin of cities: Urban theory and research in the age of the sensored and metered city, ubiquitous computing and big data. *Cambridge Journal of Regions, Economy and Society 8*(1), 27–42.
RAND Corporation. (2004). The future at work: Trends and implications. Retrieved from www.rand.org/pubs/research_briefs/RB5070.html.
REGUS. (2011). Driving growth. Retrieved from www.regus.com/images/Regus%20plc%20consolidated%20report%20and%20accounts%202011_tcm304-49762.pdf.
Rérat, P. (2012). The new demographic growth of cities: The case of reurbanisation in Switzerland. *Urban Studies 49*(5), 1107–1125.

Richter, F. (2015). Bike-sharing is taking off around the world. Retrieved from www.statista.com/chart/3325/bike-sharing-systems-worldwide/.

Sager, T. (2014). Hypermobility and the forecast-free planning of society. In S. Bergmann, T. A. Hoff, & T. Sager (Eds.) *Spaces of mobility: Essays on the planning, ethics, engineering and religion of human motion* (pp. 32–58). New York: Routledge.

Securepay. (2014). Four trends shaping Australian e-commerce. Retrieved from www.securepay.com.au/insights/articles/four-trends-shaping-australian-e-commerce.

Sessa, C., Fioretto, M., Alessandrini, A., Delle Site, P., Holguin, C., Flament, M., Csepinszky, A., Hoadley, S., & Friis, G. (2013). Blueprint of alternative city cyber-mobility take-up scenarios. Retrieved from www.citymobil2.eu/en/upload/Deliverables/PU/D27.1%20-%20Blueprint%20of%20Alternative%20City%20Cyber-%20mobility%20Take-up%20Scenarios_Final-2.pdf.

Shaheen, P., & Cohen, A. (2015). Innovative mobility carsharing outlook. Retrieved from http://tsrc.berkeley.edu/sites/default/files/Summer%202015%20Carsharing%20Outlook_Final%20(1)_0.pdf.

Sheehan, R. (2015). Communications: Intelligent transportation systems joint programs office. Retrieved from www.its.dot.gov/factsheets/v2isafety_factsheet.htm.

Singh, S., & Saini, J. (2013). New mega trends: Impacts of mega trends on future of car retailing. Retrieved from www.slideshare.net/FrostandSullivan/future-of-car-retailing-frost-sullivan.

Stephens, D. (2014). The future of retail: Experiences per square foot. Retrieved from www.retailprophet.com/blog/the-future-of-retail-experiences-per-square-foot/.

United Nations. (2015). World population ageing 2015. Retrieved from www.un.org/en/development/desa/population/publications/pdf/ageing/WPA2015_Report.pdf.

University of Wollongong. (2016). UOWx interactive seminar series. Retrieved from www.uow.edu.au/student/life/uowx/uowxinteractiveseminaroverview/index.html.

Vasus, D., & Qu, L. (2015). Demographics of living alone. Retrieved from https://aifs.gov.au/publications/demographics-living-alone.

Veerasawmy, R., & Ludvigsen, M. (2010). *Designing technology for active spectator experiences at sporting events*. Paper presented at the 22nd Conference of the Computer–Human Interaction Special Interest Group of Australia on Computer–Human Interaction, Brisbane.

Walsh, B. (2011). Masdar City: The world's greenest city? Retrieved from http://content.time.com/time/health/article/0,8599,2043934,00.html.

Whitman, T., Reid, C., Klemperer, J. v., Radoff, J., & Roy, A. (2008). *New Songdo City: The making of a new green city*. Paper presented at the 8th World Congress Council on Tall Buildings and Urban Habitat, Dubai. Retrieved from http://global.ctbuh.org/resources/papers/download/1297-new-songdo-city-the-making-of-a-new-green-city.pdf.

Yvkoff, L. (2015). One step closer to autonomous cars: 10 automakers to make automatic emergency braking standard. Retrieved from www.forbes.com/sites/lianeyvkoff/2015/09/11/automatic-emergency-braking-to-be-standard-on-10-manufacturers/#48379e9456f1.

Zhao, H. (2016, July 18). Pokémon Go attracts diverse crowd of gamers, study suggests. *Los Angeles Times*. Retrieved from www.latimes.com/business/la-fi-tn-pokemon-demographics-20160718-snap-story.html.

EPILOGUE

ETHNOGRAPHY OF PLACE AND MOVEMENT

Fast forward to the year 2050.

The global population has exceeded the nine billion mark. Around 70 percent of the world's citizens live in cities. The demographic explosion has reached its apogee. There are as many people above the age of 65 as there are under 15. Most of the urban growth has occurred in the Global South, the region that in 2017 included many developing and less developed economies. Cities in this region work hard to develop strategies to provide better opportunities for the youth and the poor. At the same time, a shrinking labor force and the need to provide resources for healthy and active living are the challenges faced by the Global North.

The urban environment has been reshaped, with shorter distances between mixed-use, denser, demographically diversified, high-quality, and connected urban places. This makes it quicker, safer, and cheaper for people to access destinations. People-oriented greenways, pedestrian areas, bike lanes, and public parks abound. High-quality, high-capacity public transport corridors attract concentrated growth and have successfully brought movement and place functions together. The connected place has encouraged a modal shift to public transport, cycling, and walking. Shifts in fuel technology and clean energy have also aided in the reduction of lifecycle emissions of transport systems. Inner-city areas that had experienced a land use shock have been reinvented as livable, connected places that attract creative knowledge economies. Far-flung disconnected suburbs have been transformed into compact, high-quality places to work, live, and play, through reconnection with urban centers via fast, sustainable transport systems.

A new age of accessible autonomy has arrived. With the growth in car sharing and breakthroughs in driverless cars, affordable mobility is within reach of the masses. The increasing shift from personal vehicle ownership to shared vehicle and public transit use has improved asset use efficiency. The average cost per mile has decreased, mainly due to the saved value of the driver's time. The Internet of Things has become a reality rather than a 'buzzword',

EPILOGUE

saving labor and time and redefining domestic and urban landscapes as smart homes and smart cities.

The city is not the anonymous place that was predicted some 35 years ago, but a place for civic engagement. Connected places are being crafted as gathering spaces. Walking and socializing with others, sharing the everyday rhythms of places, sounds, smells, collective memories, and stories, has encouraged place making as an ongoing activity with community involvement, interaction, and intellectual engagement. A sense of safety and well-being prevails.

While virtual cafés and networks abound, the use of public spaces has increased. Young people are experiencing a deeper sense of connection to the real world. In the process of hunting virtual monsters through the immersive media, families venture into neighborhoods where they had never ventured before, noticing the landmarks, paintings, and statues, and become more connected to the real world. These gaming applications make it much easier and more common to interact with new places and new people, and stronger bonds develop within families and communities. People are experiencing and capturing the stories and meanings of forgotten heritage places via augmented reality applications.

ICT applications are increasingly used by local communities to reframe local issues with a potential for global significance. Grassroots urban activism has become an outcome of democratic political discourse. Local communities are highly engaged in decisions about their physical environment, and are helping increase social capital.

Benchmarking people, place, and transport connectivity through the Connected Places Audit Tool has become the norm. Continual checks quickly identify problems or inadequacies in approaches, procedures, policies, and implementation measures, and remedial action is taken to address current and future needs.

Government provides an enabling environment for investment in sustainable transport infrastructure, thus influencing private-sector investment. Transport and land development challenges are addressed with innovation and education. Political, ideological, and disciplinary differences are mediated through awareness campaigns, outreach programs, and collaborative stakeholder approaches. Urban professionals have taken their studios and offices into the streets, and are understanding communities' needs and everyday practices through their own embodied experience of urban places, making it easier to comprehend and analyze urban issues. They have become urban ethnographers. Ethnography of movement and place has emerged as a new discipline. Connecting places, connecting people has been established as a paradigm.

INDEX

Page numbers in *italic* indicate figures and in **bold** indicate tables, end of chapter notes are indicated by a letter n between page number and note number.

Abu Dhabi 149, 150, 152, 153, 154
accessibility 3, 102–3, *103*, *104*
Adopt-a-Station Project, Chicago 48
affordable housing 18–19, 62, 67, 71, 73, 131
affordable public transport 131
aging population 147–8
Ahmedabad, India 44–5, 46
AirBnB 143
air pollution 132–3; *see also* greenhouse gas emissions
AlixPartners 144
Amsterdam, Netherlands 144
Appleyard, D. 21
applied ethnography 90–1
art *see* public art
Audit Tool 97–120, **99**, *100*; city and neighborhood structure 98, **99**, **107**; connectivity 102, *103*; cycling and cyclability 98, **99**, **109–10**; density 100, **101**; diversity 98, **99**, **108**; diversity of block sizes 100–2, *102*; King Street, San Francisco 106–7, *107*, **107–13**; Nehru Place, New Delhi, India 106, 114–19; ped-shed accessibility 102–3, *103*, *104*; permeability index 102–3, *103*, *104*, 120n5; place making 98, **99**, **111–12**; public art 105, *106*; solid:void ratio 103, *104*; transport 98, **99**, **113**; urban massing 103–5, *105*; walking and walkability 98, **99**, 106, **109–10**, 114–19
augmented reality 147
Austin, Texas 45
Australia 15, 19; car sharing 143–4; graffiti management 105, *106*; Melbourne 63–7, *64*, *65*, *66*, 103, *104*, *106*, 143–4; Perth 36, *36*, 67–9, *68*, *69*, 85–6, 87, 100–2, *102*, *103*
Australian Transport Safety Bureau 15
automatic driving 145, 148
automatic emergency braking (AEB) 145–6
average gross residential density within a station area 100, **101**
Avoid, Shift, Improve, and Finance (ASIF) paradigm 68

Ballajura, Perth, Australia 103, *103*
Bangalore, India 86, 102, *103*
Barcelona *22*
Barter, P. 138
Bates, D. 4
behavioral change 84–6
Bell, M. 20
Bella Terra, Huntington Beach, California 70
Belmar, New Jersey 40
bike sharing 143, 144–5
Bilsborough, Darren 56
Birmingham City Council, UK 37
BMW 145
Bogotá, Colombia 131, 135–8
Bollore Group 144

Boston 45, 148
Boulder, Colorado 34–5, *34*
boulevards 32
Bradbury, Ray x
Bray, D. J. 84
Brazil 47–8, 84, 132
Bristol, UK 21
Broward County, Florida 35–6, *35*
Brown, M. A. 32
brownfield developments 45, 49n6
bus rapid transit (BRT) systems 44, 47, 90, 130, 131, 137

Cadillac 145
California 19, 21, *22*, 90, 91, 148; Crossings, Mountain View 70–2, *70*, *71*; Hollywood/Vine station, Los Angeles 46–7; King Street, San Francisco 105–6, *106*, **107–13**; parklets 39–40, *40*
Cannington, Perth, Australia 100–2, *102*
canyon effects 62, *63*
Cape Town, South Africa 129–31, *130*, *131*
Car2go program 144
carbon dioxide emissions 56, 68, *68*, 69, 73, 132–3
carbon footprint 4, 32
carbon monoxide 133
carbon neutral 74, 149
car dependence 1, 19; changing behavior 84–6; *see also* car-oriented city design
car-disconnect state 55, 97
car-free zones 41, *41*, 47
car-oriented city design 13, 15, *15*, 31–2, 55–6, 72, *72*; Global South 127–8
cars: electric 144; self-driving 145, 148
car sharing 143–4
Cervero, R. 37, 90
Champs Élysées, Paris 32
Chicago 46, 48
chicanes 16, *16*
China 4, 42, *42*, 128, 132, 134, 138–9
CicLAvia, Los Angeles 91
Ciclovia 135–6, 138
Circle, Uptown Normal, Illinois 14
city and neighborhood structure: Audit Tool 98, **99**, **107**; and technology mega-trends 151
Ciudad Guayana, Venezuela 21
Clean Air Asia 92, 106, 134
collaborative consumption 143–5, 156n1
collaborative planning 84
collaborative stakeholder dialogue (CSD) 86–8, 92–3
collectivos 132
Colombia 131, 135–8, 156
Colorado 34–5, *34*
communities 5, 13–23, *14*; equitable 20–1; healthy 17–18; identity 21–2; prosperous 18–19; safe 15–17, *16*

| 165

INDEX

community non-acceptance and outrage 6–7, 40
community outreach 7
community participation *see* public involvement
commuting 14–15
Compact City 5
Complete Streets movement 39
Complete Streets Thoroughfare Assemblies Smart Code Module 33–4
computer programs 89–90
congestion charging 85, 86
connectivity, Audit Tool 102, *103*
consumerism 70
Context Sensitive Solutions in Designing Major Urban Thoroughfares for Walkable Communities (CSS) 34
creative class 5
Creedon, J. 91–2
crime, safety from 17, 118, **118**
crime prevention through environmental design (CPTED) 17
crisis 4–5
Crossings, Mountain View, California 70–2, *70*, *71*
Curitiba, Brazil 47–8, 84
Curtin University, Perth, Australia 67–9, *68*, *69*, 91–2
cyberspace 146–7, 148–9
cycling and cyclability 17, 18, 34–5, *34*, 39, 41, *41*, 44, 91, 127, 133; Audit Tool 98, **99**, **109–10**; bike sharing 143, 144–5; Global South 134–5, *135*, 137; and technology mega-trends 152

Daimler 145
Dallas, Texas 57–60, *58*, *59*, *60*
Dallas Area Rapid Transit (DART) system 58
de-industrialization 57
deliberative stakeholder engagement 86–8, 92–3
demographic trends 147–9
Denmark 17
density 129; Audit Tool 100, **101**; *see also* high-density development
Density, Diversity, and Design model 68
density bonus, California 19
Department of Transportation, US 146
desirable density 100, **101**
developing world *see* Global South
Dialogue with the City tool 87
disabilities 21
disadvantaged social groups 20–1; *see also* informal settlements
diversity 13, 19, 62, 67, 73; Audit Tool 98, **99**, **108**; and technology mega-trends 152
diversity of block sizes 100–2, *102*
docklands, reconfiguring 62–7, *64*, *65*, *66*
Dorchester, Boston 45
Dovey, K. 6
driverless cars 145, 148
Dudley Village Project, Dorchester, Boston 45

East Japan Railway Company 45–6
EcoDensity Program, Vancouver 19
e-commerce 146
economic benefits: inner-city redevelopment 56; transit-oriented developments 48–9; walking and cycling 19

edge city 128; retrofit 72–4, *72*, *74*
elderly 20, 21, 148
electric vehicles 144
Embarcadero Boulevard, San Francisco 105–6
Embarq India 136
employment densities 100, **101**
empowerment *see* public involvement
engagement *see* public involvement
engagement tools 88–92; ethnographic methods 90–2, 93; online deliberation 89–90; photo-simulations 90
Enquiry by Design workshops 87–8
environmental justice 20
equitable communities 20–1
ethnographic engagement methods 90–2, 93
experimental ethnography 91

face-to-face contact 4
Fairfax County, Virginia 72–4, *72*, *74*
FAR *see* floor area ratio (FAR)
Federal Highway Administration, US 146
Federal Ministry of Transport and Digital Infrastructure, Germany 20
Finchem, Tim 3
Five Oaks project, Ohio 17
flood mitigation 61
floor area ratio (FAR) 43, 44–5, 129, 138
Florida 17, 35–6, *35*
Florida, R. 148
footpaths, India 86, 134–5, *135*
Ford 145
Form-Based Codes 57
Fox, Anthony 145
Freemark, Y. 46
freeway deconstruction projects 37–9, *38*, *39*
Freiburg, Germany 17, 41, *41*
Friesland, Netherlands 33
FRUIT (fear of revitalization urban-infill and towers) attitude 6–7
Fruitvale, California 21, *22*
FUS-ion (Function, Universality, Scale) model 36, *36*
Future Cities Summit 156

Gaithersburg, Maryland 70
gamification 147
Garden City movement 70
gender 20–1
gentrification 15, 56, 60, 62, 148
Germany 17, 20, 41, *41*, 85
Global Commission on the Economy and Climate 56
global demographic trends 147–9
global population growth 127, 128, 129
Global South 9n2, 127–39; amenities for pedestrians and cyclists 134–6, *135*, 137; Bogotá, Colombia 131, 135–8; formal and informal peri-urban developments 128–31, *130*, *131*; informal public transport 131–2; private two-wheelers 132–4, *133*
GoGet 143–4
Google 145
graffiti 105, *106*
Grappling with Graffiti strategy, Victoria, Australia 105, *106*

INDEX

green connectors and spaces 18, 37–9, *39*, 47–8, 62, 73, 137; reconfiguring 41–3, *42*, *43*
greenfield developments 45, 49n7
greenhouse gas emissions 56, 68, *68*, 69, 73, 132–3
green rail trails 42–3, *43*
Guerra, E. 90
Gujarat, India 46
Gurgaon, India 136

Hanoi, Vietnam 132, *133*
Harbordale, Florida 17
Hayes Valley Neighborhood Association 37
healthy communities 17–18
height to width ratios 103–5, *105*
high-density development 44, 47, 56–7, 59, 71, 73, 74, 129, 138; photo-simulations 90
High Line Park, New York 42–3, *43*
Hoboken Yard Redevelopment Area, New Jersey 60–2, *61*, *63*
Hollywood/Vine station, Los Angeles 46–7
home working 147, 148
Home Zones Program, UK 33
Hong Kong 20, 44, 129
housing, affordable 18–19, 62, 67, 71, 73, 131
Hubbert, Marion King 81
Hughes, Ken 58, 59
Human Development Index (HDI) 9n2, 127, 139n1
Huntington Beach, California 70

identity, community 21–2
IKEA 146
in between spaces 4; nature of 31–2; *see also* movement reconfiguration
India 44–5, 46, 128, 131; Audit Tool 106, 114–19; connectivity 102, *103*; informal public transport 132; Space Reclamation movement 135–6; walking and walkability 86, 87–8, 91–2, 106, 114–19, 134–6, *135*
IndiMark Program 85
Indira Nagar, Bangalore, India 102, *103*
Indonesia 132, 134
Industrial Revolution 55
industrial zones, reconfiguring 57–60, *58*, *59*, *60*
informal public transport 131–2
informal settlements 129–31, *130*, *131*, 156
information communication technology (ICT) *see* technology mega-trends
information dissemination programs 85–6
inner-city redevelopment *see* place reconfiguration
Insurance Institute of Highway Safety 145–6
internet commerce 146
Internet of Things 1–2, 156, 157n6

Jacobs, A. 21
Jacobs, Jane 4, 56
Jamaica 132
Janmarg Bus Rapid Transit (BRT), Ahmedabad, India 44–5
Jayanagar, Bangalore, India 86
JCDecaux 145
jobs 18

Kenya 20, 132
King Street, San Francisco 106–7, *107*, **107–13**

Klipfontein Corridor, Cape Town, South Africa 129–31, *130*, *131*
knowledge economy 148
Kott, J. 106, **107–13**

land-banking programs 131
land consolidation techniques 45–6
land densification *see* high-density development
land use efficiency 100–2, *102*, 120n3
LaTorre, Dan 147
leadership 47–8
Lerner, Jaime 47–8
life expectancy 147–8
Livable Streets concept 33
Liveable Neighbourhoods 5
London 20, 37, 48, 144
London Underground 48
Los Angeles 46–7, 91, 148
Lugo, Adonia 91

Maginn, P. J. 90–1
Malaysia 132
malls *see* shopping centers
Manning Road, Perth, Australia 36, *36*
Maryland 70
Masdar, Abu Dhabi 149, 150, 152, 153, 154
Mass Transit Railway (MTR), Hong Kong 44
matututs 132
Meddin, Russell 145
Medellín, Colombia 156
Melbourne, Australia 103, *104*, *106*, 143–4; Docklands 63–7, *64*, *65*, *66*
Mercedes-Benz 144
Metrovivienda initiative, Bogotá, Colombia 131
Mexico City 132
Mockingbird Station, Dallas, Texas 57–60, *58*, *59*, *60*
Monderman, H. 33
Mongolia 134
mono-use zones, reconfiguring 67–9, *68*, *69*
Moos, Markus 148
motorcycles 132–3, *133*
motorists' behavior 119
motorized two-wheelers 132–4, *133*
Mountain View, California 70–2, *70*, *71*
Mount Lawley, Perth, Australia 100, *102*
movement reconfiguration 5, 31–49; green connectors 41–3, *42*, *43*; public transport 43–9; streets and corridors 33–41, *34*, *35*, *36*, *38*, *39*, *40*, *41*
Multi-Family Tax Exemption Program, Seattle 19
municipal governance 48

Nairobi, Kenya 20, 132
natural surveillance 4, 17
Nedlands, Perth, Australia 103, *103*
Nehru Place, New Delhi, India 91–2, 106, 114–19
neighborhood structure *see* city and neighborhood structure
Nepal 134
Netherlands 33, 49n2, 144
Network City planning strategy, Perth, Australia 87
New Climate Economy Project 56
New Delhi, India 91–2, 106, 114–19, 131

| 167

New Jersey 40, 60–2, *61*, *63*
Newman, Peter 56
New Urbanism 5, 6, 33–4, 57, 74
New York 42–3, *43*, 148, 149
NIMBY (not-in-my-back-yard) attitude 6–7, 83
non-motorized modes of transport (NMT) 134–6, *135*; *see also* cycling and cyclability; walking and walkability
Northern Ireland 20

obesogenic environments 17
Octavia Boulevard, San Francisco 37–8, *38*
Odense, Denmark 17
Ohio 17
older people 20, 21, 148
one-person households 148
online deliberation 89–90
online retail 146
Open Space Technology 87–8
Optimization Tool 89
Oudehaske, Netherlands 33

Pakistan 134
Paris 32, 143, 145
parking areas: and car sharing 144; transit-oriented developments 46
parklets 39–40, *40*
pedestrianized streets 47
pedestrians *see* walking and walkability
ped-shed accessibility 102–3, *103*, *104*
Peñalosa, Enrique 137
people connectivity 97, 98; *see also* Audit Tool
permeability index 102–3, *103*, *104*, 120n5
Personalised Travel Planning (PTP) Program 85, 86
personal rapid transit (PRT) systems 154
personal travel planning 85–6
persuasion tactics 85, 86
Perth, Australia 36, *36*, 67–9, *68*, *69*, 85–6, 87, 100–2, *102*, *103*
Philippines 132, 134
photo-simulations 90
Place and Link 37, 49n4
place connectivity 97, 98; *see also* Audit Tool
place making 1, 3, 5–7, 21–2; Audit Tool 98, **99**, **111–12**; and technology mega-trends 153
place reconfiguration 5, 55–75; edge city retrofit 72–4, *72*, *74*; mono-use zones 67–9, *68*, *69*; redundant docklands 62–7, *64*, *65*, *66*; redundant industrial zones 57–60, *58*, *59*, *60*; shopping centers 70–2, *70*, *71*; unused rail yards 60–2, *61*, *63*
Platform for Art program, London Underground 48
Pokémon Go game 147
pool loan bikes 86
population growth 127, 128, 129
pop-up parks 73–4, *74*
post-industrialization 57
private two-wheelers 132–4, *133*
Project for Public Spaces (PPS) 5, 7, 147
property tax revenues 42, 46, 71
prosperous communities 18–19
proximity factor 4
psychological traffic calming 33
public art 48, 66, *67*, 69; Audit Tool 105, *106*

public involvement 5, 73, 83–94; collaborative stakeholder dialogue (CSD) 86–8, 92–3; contextualizing 83–4; engagement tools 88–92; ethnographic methods 90–2, 93; Melbourne Docklands 66, *67*; Nehru Place, New Delhi, India 106, 114–19; online deliberation 89–90; photo-simulations 90; soft policy measures and behavioral change 84–6, 92
Public Participation Geographic Information System (PPGIS) 89
public–private partnerships (PPPs) 46
public spaces 13–14, 62; Bogotá, Colombia 135–6, 138; Melbourne Docklands 66, *67*; Space Reclamation movement 135–6; Tysons Corner 73–4, *74*; *see also* movement reconfiguration
public transport 17–18, 19, 31, 127; affordability 131; Bogotá, Colombia 131, 136–8; bus rapid transit (BRT) systems 44, 47, 90, 130, 131, 137; and equity 20–1; informal 131–2; and informal settlements 129–31, *130*, 156; and private two-wheelers 133–4, *133*; reconfiguring 43–9; *see also* transit-oriented developments (TODs)
Pune, India 87–8

Queensland, Australia 19
Quilt-Net approach 35–6, *35*

Raahgiri 135–6
rail yards, reconfiguring 60–2, *61*, *63*
RAND Corporation 148
Real Time Traffic Information app 145
rents 18, 19, 59–60, 148
residential density 100, **101**; *see also* high-density development
retail stores 146; *see also* shopping centers
right-sizing 39
Rio de Janeiro, Brazil 132
road dieting 39
road safety 15–17, *16*, 35, *35*, 127; accidents 15, *16*, 35, 38, 39, 127, 132, 145–6; fatalities and injuries 15, *16*, 35, 38, 127, 132
Roads Task Force, London 37
road tolls 86

safe communities 15–17, *16*
San Antonio Transit Center, Mountain View, California 70–2, *70*, *71*
San Francisco: King Street 106–7, *107*, **107–13**; parklets 39–40, *40*
Seattle *16*, 16, 19, 39, 148
self-driving vehicles 145, 148
sense of enclosure 103–5, *105*
Seoul, South Korea 38–9, *39*, 44, 129
Shanghai 42, *42*, 128, 138–9
shared space 16, 33
shopping centers 70–2, *70*, *71*
sidewalks 18; *see also* footpaths
Singapore 129, 138–9
slum settlements 129–31, *130*, *131*, 156
SMART (safe, mixed-income, accessible, reasonably priced, transit-oriented) housing program 45
Smart Codes 57
Smart Growth 5, 6

INDEX

smartphone games 147
social diversity 13, 19, 62, 67, 73; Audit Tool 98, **99, 108**; and technology mega-trends 152
social inclusion 32
social interaction 14–15, 21–2
social justice 15
soft policy measures 84–6, 92
software programs 89–90
solid:void ratio 103, *104*
solo living 148
Songdo, South Korea 149, 150, 151, 152, 153, 154
South Africa 129–31, *130*, *131*, 132
South Korea: Seoul 38–9, *39*, 44, 129; Songdo 149, 150, 151, 152, 153, 154
Space Reclamation movement 135–6
special needs infrastructure 117, **117**
Sri Lanka 134
'Steer to Safety' studies 92
Stockton, California 90
Stone Way North, Seattle 39
stormwater management 61
strategic communication 84
streets and corridors, reconfiguring 33–41, *34*, *35*, *36*, *38*, *39*, *40*, *41*
Su, F. 20
suburban transformations *see* place reconfiguration
super-smart cities 1–2
surveillance, natural 4, 17
Sydney, Australia 143–4

technology mega-trends 143–56; collaborative consumption 143–5, 156n1; and connecting places, connecting people attributes 149–55, *151*, *154*, *155*; and demographic trends 147–9; vehicle technology innovation 145–6, 148; virtual spaces 146–7, 148–9
teleworking 147, 148
Texas 45, 57–60, *58*, *59*, *60*
Thailand 132
third spaces 147
TODs *see* transit-oriented developments (TODs)
Tokyo 45–6, 129
Tokyo Station City 45–6
Toyota 145
traffic calming measures 16, *16*, 17, 33, 39, 40, 71; *see also* shared space
traffic congestion 4, 15
traffic safety 15–17, *16*, 35, *35*, 127; accidents 15, 16, 35, 38, 39, 127, 132, 145–6; fatalities and injuries 15, 16, 35, 38, 127, 132
transit-oriented developments (TODs) 6, 44–9, 61–2, 65, 68, *68*, 73, 74, 134
TransMilenio BRT system, Bogotá, Colombia 131, 137
transport 3, 19; Audit Tool 98, **99, 112–13**; carbon footprint 32; car dependence 1, 19, 84–6; car sharing 143–4; changing behavior 84–6; collaborative planning 84; electric cars 144; electric vehicles 144; and equity 20–1; private two-wheelers 132–4, *133*; self-driving cars 145, 148; and technology mega-trends 153–4; *see also* car-oriented city design; cycling and cyclability; public transport; transit-oriented developments (TODs)

transport connectivity 98; *see also* Audit Tool
TravelSmart Program 85–6
triangulating functions 14
Trubka, Roman 56
two-wheelers, motorized 132–4, *133*
Tysons Corner, Fairfax County, Virginia 72–4, *72*, *74*

Uber 144
United Arab Emirates 128
United Kingdom 20, 21, 33, 37, 48, 85, 144
United Nations 148
United Nations Development Program (UNDP) 9n2, 139n1
urban and suburban transformations 55–75
urban growth 31, 127, 163; compact 56–7
urban heat island effect 39
Urban Land Institute 5, 70
urban massing 103–5, *105*
urban protestors 6–7
urban reconfiguration 5–7; *see also* movement reconfiguration; place reconfiguration
Urban Renaissance 57
urban structure *see* city and neighborhood structure
Utter, M. A. 47

Vancouver 19
Vauban, Freiburg, Germany 41, *41*
vehicle technology innovation 145–6, 148
vehicle-to-infrastructure (V2I) communications 145, 146
vehicle-to-vehicle (V2V) communications 145, 146
Vélib 143, 145
Venezuela 21
Victoria, Australia 105, *106*; *see also* Melbourne, Australia
Victorian Greater Alpine region, Australia 89
Vietnam 132, 133, 134
Virginia 72–4, *72*, *74*
virtual spaces 146–7, 148–9
volatile organic compounds 133
Voluntary Green Pathway Program, Berkeley 19

walking and walkability x, 17–18, 19, 20, 21, 33–4, 35, 127; Audit Tool 98, **99**, 106, **109–10**, 114–19; Global South 134–6, *135*; India 86, 87–8, 91–2, 106, 114–19, 134–6, *135*; and technology mega-trends 152
Washington Center, Gaithersburg, Maryland 70
water-sensitive urban design techniques 41–2, 61, 62
wicked problems 83
women 20–1
Woodcock, I. 6
woonerf concept 33, 49n2
World Bank 139n1
World Health Organization 127, 132

xeriscaping 42, 49n5

young people 148, 149
youthification 148

zero carbon 149
zoning regulations 19, 44, 47, 57

| 169